GETTING TO THE TABLE

Perspectives on Security
Richard Ned Lebow, Consulting Editor

Psychology and Deterrence
  Edited by Robert Jervis, Richard Ned Lebow, and Janice Gross Stein
Getting to the Table: The Processes of International Prenegotiation
  Edited by Janice Gross Stein

Getting to the Table

The Processes of International Prenegotiation

EDITED BY JANICE GROSS STEIN

THE JOHNS HOPKINS UNIVERSITY PRESS
BALTIMORE AND LONDON

Reprinted from *International Journal*, volume 44 (Spring 1989),
by permission of the Canadian Institute of International Affairs
(© 1989). A nonpartisan, nationwide forum for informed discussion and analysis of international affairs, the Institute as such is
precluded from expressing an opinion on any aspect of world
affairs. The views expressed in its publications are therefore
those of the authors.

The Johns Hopkins University Press
701 West 40th Street, Baltimore, Maryland 21211
The Johns Hopkins Press Ltd., London

The paper used in this publication meets the minimum
requirements of American National Standard for Information
Sciences—Permanence of Paper for Printed Library Materials,
ANSI Z39.48-1984.

Library of Congress Catalog Card Number 89-45453
ISBN 0-8018-3919-X (hardcover)
ISBN 0-8018-3920-3 (paperback)

To Isaac and Gabriel, whose prenegotiating skills before they get to the table are unsurpassed

Contents

Preface and Acknowledgments

We do not know enough about when, why, and how parties get to the negotiating table. Most analyses of international negotiation begin at the table and explore the determinants of and obstacles to agreement among the participants. More recently, however, analysts and practitioners alike have recognized the importance of investigating the conditions and processes that encourage the parties to consider negotiation. Harold Saunders, who participated in many fruitless attempts to get the parties to the Arab-Israeli conflict to the table, and William Zartman have both called for a broader theory of negotiation which encompasses the processes that permit parties to a protracted conflict to agree to negotiate.[1] This volume explores the process of getting to the table.

Professor of Political Science, University of Toronto, Toronto, Ontario, and co-ordinator of the Project on Prenegotiation of the Canadian Institute of International Affairs and the Centre for International Studies of the University of Toronto.

1 Harold Saunders, 'The pre-negotiation phase,' in D.B. Bendahmane and J.W. McDonald Jr, eds, *International Negotiation: Art and Science* (Washington: Foreign Service Institute, Department of State, 1984); 'We need a larger theory of negotiation: the importance of pre-negotiating phases,' *Negotiation Journal* 1(July 1985), 249-62; 'International relationships – it's time to go beyond "we and they," ' *Negotiation Journal* 3(July 1987), 245-74; and *The Other Walls: The Politics of the Arab-Israeli Peace Process* (Lanham MD: University Press of America 1985). See also I. William Zartman, 'Ripening conflict, ripe moment, formula, and mediation,' in D.B. Bendahmane and J.W. McDonald Jr, eds, *Perspectives on Negotiation: Four Case Studies and Interpretations* (Washington: Foreign Service Institute, Department of State, 1986); I. William Zartman and Maureen R. Berman, *The Practical Negotiator* (New Haven CT: Yale University Press 1982); and I. William Zartman, 'Power strategies in de-escalation,' in Louis Kriesberg, ed, *Timing and De-Escalation in International Conflicts* (Syracuse NY: Syracuse University Press, forthcoming).

We conceive the process of getting to the table as 'prenegotiation,' or negotiation about negotiation. We consider this process important. Most obviously, if prenegotiation does not succeed, negotiation does not occur. If prenegotiation does succeed, we expect that it will have important consequences for negotiation at the table; indeed, we suggest that prenegotiation defines the boundaries, shapes the agenda, and affects the outcome of negotiation. Finally, prenegotiation may have important consequences even if the participants do not get to the table. Significant learning may occur during the process which permits the parties to reconceive their relationship. At times, moreover, parties may enter into a process of prenegotiation with the expectation that they will not get to the table but that participation in the process will bring important political benefits independent of the outcome.

The process of prenegotiation begins when one or more parties considers negotiation as a policy option and communicates this intention to other parties. Prenegotiation ends when the parties agree to formal negotiations or when one party abandons the consideration of negotiation as a policy option. This delimitation of the boundaries of the process builds in several important assumptions about a broader theory of negotiation.

By defining prenegotiation as a process, we treat it as analytically distinct and prior to the process of negotiation. At times, the two processes may overlap: if prenegotiation succeeds, the parties may negotiate one set of issues and simultaneously explore the possibility of broadening the agenda and initiating additional negotiations. Parties may also move back and forth from one process to another: they may get to the table, encounter serious obstacles, suspend negotiation, and return to prenegotiation to consider other negotiating formats and options. Even though the two processes may overlap or regress in time, we conceive of the process of getting to the table as distinct, with triggers, stages, functions, and consequences that are separable from those found in negotiation. Prenegotiation as a process frames negotiation; the two are linked but analytically distinct.[2]

Analyses of prenegotiation as a process have concentrated largely on two aspects of its effect on subsequent bargaining. They have explored the impact of the process of getting to the table on the formation of agendas and positions. Experiments with agenda formation have suggested that negotiators will undertake 'protective contracts' during the process of prenegotiation to ensure that each party bargains in 'good faith.' Analyses of position formation have examined the impact of a focus on tactics, issues, and values on subsequent negotiations.[3]

This volume casts its net more widely to address five central questions. First, why does a process of prenegotiation begin? Why do leaders seriously consider the option of negotiation and communicate their interest to other leaders? Second, what are the stages of prenegotiation? Are these stages distinct from those of a process of negotiation? Third, what are the functions of a process of prenegotiation? Fourth, when does prenegotiation culminate at the table? Finally, what are the consequences of prenegotiation, both when the parties proceed to the table and when they do not? Are there important side-benefits, independent of the table? Indeed, how do we define the 'success' of a process of prenegotiation?

2 Daniel Druckman, 'Prenegotiation experience and dyadic conflict resolution in a bargaining situation,' *Journal of Experimental Social Psychology* 4(1968), 367-83, and Daniel Druckman and P. Terrence Hopmann, 'Behavioral aspects of negotiations on mutual security,' in Paul Stern, Jo. L. Husbands, Robert Jervis, Philip Tetlock, and Charles Tilly, eds, *Behavior, Society, and Nuclear War* (New York: Oxford University Press 1989, forthcoming). In this volume, we treat prenegotiation as process rather than as context. Context refers to the structures, interactions, and events in the broader system within which negotiation occurs. It also comprises the relatively enduring aspects of nation-states and their relationships that impinge on the negotiating process.

3 Jo. L. Husbands, 'Domestic factors and de-escalation initiatives: boundaries, process, and timing,' paper prepared for the Conference on Ripeness and Deescalation of International Conflicts, Maxwell School of Citizenship and Public Affairs, Syracuse University, 28-29 March 1988, and Daniel Druckman, Benjamin Broome, and Susan Korper, 'Value differences and conflict resolution: facilitation or delinking?' unpublished paper, 1988.

The studies in this volume, although they differ substantially in their emphases, all examine why the parties considered going to the table, how they got there if indeed they did, and whether the process of getting to the table influenced what they did once they got there. Finally, we ask if getting to the table was the only important purpose and consequence of a process of prenegotiation.

In the introductory article to the volume, I. William Zartman reviews the analysis of prenegotiation and sets the agenda for the case-studies that follow. He examines prenegotiation as a phase of negotiation and defines its essence as the attempt to persuade another that a joint solution to a common problem is possible. Brian Tomlin traces five stages in the process of prenegotiation between the United States and Canada on free trade. These stages include the decisional activity that precedes the communication of the intention to negotiate as well as the process of prenegotiation itself; they give content to the phase of prenegotiation identified by Zartman. Tomlin then examines the turning points which moved both parties through the five stages of the process to the negotiating table. Gilbert Winham explores a multilateral process of prenegotiation within a highly institutionalized régime, the General Agreement on Tariffs and Trade. He analyses the triggers, the process, and the consequences of the complex prenegotiation to the multilateral negotiation of the Uruguay Round.

Attention then shifts from economic to security issues. Franklyn Griffiths examines the actions of the Soviet Union in four processes of prenegotiation on arms control. He analyses each as a turning point in the readiness of the Soviet leadership to come to terms with a world it was sworn to transform. He assesses the impact of prenegotiation on the subsequent negotiation at the table and, more importantly, on the texture of the Soviet-American relationship. Fen Osler Hampson examines the participation of the United States in four processes of prenegotiation on arms control and assesses why prenegotiation began and how and why the United States got to the table.

Janice Gross Stein examines the multilateral processes of pre-negotiation between Arabs and Israelis that culminated at Camp David. She argues that in a protracted and bitter conflict, pre-negotiation is extraordinarily important in framing the negotiation that follows. Moreover, she concludes, the process had significant and unanticipated consequences both when the parties failed to get to the table and when they succeeded.

The optic then shifts from analyses of particular cases to a broader consideration of the analysis and policy relevance of prenegotiation. Ronald Fisher considers the potential of problem-solving approaches to enhance the prospects of getting to the table, particularly in cases of protracted conflict. He argues that problem-solving strategies can be especially effective in improving an adversarial relationship before the parties get to the table.

In the conclusion to this volume, Janice Gross Stein draws on the comparative analysis of cases to address the questions of why prenegotiation began and how the parties got to the table. She then considers the importance of prenegotiation, both to the negotiation that followed and to the broader relationship among the parties. Finally, she assesses the consequences of prenegotiation for the management of conflict among adversaries and its capacity to promote change in relationships of enduring conflict. Analysis of prenegotiation focusses attention in the first instance on preparation for substantive negotiation. More broadly, it looks at the political preconditions of negotiation and at the series of steps that is necessary to build a commitment to negotiate. The process of 'getting to the table,' she concludes, may be even more important than the table itself.

This volume is the product of an interdisciplinary seminar on international negotiation sponsored by the Canadian Institute of International Affairs and the Centre for International Studies at the University of Toronto. Funding for the seminar was provided by a grant from the John D. and Catherine T. MacArthur Foundation of Chicago to the Canadian Institute of International Affairs and by a grant from the Canadian Institute for International Peace and Security to the Centre for International Studies at the University of Toronto.

In the first year of the project, the contributors to this volume invited representatives from different disciplines to think afresh about the analysis of international negotiation. Those papers were subsequently published in *Negotiation Journal*, under the title: 'International negotiation: a multidisciplinary perspective.'[4] In the second year of the colloquium, the participants considered the process of getting to the table. This volume is the result of our discussions together. Daniel Druckman, Jeffrey Rubin, and Harold Saunders read parts of the manuscript and provided valuable advice. We would like to acknowledge especially the constructive criticism of I. William Zartman on all the chapters and the assistance of Robert O. Matthews and Charles Pentland, the editors of *International Journal*. The *Journal*'s associate editor, Marion Magee, edited the manuscript with sensitivity, skill, and a firm hand.

4 *Negotiation Journal* 4(July 1988): Janice Gross Stein, 'International negotiation: a multidisciplinary perspective,' David V.J. Bell, 'Political linguistics and international negotiation,' Philip H. Gulliver, 'Anthropological contributions to the study of negotiations,' Aaron V. Cicourel, 'Text and context: cognitive, linguistic, and organizational dimensions in international negotiations,' Robert Rosenthal, 'Interpersonal expectancies, nonverbal communication, and research on negotiation,' Deborah Welch Larson, 'The psychology of reciprocity in international relations,' and Max H. Bazerman and Harris Sondak, 'Judgmental limitations in diplomatic negotiations.'

1. *Prenegotiation: Phases and Functions*

I. WILLIAM ZARTMAN

After all these years, we still have trouble living with concepts. Unlike tangible realities, such as a dog, concepts have no clear beginnings and ends, no unambiguous middles, and not even a usefulness that is beyond debate. A dog – which does not exist to the left of its nose or the right of its tail, is clearly distinguishable from a car or even a cat, and would require a name if it did not have one – offers none of these problems. We may try to dodge the boundary problem and focus on the essential or functional nature of the concept, but that will only satisfy philosophers, who have less trouble with concepts than most of us anyhow, and not practitioners. A phase is a particularly troublesome form of concept because a time dimension is added to its other elusive qualities and because other relational questions are raised. Is a phase part of subsequent phases, for example, and is the sequence of phases a one-way street or can there be backtracking and even leapfrogging? None of these questions ever arises about the good old dog!

Prenegotiation is such a troublesome phase concept. There is no doubt that there is something before negotiation, but it is less clear whether it is a prelude to or a part of negotiation, whether there is a difference in nature between these two, how sharp the boundaries are and how reversible the flows, or what the relation is to other contextual events such as crises and régimes. These are questions that this volume seeks to confront

Jacob Blaustein Professor of International Organization and Conflict Resolution at the School of Advanced International Studies, Johns Hopkins University, Washington, DC.

and elucidate. This attention to prenegotiation is timely and appropriate, for while a number of writers have identified it as an important element of the overall process of negotiation, few have developed the concept. Practitioners, in particular, emphasize that the usual academic treatment of negotiation as beginning when the parties sit down at the table in fact takes no account of the most challenging phase of preparations and therefore misses an important aspect of the process of narrowing disagreement between parties.

PHASES

Harold Saunders has most eloquently drawn attention to the need to 'reach back and more extensively into the period before the decision to negotiate is made, and analyse what can be done to help parties reach that decision.'[1] His starting point, however, is the decision of third parties to pursue negotiation, and his prenegotiation period covers two functional needs, 'defining the problem' and 'developing a commitment to negotiation on the part of the parties,' which are followed by a third phase, 'arranging the negotiations.' The first two phases centre about the creation of a political commitment to solve a problem which has been defined in such a way as to be susceptible of mutually satisfactory management. The fourth phase, negotiation itself, involves efforts to come to closure or to crystallize the previous intent or search in a concrete agreement. However, even then, 'it is apparent that, in many ways, negotiation has already begun in the earlier stages of the process.'[2] Hence, the word 'negotiation' is being used, as it often is, in two ways, referring both to the whole process, including the preliminaries to itself, and to the ultimate face-to-face diplomatic encounters.

---

1 Harold Saunders, 'We need a larger theory of negotiation: the importance of pre-negotiating phases,' *Negotiation Journal* 1(July 1985), 250, and *The Other Walls: The Politics of the Arab-Israeli Peace Process* (Lanham MD: University Press of America 1985), 22 et passim.
2 Saunders, *The Other Walls*, 35.

William Zartman and Maureen Berman identify the first of the three phases of negotiation as the 'diagnostic stage,' the phase of 'bringing about negotiations ... long before the first formal session opens.' Admitting that the beginning moment of the phase is usually not clear-cut, they see it going on until the 'turning point of seriousness,' when each party has perceived the other to be serious about finding a negotiated solution and the second or 'formula phase' begins. However, they warn that phases tend to be grey around the edges, that in fact the work of each phase continues underneath its successor, and that backtracking is possible, indeed desirable, when the succeeding phase finds itself ill prepared by its predecessor.[3] Zartman later focussed exclusively on the diagnosis phase and its appropriate contextual conditions. Similarly, Richard Haass has adopted the notion of the ripe moment and has written insightfully about measures to be taken when the moment is not yet ripe.[4]

Recently, a group has begun to look at the specific problem of initiating negotiations in relation to the notion of de-escalation.[5] For the most part, Louis Kriesberg and his colleagues consider prenegotiation (without using the name) as the phase in which conflict is transformed into a search for a co-operative agreement by measures inducing a lowering of conflict (de-escalation), a redefinition of relationships, a re-evaluation of the appropriate means or of the effectiveness of alternative means to an end, and a consideration of potential third-party roles. All of these are useful and even necessary components

3 I. William Zartman and Maureen R. Berman, *The Practical Negotiator* (New Haven CT: Yale University Press 1982), especially 42 et passim and 87 et passim.
4 I. William Zartman, *Ripe for Resolution: Conflict and Intervention in Africa* (New York: Oxford University Press 1985); I. William Zartman, ed, *Positive Sum: Improving North-South Negotiations* (New Brunswick NJ: Transaction Books 1987); Richard Haass, *Conflicts without End* (New Haven CT: Yale University Press 1989).
5 Louis Kriesberg, ed, *Timing and De-Escalation in International Conflicts* (Syracuse NY: Syracuse University Press forthcoming).

of the preparation for negotiation, and they suggest defining components of the phase although they do not identify it or define it per se.[6]

Out of all these elements, it is important to focus on some basic items if one is to understand the concept of prenegotiation: a definition of the phenomenon, an identification of its component characteristics, and an indication of its function (usefulness) in the process through which parties achieve conflicting goals. While other studies have raised questions about the nature of prenegotiation and discussed aspects of it, they have left room for one whose focus is on this phenomenon, investigating its dynamics and testing the strength of the concept as a tool for the analysis of diverse, specific events.

The present study has already justified its existence by proposing a definition of prenegotiation: Prenegotiation begins when one or more parties considers negotiation as a policy option and communicates this intention to other parties. It ends when the parties agree to formal negotiations (an exchange of proposals designed to arrive at a mutually acceptable outcome in a situation of interdependent interests) or when one party abandons the consideration of negotiation as an option. This definition leaves the essential characteristics of prenegotiation implicit, however, because it concentrates on the limiting characteristics. In essential terms, prenegotiation is the span of time and activity in which the parties move from conflicting unilateral solutions for a mutual problem to a joint search for cooperative multilateral or joint solutions. From both definitions, it is clear that the nature of the activity lies not in conducting the combined search for *a/the* solution but in arriving at and in convincing the other party to arrive at the conclusion that *some* joint solution is possible. If that appreciation creates a better

---

6 Others who looked at negotiation as a succession of phases have examined some of the functions of prenegotiation, but without defining the concept per se: see P.H. Gulliver, *Disputes and Negotiations: A Cross-Cultural Perspective* (New York: Academic Press 1979) and Charles Lockhart, *Bargaining in International Conflicts* (New York: Columbia University Press 1979).

understanding of prenegotiation, however, its sharpness should not be overdrawn, tempting though sharpness may be. It is impossible to perceive a potentiality for a joint solution without considering potential joint solutions and discarding some of them. This is the importance of Saunders' first stage, summarized in his good phrase, 'getting one's mind around the problem.'

At the same time, it should be clear that whatever parties do differently during prenegotiation, that activity is part of the general process of coming to agreement out of conflict and hence of negotiation itself. Once again, sharpness should not be exaggerated. Ultimately, life is a seamless web, and analysis, indeed knowledge, is basically a matter of making order and distinctions out of it. Indeed, what happens prior to prenegotiation is related to negotiation too. But the initiation of the prenegotiation process, by definition and by nature, begins when one side considers the multilateral track as a possible alternative to the unilateral track to a solution in a conflict, and it continues into the next phase when both parties reach this conclusion. (Saunders' opening moment which focusses on third-party perceptions and behaviours extends the period a bit but does not affect either the essential nature of the activity or its position as part of the larger negotiation process.)

The question then is not the absolute distinction between two parts of the same and evolving process, but how to get to negotiation. The definitions we have already examined make some assumptions about elements in the answer. They hypothesize that parties arrive at the decision to negotiate separately, differently, and not concomitantly; that they shift from, or at least add a multilateral track to, their previously exclusively unilateral strategy; and that there is an identifiable decision for which a cause may be sought, explained, and, indeed, eventually produced.

Partial answers and further hypotheses are also available from the early literature on prenegotiation. The decision to negotiate is found to be associated with 'a plateau and a precipice' – a mutually hurting stalemate combined with a recent or impending catastrophe.[7] The nature and perception of the stalemate, the role of escalation, and the positioning of the catastrophe or crisis are all matters to be pursued. Parties shift from unilateral solutions towards multilateral or negotiated ones when the unilateral track is blocked or overly costly or when the alternative track is more promising or comparatively cheaper.[8] The comparative effectiveness of negative and positive sanctions and inducements has been investigated only preliminarily and needs more work.[9] Parties often decide to negotiate when they perceive the distribution of power between them moving towards equality.[10] Relations between perception and reality and increases in the efficiency of perception are yet further issues to be developed.

FUNCTIONS

All these questions and hypotheses, and others that flow from them, have both an explanatory and a practical value. All are causative questions, susceptible of comparative investigation so that causal sequences and correlations as well as intervening variables can be identified. But, by the same token, all are important questions for practitioners, providing general guidelines for the improved conduct of negotiations. Furthermore, both policy-makers and academics benefit from the same syllogisms and causative statements, a point often missed on both sides but most frequently by practitioners delighting in the use

7 Zartman, *Ripe for Resolution*, 232f; Zartman and Berman, *Practical Negotiator*, 57ff, 74ff; Saadia Touval and I. William Zartman, eds, *International Mediation in Theory and Practice* (Boulder CO: Westview 1985), 16.

8 Zartman, *Ripe for Resolution*, 233ff; Zartman and Berman, *Practical Negotiator*, 52ff, 62ff, 70ff; Saunders, *The Other Walls*, 25ff; Kriesberg, ed, *Timing and De-Escalation*.

9 David Baldwin, 'The power of positive sanctions,' *World Politics* 24(October 1971), 19-38; Louis Kriesberg, 'Non-coercive inducements in U.S.-Soviet conflicts,' *Journal of Military and Political Sociology* 9(spring 1981), 1-16; I. William Zartman, 'Power strategies in de-escalation,' in Kriesberg, ed, *Timing and De-Escalation*.

10 Zartman, *Ripe for Resolution*, 234; Zartman and Berman, *Practical Negotiator*, 48ff, 54ff; Saunders, *The Other Walls*, 30f.

of 'academic' in its derivative and disparaging meaning. The academics' question 'What causes A?' is the mirror image of the policy-makers' question 'what will happen if I do B?' and the same as the latter's question 'How can I help bring about A?' An answer to any of them is a step to answering the others. The search for answers in this volume is useful to both audiences.

The first and clear answer that this volume yields is that prenegotiation is necessary. In each of the case-studies, prenegotiation is not just a definitional construct but a preparatory phase without which the negotiation would not have taken place. But there are other uses in the identification of prenegotiation and an understanding of its characteristics. If one turns the definition into an attempted explanation and asks *how* does prenegotiation lead to negotiation, one can discover both ramifications of a process and prescriptions for behaviour. Prenegotiation is a purposive period of transition that enables parties to move from conflicting perceptions and behaviours (unilateral attempts at solutions) to co-operative perceptions and behaviours. Where they once saw only an enemy, bound on undoing its opponent and untrustworthy in any joint efforts (and behaved accordingly themselves, thus justifying a similar perception on the part of the opponent), by the end of the period they have to be able to see an adversary who is nonetheless capable of co-operative behaviour and of some trust (and to reflect such characteristics themselves). Where each party regarded the problem with a winning mentality, seeking only ways to overcome and get what it wanted, by the end of the transition they must shift to a conciliatory mentality, believing the solution is to be found with, not against, the adversary and preparing to give a little to get something, to settle for an attainable second-best rather than hold out for an unattainable victory. These are significant shifts, often greater than anything involved in finding the final agreed outcome, but necessary preconditions to that search. These shifts are not unshakable, it must be emphasized; they are continually being tested in the actual negotiation and from time to time may need explicit reaffirmation.

But they are the necessary substance of the prenegotiation period. How are they brought about? There are at least seven functions of prenegotiation, to be performed in no special order.

Risks

Because negotiation, as an exercise in mutual power, involves the exchange of contingent gratifications and deprivations ('I will do this, if you will do that'), it is a very risky undertaking. Before prenegotiation, the risk is too high to be affordable. Prenegotiation may lower the risks associated with co-operation and may prepare escape hatches in case things go wrong (as Franklyn Griffiths' article shows). But, above all, it makes the extent of the risk clearer. Because exit costs are lower in prenegotiation, where no engagements have actually been made as yet, parties can be freer about stating maximum terms and real interests clearly. The exchange of information reduces the unknown and hence the risks of eventual concessions. The parties come to know what to expect.

Costs

Prenegotiation allows the parties to assess and come to terms with the costs of concessions and agreement, and also with the costs of failure, before firm commitments are made. One major element of power in negotiation and also a reference point which helps establish the value of the final agreement is the security point – the value of what is obtained by each party without an agreement. Outcomes must be better than security points to be worthwhile, but both outcomes and security points have costs. The costs and benefits of various agreements as well as of no agreement must be estimated by the parties. Like risk and reciprocity, costs can be estimated without ever meeting the adversary but those estimates will be based on poorer information than that a party could obtain by meeting in prenegotiation. A clearer idea of costs works back to lower risks, because the risk and cost of the unknown can be reduced. As Griffiths makes clear in his article, prenegotiation is necessary to enable or oblige the parties to sort out their *own* motives for negotiating in the given context.

Requitement

Studies have shown that beyond hurting stalemate, requitement or a belief in reciprocity is the second most important element in beginning negotiations. It does no good to see one's unilateral path to a solution blocked, if one is sure that the other side will not repay concessions with concessions.[11] But fear of reciprocity is its own undoing: one does not make concessions because one is sure the other side will not repay and the other does not repay concessions because it is sure that the other will not either. Prenegotiation is the time to convince the other party that concessions will be requited, not banked and run away with. Such exchanges and assurances are less risky during this phase because they are indicative of future behaviour rather than commitments. They are taken to be credibly indicative, however, because a promise of requitement that was not honoured in the negotiation period itself would be considered a strong case of bad faith, harmful to the party's reputation. The chance to explore requitement not only allows parties to see if concessions are possible but also allows responding conceders to see what would happen and where they would be if counter-concessions were offered. All this information is necessary to the decision to negotiate. Requitement is basic to both of Brian Tomlin's procedural phases – commitment to negotiate and decision to negotiate.

Support

Prenegotiation allows each party to estimate and consolidate its own internal support for an accommodative policy, to prepare the home front for a shift from a winning to a conciliatory mentality. This involves not only changing the public image of

---

11 Dean Pruitt, 'The escalation of conflict: project proposal,' 1988; Deborah Welch Larson, 'Game theory and the psychology of reciprocity,' 1986; Zartman, *Ripe for Resolution* (2nd ed; New York: Oxford University Press 1989).

the adversary but also putting together a domestic coalition of interests to support termination rather than conduct of conflict. As elsewhere, the first step is to prepare for change in the conflict policy, a step related but prior to a determination of the new outcome. Like the other aspects of prenegotiation, the construction of domestic support should not be merely the affair of each side. Each party has a role to play in the other's politics, and that party which has first concluded that negotiation is a conceivable outcome has an especial challenge to reach into the domestic political processes of the other and help build a supportive coalition for accommodation.[12] Griffiths characterizes this activity as informal coalition-building with counterparts on the other side, and Janice Gross Stein and Fen Osler Hampson show the importance of heading off or building on domestic opposition as a key activity in determining the course of prenegotiation.

Alternatives

The core function of prenegotiation involves turning the problem into a manageable issue susceptible of a negotiated outcome. Three of Tomlin's prenegotiation phases break down the agenda-setting functions. Identifying the problem, searching for options, and setting the parameters are steps along the path to finding a formula. The process involves inventing and choosing among alternative definitions of the problem, inventing and choosing among alternative ways of handling the problem so defined, and setting the themes and limits – parameters and perimeters – that are necessary to guide a solution. Indeed, the whole process of multilateral conflict resolution can be considered as one of eliminating alternatives, until only one solution remains. (This is in itself a useful approach to the analysis of the situation and diametrically different from the usual one which consists in studying negotiation as a process of selection.) Even though selection and elimination go hand in hand in real-

---

12 Saunders, *The Other Walls*, chaps 9 and 10; Harold Saunders, 'International relationships,' *Negotiation Journal* 3(July 1987), 245-74.

ity, formal negotiation can be considered to be more the selection phase and prenegotiation the elimination phase. It is in the latter phase that parties put aside some of the salient possibilities for agreement, avoid worst alternatives, and begin to focus on a few that appear most promising.

Any conflict can be defined in several ways, some of them more susceptible of resolution than others. One part of the shift from a winning to a conciliatory mentality consists in coming together on more resolvable definitions of the problem and eliminating competing zero-sum definitions and their inherently one-sided solutions. But even among the other variable-sum solutions, there are some which imply greater difficulties, complex ramifications, and more costs than others, and successful prenegotiation works to eliminate these, leaving only a few definitions and alternatives in place to deal with in depth in the formal negotiation.

Thus, there are two possible patterns of formal negotiation: one in which the parties work out the diagnosis and formulas of successive alternatives, as shown by Stein on the Middle East, and one in which the dynamic is centred on a competition between a few salient alternatives; both are identified in the articles by Griffiths and Hampson on arms control. In either case, prenegotiation is concerned with the setting of the agenda, the elimination of some issues, and the selection of those encompassed by the mutually acceptable definition of the problem, as Gilbert Winham's discussion of the General Agreement on Tariffs and Trade (GATT) shows. But these same studies also show that agenda formation is determined not just by its own substantive concerns but also by its links with the previous function, that of gathering support – shaping an agenda that brings internal forces on board, as Griffiths sees it.[13] Prenegotiation is as much a process of finding a solution that is supportable as of finding support for an ideal solution.

However the process of selecting and discarding alternatives

13 Robert Putnam, 'Diplomacy and domestic politics: the logic of two-level games,' *International Organization* 42(summer 1988), 427-60.

is conducted, it is a process of establishing boundaries to the issues to be considered and of setting agendas, or, in a less two-dimensional image, of 'getting one's mind around the problem.' If it is not clear how the problem is defined, what the limits to the negotiable issues are, and what the agenda for the negotiation is, prenegotiation has not done its job and, indeed, is not over.

Participants

Just as a certain amount of selection needs to be done among the alternative definitions of and solutions to the conflict during prenegotiation, so it may also be necessary to select those who are susceptible of coming to agreement from among the participants to the conflict. Just as all aspects of the conflict are not likely to be solved, so it may not be possible to include all parties in an agreement. As parties crystallize their positions, they may find themselves confronting a choice about whether to join the growing coalition or not, just as the coalition will face the choice of whether to stretch its own boundaries to include a particular party or not. Like the range of alternatives, the number of participants to an agreement has to be judged carefully, lest there not be enough of them to create a lasting settlement. Leaving out either the major contender or the major issue may produce an agreement but not a solution.

In between the dilemma of comprehensiveness versus compatibility is the tactic of building a coalition large enough to make a stable agreement no broader than necessary to cover the bases, a tactic of participant incrementalism.[14] A core group of agreers can come together and gradually expand its membership, co-ordinating its selection of participants with its selection of issues and definitions of the conflict. Although this may sound like a multilateral process not relevant to bilateral conflicts, its logic can also be extended to the multiple components that usually make up any party. In the building of

14 Zartman, ed, *Positive Sum: Improving North-South Negotiations*, 292-4.

domestic support both by the negotiating party and by its adversary, a party must choose those to include in its participating coalition and those to accept in the other party's coalition as well.[15] Thus, as much as setting the agenda, prenegotiation selects the participants at the table (and perhaps even begins to look to their seating arrangements). These considerations are crucial in multilateral prenegotiation, as Winham's and Stein's articles on the GATT and on the Middle East (and interested outside powers) show. They are much less of a factor in bilateral prenegotiation, as Tomlin, Griffiths, and Hampson show, but that is only because the two participants have already decided to leave out other parties whose claim on the action is based on different criteria.

Bridges

The principal function of prenegotiation is to build bridges from conflict to conciliation, with the changes in perception, mentality, tactics, definitions, acceptability levels, and partners that have already been discussed. While these other measures all cover important aspects of that shift, prenegotiation also sets up temporary mechanisms that provide for the change itself on a transitional and provisional basis. One is a temporary suspension of conflict activities. Although the ceasefire is the best-known form of this change, its functional equivalent can also be found in trade disputes where conflicting practices would be suspended, as Winham discusses below, or in arms control situations where moratoriums on testing or on production would be introduced, as Griffiths and Hampson discuss. Ceasefires and moratoriums are downpayments on confidence; temporary, vulnerable, provisional concessions that at the same time form the basis of potential threats. They remove the danger of misinterpretation of intentions, but they also remove the possibility of unilateral acts either to effect or to affect a solution. As such, they are more likely to conclude than to open pre-

15 Putnam, 'Diplomacy and domestic politics.'

negotiation. The resolution process must be brought to the point where the power structure is no longer in doubt and unilateral efforts to gain advantage are no longer permissible for a ceasefire to receive the parties' support. Beyond that point, a refusal of a ceasefire is a sign of bad faith, and before that point it is not.

A second measure is the building of trust, the need and methods for which are treated by Ronald Fisher. Before prenegotiation, parties in general can be expected (and can expect) not to trust each other, because each is looking for unilateral advantage; by the end of a negotiation they must have established some mutual trust to be able to make an agreement. The initial steps of the shift are made in prenegotiation, as parties conduct small tests of trust and construct mechanisms by which trust can be shown and monitored.[16] It is wrong to expect that trust will or must be firmly in place for formal negotiation to begin. Parties will and should be wary of each other from the beginning to the very end, because we know that it is rational to defect or cheat at the last moment (in the phenomenon of crest or end game), and, in any case, neither cheating nor agreement would be possible if trust were not the norm.[17]

An understanding of the nature and components of prenegotiation is an worthwhile objective in itself. Because there is a need for a preparatory transition between the conflict and conciliation processes, there is a need to analyse it and to test the structures and functions involved. Once they are established and their workings better understood, such knowledge becomes useful to those who practise negotiation as well as to those seeking to explain how and why specific cases worked out the way they did.

FRAMEWORKS

A better understanding of the functions of prenegotiation can also throw light on other – sometimes competing – concepts

16 Zartman and Berman, *Practical Negotiator*, 27-41.
17 Otomar Bartos, *Process and Outcome of Negotiations* (New York: Columbia University Press 1974).

that inform current studies of co-operation and conflict. Much of the contemporary analysis of co-operation among selfish states takes place within the concept of régimes, the minimal and often implicit rules and routines governing interaction.[18] Prenegotiation performs many of the same functions as a régime, or vice versa. On issues covered by régimes, therefore, one might expect that prenegotiation would be less necessary, shorter, or different in nature; even conflict régimes, which provide rules of the game for the conduct and limitation of hostilities, would offer a framework for building and assessing many of the prenegotiation functions. Yet régimes cover large areas of interaction, whereas the success of negotiation depends on the identification of specific definitions of problems, the selection of participants and alternatives, and the establishment of parameters and agendas. Each of these activities involves at least potential conflict, not of the armed type, of course, but of the basic type related to incompatibilities of interests. Thus, even within régimes, prenegotiation is necessary to focus the ensuing process of agreement on appropriate items, but this process should benefit from some of the work already being done through the régime. One would want to avoid the illusion that prenegotiation would therefore be 'easier' on issues covered by régimes; it is hard to use a comparative because there are no control cases for the comparison, and the prenegotiation may be difficult nonetheless. Indeed, prenegotiation within régimes may well be 'easier' only in the sense that it would not have been possible at all if the terrain had not been prepared by the régime. That indeed is the purpose of régimes, as Winham's study of the GATT and Fisher's of the Commonwealth show. Proof of such statements would have to lie in logic rather than in empirical testing, because of the difficulties of comparison, but even on that basis a case could be made for the usefulness of régimes to the negotiation process.

The value of such questions lies in the linkage they establish

18 Stephen Krasner, *International Regimes* (Ithaca NY: Cornell University Press 1983); Robert Axelrod, *The Evolution of Cooperation* (New York: Basic Books 1984).

between two major fields of inquiry that have communicated too little – the search for broad frameworks of analysis such as régimes and the study of processes and activities of interaction such as negotiation. Such works as do exist are for the most part in the field of North-South economic negotiations,[19] but the interpenetration of the two fields of inquiry should be much broader. Prenegotiation provides the link. As Winham's study of prenegotiation within the GATT shows, prenegotiation within explicit régimes can subsume certain functions such as those dealing with risk, cost, and requitement and focus within already established routines and rules on those dealing with alternatives, participants, support, and bridges. Without the functional economies that the GATT provided, it might not have been possible to get through the prenegotiation of a Uruguay Round.

The other field of inquiry into types of events similar to those covered by prenegotiation is centred on crises. The study of crises has provided a focal point for much otherwise disparate material involved in international relations; in a crisis-ridden world, the management of crises when they occur and the prevention of crises before they do occur are realistic concerns and conceptual challenges. Prenegotiation comes to the rescue. Not only is it necessary to the management and prevention of crises, so that negotiations themselves may be more effective and efficient, but it also stands in a creative, if uncertain, relationship to crisis.

Prenegotiation is crisis avoidance. While at first glance it may appear unclear whether crisis precedes prenegotiation or

19 See Beverly Crawford, 'Stabilizing factors in international conflict resolution,' *Negotiation Journal* 3(October 1987), 333-45; Vincent Mahler, 'The political economy of North-South commodity bargaining: the case of the International Sugar Agreement,' *International Organization* 38(autumn 1984), 709-32; Vinod K. Aggarwal, 'The unraveling of the Multi-Fiber Arrangement 1981: an examination of international regime change,' *International Organization* 37(autumn 1983), and *Liberal Protectionism* (Berkeley: University of California Press 1985); Robert Rothstein, *Global Bargaining: UNCTAD and the Quest for a New International Economic Order* (Princeton NJ: Princeton University Press 1979); Zartman, ed, *Positive Sum*.

whether prenegotiation staves off crisis, it soon becomes apparent that the only reason why negotiation should follow crisis is that human beings tend to disagree on the reality of an impending crisis and only lock the stable door after the horse has bolted. But they lock it at all, and negotiate under the shock of a crisis, only because they fear another one. The last crisis has brought us to our senses and made us negotiate (and hence prenegotiate) because we fear the next one. The study of Middle East prenegotiation, as in Stein's chapter, shows the effect of a recent and again looming crisis, as does Hampson's study of American arms control negotiations. More striking is the role of crisis avoidance even within a régime such as the GATT, in Winham's analysis of prenegotiation.

There may be other fields of study in international relations which can benefit from the attention given here to prenegotiation. Régimes and crises are only two important examples of concepts that stand in some relationship to prenegotiation and suggest useful questions about its role and functions. The following studies on a wide range of cases address these questions, explore these functions, and investigate the nature of prenegotiation. The reasons parties turn to negotiation, the stages of the prenegotiation process, the functions of prenegotiation, the explanation of outcomes of prenegotiation – these are the general questions that each case examines, with results that are gathered together in the conclusion to the book. The concept may not emerge as concrete as a canine, but this work brings out the inherent reality and importance of prenegotiation.

2. The Stages of Prenegotiation: The Decision to Negotiate North American Free Trade

BRIAN W. TOMLIN

On 3 October 1987 Canada and the United States concluded their negotiation of the basic principles of a free trade agreement. Although agreement on the final details of the arrangement would require another two months of intense discussion, the October breakthrough brought to a successful conclusion the formal talks that had begun almost eighteen months before, on 21 May 1986.

An adequate understanding of this negotiation must include an analysis of the decisions and interactions that preceded the start of the formal negotiation in 1986. Not only is such an analysis required to explain how the parties came to negotiate in the first instance, but it is also necessary to an understanding of the process and outcomes of the negotiation itself. This is so because the dynamics of the prenegotiation process contribute to the establishment of the parameters within which formal negotiation subsequently unfolds. These parameters may be more or less precisely defined, and they are not immutable once negotiation is under way, but the initial definition of their scope in the prenegotiation phase may have important effects on both the process and outcomes of negotiation. Although the prenegotiation and formal negotiation phases must ultimately be

Professor of international affairs and political science and director of the Centre for International Negotiation in The Norman Paterson School of International Affairs, Carleton University, Ottawa, Ontario.

This paper is based on research funded by a grant from the Social Sciences and Humanities Research Council of Canada. G. Bruce Doern is also a principal investigator on the project. I am grateful to Claire Turenne Sjolander for research assistance.

linked analytically to determine these effects, a first step in this direction is the conceptualization and description of the pre-negotiation process.

Analysis of the prenegotiation phase of the negotiation resulting in the Canadian-American free trade agreement is important as well because the decision to negotiate free trade represented a rather dramatic policy shift on the part of the government of Canada, one that could not have been anticipated at the outset of the decade.[1] At the beginning of 1981, Canada's under-secretary of state for external affairs published an article heralding the resurrection in Canadian foreign policy of the Third Option, a short-lived effort in the 1970s to promote restructuring of the Canadian economy and to diversify Canada's foreign economic relations beyond North America. Allan Gotlieb, who was to be Canada's ambassador to the United States during the free trade negotiations, wrote: 'The nature of the Canadian economy and society has required government involvement to channel aspects of long-range development in beneficial ways. Similarly, it is axiomatic that the benefits of development have to be worked at by Canada. They will not fall out of a free trade, free investment, free-for-all continental economy. This is not an option for Canadian development.'[2]

Canada's movement from a revival of the Third Option to bilateral free trade in less than five years provides an important case-study of the decision to negotiate as a response to a fundamental problem of public policy. By studying the prenegotiation phase of the decision, we may not only better understand the process leading to this shift in policy, but also advance our

1 For a discussion of the recurrent debates on the free trade issue in Canadian public policy, see J.L. Granatstein, 'Free trade between Canada and the United States: the issue that will not go away,' in Denis Stairs and Gilbert R. Winham, eds, *The Politics of Canada's Economic Relationship with the United States* (Toronto: University of Toronto Press 1985).

2 Allan Gotlieb and Jeremy Kinsman, 'Reviving the Third Option,' *International Perspectives* (January/February 1981), 3. For the original Third Option paper, see 'Canada-U.S. relations: options for the future,' *International Perspectives*, special issue (autumn 1972).

knowledge about the process by which nations decide to entertain negotiation as a policy option. As a first step, the prenegotiation phase must be properly demarcated and its various stages conceptualized.

PRENEGOTIATION DEFINED

The decision to concentrate analysis on the prenegotiation phase of the negotiation process introduces the difficult question of how to define and demarcate this phase within the broader process. Certainly, the interval between a decision on the part of some or all of the parties to seek negotiations over a set of issues and the formal start of negotiating sessions should be included in any definition of the prenegotiation phase. It is in this period that the parties are most likely to try to define the initial scope of the negotiation, in an attempt to shape the agenda to suit their needs.

More problematic is the inclusion of interactions and events in the relations between parties that occurred prior to any decision to negotiate, as proposed by Harold Saunders.[3] Saunders' concern with the factors that lead parties to consider negotiation (or to reject it) as a means to resolve conflict is appropriate because prior relations between parties are potentially important in determining whether a decision will be taken to negotiate. As well, such relations may be important in influencing the course of the negotiations once undertaken. However, their inclusion in the prenegotiation phase may impede efforts to theorize about this process and its effects, by seeking to explain too much, and may lead to infinite regress in efforts to understand the negotiation process and its outcomes.

To avoid these pitfalls, the prenegotiation phase should be defined in terms that clearly mark it as a prelude to negotiation, rather than merging it with the long-term pattern of relations between the parties. To achieve this demarcation, a conception

3 Harold Saunders, 'We need a larger theory of negotiation: the importance of pre-negotiating phases,' *Negotiation Journal* 1 (July 1985), 249-62.

of the prenegotiation phase is required that distinguishes relations within the phase from those that went before. Such a conception is suggested in the work of Daniel Druckman who employs a threshold-adjustment model to describe the negotiation process.[4] Druckman conceives negotiation in terms of patterns of delayed mutual responsiveness between parties, marked by turning points that move the parties through various stages and from one stage to another in the negotiation process.

Applying these concepts to the prenegotiation phase, one would attempt to identify a turning point in the relationship between the parties that is followed by a decision on the part of some or all to consider negotiation as a means to pursue goals. In these terms, the prenegotiation phase may be conceived as that period in relations when negotiation is considered, and perhaps adopted, as a behavioural option by some or all of the parties. The onset of the phase is likely to be marked by a turning point in relations between the parties, an event or change in conditions that prompts a reassessment of alternatives and adds negotiation to the range of options being considered. We expect that the prenegotiation phase itself is also a process marked by turning points that move the parties through various stages of prenegotiation, as set out below. The phase concludes with the start of formal negotiating sessions.

The Druckman framework provides an organizing set of concepts for the examination of the negotiation process, highlighting important stages and events and indicating possible behavioural patterns. Application of the framework to the prenegotiation phase of the Canada-United States free trade negotiation will permit the superimposition of these general concepts on the case-specific details. The results will provide a systematic description of the decision processes and behaviour of the two parties during the prenegotiation phase as well as of the pattern

4 Daniel Druckman, 'Stages, turning points, and crises: negotiating military base rights, Spain and the United States,' *Journal of Conflict Resolution* 30(June 1986), 327-60.

of relations between the two as they moved towards formal negotiation.

PRENEGOTIATION STAGES

As indicated above, the prenegotiation phase centres on that period in relations between parties when negotiation is considered, and perhaps adopted, as a behavioural option by some or all of them. We expect the onset of the prenegotiation process to be marked by a turning point in their relations, when negotiation is added to the range of options being considered by one or more of the parties. The occurrence of this initial turning point in relations is best understood through a strategic analysis of the effects of the changing events or conditions on the relative array of outcome values of the parties.[5] As William Zartman notes, the explanatory value of strategic analysis lies in the comparison of decisions to negotiate with decisions not to do so in terms of the restructuring of evaluations of different outcomes by one or more of the parties.[6]

Following from this, the first stage of the prenegotiation process is *problem identification.*[7] As noted, the onset of this stage is brought about by an event or change in conditions that (1) causes a restructuring of the values attached to alternative outcomes by one or more of the parties in a relationship and (2) results in the addition of a negotiated solution to the array of outcomes under consideration by at least one of the parties. The stage is characterized by an assessment of the problem produced by changing events or conditions and a preliminary evaluation of alternative responses that may or may not add

5 F. Zagare, 'A game-theoretic analysis of the Vietnam negotiations,' in I. William Zartman, ed, *The Negotiation Process: Theories and Applications* (Beverly Hills CA: Sage 1978).
6 I. William Zartman, 'Common elements in the analysis of the negotiation process,' *Negotiation Journal* 4(January 1988), 31-43.
7 Saunders suggests ('We need a larger theory of negotiation,' 255) that 'defining the problem' constitutes the first of three stages of the negotiation process that occur before the actual negotiation begins. In Saunders' first stage the parties come to share some common definition of the problem.

negotiation to the range of policy options. If that addition does occur, then a turning point is reached, and the prenegotiation process moves to its second stage.

In the second stage of the prenegotiation phase, the *search for options*, one of the parties has under active consideration a negotiated solution to the policy problem identified in stage one. If the issue underlying the problem has been a long-standing subject of some controversy, then this stage might be characterized as 'thinking the unthinkable' as some or all of the parties attempt to come to terms with the need to negotiate. In this circumstance, the stage may well be a protracted one. In the event that negotiation is chosen as the preferred (or necessary) policy alternative, another turning point in the prenegotiation process is reached.

The third stage of prenegotiation, *commitment to negotiation*, begins the shift from 'whether' to negotiate to 'what' will be negotiated.[8] In this stage, the policy focus is still largely inner-directed as the parties address the question, 'How far will we go?' In the first instance, the answer is likely to reflect a preference for minimal solutions on the part of policy-makers as they attempt to edge incrementally into the implementation of the decision to negotiate. As a result, this stage will be characterized by the consideration of alternative negotiating scenarios, reflecting varying degrees of scope for the potential negotiation, and possibly by successive steps towards increasing commitment to a negotiated solution to the policy problem.

It is in this third stage, however, that the focus of policy-makers also becomes more outer-directed, as the preoccupation with internal decision dynamics gives way to increased concern for the other parties to the policy problem. The Druckman

---

8 Saunders conceives (*ibid*, 257) the second stage in the prenegotiation process as 'producing a commitment to a negotiated settlement.' He assumes that in this stage the parties will make the following judgments: the present situation no longer serves their interests, a fair settlement is possible and attainable, and the other party is likely to come to terms. In my view, only the first of these judgments is likely to be made conclusively in the prenegotiation phase, the others are more likely to await direct negotiation experience.

framework emphasizes the monitoring activity that is undertaken by the negotiating parties, especially when attempting to
define the scope of the negotiation. Monitoring involves determining the interests of various parties, including those of domestic agencies within the principals.[9] This inside focus is
particularly salient in stages one through three of the prenegotiation phase when the primary interest coalitions may have
to be constructed within, rather than between, parties. At some
point in stage three, however, attention will shift to a consideration of the interests of the other parties to the potential
negotiation, particularly because the desire to undertake negotiations (of still undetermined scope) is likely to be communicated to them at this stage.

It is the communication of a desire to negotiate from the
parties on one side of an issue to those on the other that marks
the turning point to stage four in the prenegotiation process,
agreement to negotiate. It is in this stage that the parties must
agree to pursue a negotiated solution to the policy problem that
divides them. Their dominant focus will be outer-directed as
they attempt to come to terms on the desirability of negotiation
as an approach to the problem while reserving any commitment
as to the scope of the negotiation itself. The achievement of an
agreement to negotiate is the turning point marking passage
to the final stage of the prenegotiation process.

As noted earlier, in Druckman's model of negotiation, the
parties engage in complex patterns of mutual responsiveness
to move negotiation through a series of turning points. The
first stage in this model consists of negotiating behaviour whereby
the parties attempt to define the scope of, or agenda for, the
negotiation. This behaviour is defined as structuring activity by
Brian Tracy,[10] in which the parties attempt to establish or alter

9 See Daniel Druckman, 'Boundary role conflict: negotiation as dual responsiveness,' in Zartman, ed, *The Negotiation Process.*
10 Brian Tracy, 'Bargaining as trial and error,' in Zartman, ed, *The Negotiation
Process.*

the parameters within which the exchange and convergence process that characterizes negotiation will occur.

In fact, structuring activity is likely to occur prior to the beginning of formal negotiation, as the parties attempt to position themselves for an advantageous start. It is this activity, intended to influence the scope or agenda of the negotiation, that predominates in the fifth stage of the prenegotiation process, *setting the parameters*. In this stage, the attention of the parties will remain directed outward in an effort to define the initial scope of the proposed negotiation and to attempt to establish the parameters, whether limited or expansive, for the negotiation process to follow. This stage also provides the parties with an important opportunity to assess the extent of congruence in their respective agendas prior to the formal negotiation. Although the parties may not reach agreement on appropriate parameters, their agreement to proceed with formal talks will mean that this final stage of the prenegotiation phase simply merges into the first stage of negotiation proper as formal negotiating sessions begin.

An integrative analysis[11] of the prenegotiation process, using the stages and turning points outlined above, will permit a reconstruction of the sequence of decisions and interactions that lead two or more parties to attempt to negotiate joint solutions on a set of issues. Thus the application of this framework of stages to the prenegotiation phase will provide order and organization to the flow of activities leading up to the formal negotiation.[12] The concept of turning points serves to focus the analysis on the transition from one stage to another in the process. It also guides the search for the events and conditions that facilitate or impede the movement of the parties through and between the stages of the prenegotiation process.

Druckman argues that the movement of the negotiation

11 Zartman, 'Common elements in the analysis of the negotiation process,' 37.
12 Druckman, 'Stages, turning points, and crises.'

process through its various stages is marked by a series of turning points. The achievement of these turning points represents progress from one stage to another, progress that may be impeded by impasse or crisis.[13] Resolution of that impasse or crisis is then necessary before progress to the next stage can occur. This notion can be applied to the stages of the prenegotiation process as well, where deadlock in the policy process (impasse) or intensification of the problem giving rise to the onset of prenegotiation (crisis) may prevent or promote movement through the successive stages towards negotiation. The present analysis, then, will focus on the events and conditions that impeded and promoted progress through the turning points of the five stages of prenegotiation.

THE DECISION TO NEGOTIATE
NORTH AMERICAN FREE TRADE

Druckman suggests that while an agreement to negotiate an issue is less problematic between friendly nations which seek to reinforce and extend their relationship, it is more of a problem when other nations seek to redefine their relationship.[14] For Canada, the decision to negotiate free trade represented a basic redefinition of its relationship with the United States, not only because of the long-standing national debate on the issue but also because of the significant asymmetry between the two countries. For this reason, the analysis of the stages of prenegotiation will place primary emphasis on decision-making in Canada. Although the principal decisions taken by the United States throughout the process will be identified, they will be examined in less detail.

The origins of the formal negotiation that began between Canada and the United States in May of 1986 to establish a free trade arrangement between the two countries may be traced to

---

13 There is considerable ambiguity in Druckman's definitions and discussion of the concepts of turning point, crisis, and impasse. This summary statement of his argument attempts to resolve the ambiguity.
14 Druckman, 'Stages, turning points, and crises,' 333.

the acute bilateral conflict that erupted in 1981 over Canadian energy and investment policies. American plans for retaliatory measures focussed on the Canadian Achilles' heel of trade dependence on the United States, producing a crisis for Canadian policy-makers. In the aftermath of the crisis, it was clear that 1981 marked a significant shift in the evolution of American trade policy, ushering in a period of great uncertainty in Canada-United States trading relations.[15]

It was this acute conflict, and the accompanying crisis for Canadian foreign policy makers, which constituted a turning point for Canada in its relations with the United States, one that led in turn to the onset of the prenegotiation phase of the bilateral free trade negotiations. American threats to the security of Canadian access to a market on which Canada was overwhelmingly dependent, and the profound implications of the threatened actions for employment and investment in Canada, produced a 'dramatic change in Canadian strategic thinking.'[16] These events stimulated a reassessment, on the part of both business and government, of the value to Canada of secure and enhanced access to the United States market, an assessment that took place in the context of the economic recession then developing.

Stage one
The 1981 conflict therefore triggered the first stage of prenegotiation, *problem identification*. What was to become the prenegotiation phase began in a relatively innocuous fashion when the Priorities and Planning Committee of the Canadian cabinet initiated a wide-ranging review of government policies in September 1981. Coming at the peak of the conflict with the United States, the review had as its mandate an evaluation of trade

15 See Stephen Clarkson, *Canada and the Reagan Challenge: Crisis in the Canadian-American relationship* (Toronto: Lorimer 1982), 34-6, 151.
16 Stephen Clarkson, 'Canada-U.S. relations and the changing of the guard in Ottawa,' in Brian W. Tomlin and Maureen Appel Molot, eds, *Canada Among Nations, 1984: A Time of Transition* (Toronto: Lorimer 1985), 153.

policy as well as an assessment of Canadian-American relations. The trade policy review was started in the Department of Industry, Trade and Commerce (ITC), while the concurrent review of the Canada-United States relationship was undertaken within the Department of External Affairs (DEA). In January 1982, however, a major reorganization of the latter department began that would integrate the trade and commerce elements of ITC into External Affairs as a new trade and economic wing, reporting to its own minister of state for international trade. Thus, in the summer of 1982 the trade policy review was shifted to a task force in External Affairs under the management of Derek Burney, assistant under-secretary for trade and economic policy.

By the time this task force had been handed the issue, the 'temporary slowdown' that had been anticipated in the United States economy for 1981 and part of 1982 had blossomed into the most severe recession experienced by the Canadian and American economies since the 1930s. Thus, as the task force conducted its review during 1982, a second crisis, this time in the economy, made it certain that the threat to secure access to the American market for Canadian exports would be defined as the central problem for Canada's trade policy.

It was the recession that marked the onset of the problem identification stage for the United States as well. The decline in trade that accompanied the recession made trade policy a preoccupation for the Reagan administration, and the 'unfair' trade practices of others were identified as the root of the American problem. Protectionist pressures had increased during the 1970s as the United States lost its competitive edge in the world trading system. The recession increased these pressures significantly, prompting a greater willingness on the part of the United States administration to move more aggressively to curb imports. Ironically, the accompanying American disenchantment with multilateralism also led to greater interest in bilateral trade agreements.

The External Affairs task force began its trade policy review in the late summer of 1982 with a series of consultations with representatives of the Canadian business community and with the provincial governments. In these consultations, the task force was repeatedly told that the government must 'get the Canada-United States relationship right': the United States market was fundamentally important to Canadian economic well-being and preservation of that market required stability in the Canada-United States relationship.[17] In particular, the government had to find a means to deal with the contingency protection provisions of United States trade law in order to make secure Canada's principal export market.

The position of Canadian business was put forward most forcibly by the Business Council on National Issues (BCNI), made up of major corporations operating within the Canadian market. During 1982 and 1983 the BCNI was active in advocating free trade negotiations as a means to guarantee access to the United States market.[18] Equally important, however, was the decision of the influential Canadian Manufacturers' Association to reverse its long-standing opposition to free trade with the United States.

In this first stage of the prenegotiation phase, the economic crisis ensured that the problem identified in the Canadian-American relationship was that of secure access to the United States market, and the Canadian business lobby saw to it that the negotiation of some form of trade liberalization arrangement was put forward as an option for consideration by the task force. When the task force added this option to the alter-

17 The concurrent review of the Canada-United States relationship under way in External Affairs was being prepared for the deputy minister for foreign policy, rather than the minister for international trade, and was not based on broad consultations. A similar review in the aftermath of a comparable conflict with the United States in 1971 recommended the adoption of the Third Option, and its basic tenets were reaffirmed in the 1982 review. It was the trade policy review that provided the opening for fundamental change in the bilateral relationship.

18 See Duncan Cameron, 'Introduction,' in Cameron, ed, *The Free Trade Papers* (Toronto: Lorimer 1986); and D. Langille, 'The Business Council on National Issues and the Canadian state,' *Studies in Political Economy* 24(autumn 1987).

natives that it was evaluating, the prenegotiation phase reached the turning point to its second stage.

For the United States, the problem identified was rather different, namely, the unfair trading practices of its major trading partners, a problem made more serious, or visible, by the severity of the recession. Nevertheless, the United States prenegotiation process moved to its second stage when the administration identified bilateralism as one possible approach to the trade liberalization it sought to achieve. The prospect of bilateral trade agreements was advanced as a potential alternative to the multilateral negotiations the Americans were unsuccessfully promoting with their Japanese and European trading partners. The bilateral option was subsequently formalized in a legislative bill authorizing the administration to negotiate bilateral trade liberalization agreements. Although not specifically addressed to Canada, the legislation named only Canada and Israel as prospective parties to such bilateral agreements.

Stage two

In its *search for options*, the External Affairs task force reaffirmed the central importance for Canada of multilateral trading relationships and diverse trading partners. Secondarily, it raised the prospect of pursuing sectoral free trade arrangements with the United States as an additional option for the government to consider. The sectoral option was not without precedents because Canada already had three sectoral free trade arrangements with the United States, covering automotive products, defence materials, and agricultural machinery. Nevertheless, free trade was a sensitive political issue in Canada, and the central place given in the task force report to the continuation of multilateralism in Canadian trade policy eased the task of the new minister for international trade, Gerald Regan, who received the report and saw to its acceptance by cabinet.

With the publication of this report, the first-ever government statement on trade policy and its importance for Canada's economic well-being,[19] the government's willingness to pursue a limited free trade agreement with the United States received widespread public attention. This was partly due to the acuity of Mr Regan who seized on the report's most controversial element as a means to capture public attention while presenting it to a press conference during the news doldrums of August 1983. In this way, sectoral free trade negotiations became the preferred option of the government of Canada. Another turning point in the prenegotiation process was reached when, immediately following the Regan announcement, the United States trade representative, William Brock, endorsed the Canadian proposal.

Stage three
Canada's decision to pursue sectoral free trade, and American willingness to explore the initiative, led the prenegotiation phase into its third stage as the two parties moved towards a *commitment to negotiation*. This stage of the prenegotiation process was protracted, extending from September 1983 to September 1985, as the Canadians edged incrementally into the implementation of the decision to seek negotiations. In February 1984 Regan and Brock agreed on four areas for preliminary discussion on sectoral free trade by officials from the two countries. The Americans had strong reservations about sectoral arrangements, however, preferring to aim for a more comprehensive free trade arrangement.[20] As a result, by June of 1984 little progress had been made in the preliminary discussions, and nothing further had been decided on the question of whether and when to begin formal negotiations.

Following the coming to power of the Conservatives in the September 1984 federal election, Canadian prenegotiation ac-

19 *Canadian Trade Policy for the 1980s: A Discussion Paper* (Ottawa: Department of External Affairs/Supply and Services Canada 1983).
20 According to the deputy United States trade representative, Michael Smith, in 'Sectoral free trade with Canada,' *International Perspectives* (May/June 1984), 17.

tivity turned inward again as the new government assessed the Liberal legacy in this area of policy. Ministers were cautious at the outset. The new minister for international trade, James Kelleher, indicated in a September speech that Canada was prepared to continue discussions with the United States to identify potential areas for action on trade relations between the two countries, but not 'to create fortress North America.'[21] Similarly, the secretary of state for external affairs, Joe Clark, following his first meeting with the United States secretary of state, George Shultz, would do no more than announce the need to study the implications of opening up more products for free trade across the border before entering into any agreements.

There was no doubt, however, that a central element in the foreign policy of the new government would be improved relations with the United States and that market access would be a principal goal. As a result, policy development on the free trade issue continued within External Affairs, again under the direction of Derek Burney, now assistant deputy minister for United States affairs. The sectoral initiative was reassessed, and found wanting, and another trade policy review was undertaken, this one to include comprehensive free trade among the various options to be presented to ministers.

The United States, meanwhile, continued down its own prenegotiation path. During the autumn of 1984, the Senate and House of Representatives passed the bill authorizing trade liberalization negotiations with Canada and Israel. In addition, the Reagan administration asked the United States International Trade Commission to study the likely effects of sectoral free trade with Canada, and the commission subsequently held hearings on the issue, as did the Office of the United States Trade Representative.

Pressures also mounted inside Canada for the new govern-

---

21 James Kelleher, 'Notes for a speech to the 55th annual meeting of the Canadian Chamber of Commerce,' Toronto, 25 September 1984.

ment to pick up the free trade agenda. A substantial lobbying effort was undertaken by Canadian business to solidify support for a comprehensive free trade arrangement, and this position received serious government attention.[22] The negotiation option received perhaps its most substantial boost in November 1984, however, when Donald Macdonald, a former Liberal cabinet minister and chairman of the Royal Commission on Economic Union and Development Prospects for Canada, announced that he favoured free trade between Canada and the United States as the principal long-term solution to Canada's economic problems.[23]

Because the royal commission was bipartisan and seemingly authoritative, the chairman's conversion to comprehensive free trade provided important momentum to the free trade option at a critical juncture in the decision-making process – as the new government was considering its options. This endorsement was followed by a series of government reports and statements that moved the Mulroney cabinet ever closer to a final commitment to negotiation.

The first of these reports was tabled in January 1985.[24] This government discussion paper, while emphasizing the importance of multilateral trade liberalization, confirmed the centrality of the goal of enhanced and secure access to the United States market. To this end, the paper suggested that some form of bilateral trade arrangement should be considered and set out the options available to Canada as follows: the status quo, sectoral arrangements, a comprehensive trade arrangement (the

22 James Kelleher, 'Notes for an address to the Centre for International Business Studies trade conference,' Dalhousie University, Halifax, 1 November 1984.

23 Appointed by the Liberal prime minister, Pierre Elliott Trudeau, in 1982, the Macdonald Commission was examining Canada-United States free trade as part of its study of trade policy. At the time of Macdonald's announcement, however, the commission had neither completed its studies nor framed its conclusions.

24 *How to Secure and Enhance Access to Export Markets* (Ottawa: Department of External Affairs 1985).

Conservative euphemism for free trade), and a bilateral framework to discuss means to improve and enhance trade relations
(a BCNI proposal). Although the paper avoided the identification of a preferred option, it rejected the status quo as inadequate, sectoral arrangements as unattainable, and the BCNI
framework as unnecessary.[25] Clearly the government was edg-
ing down the path to comprehensive free trade negotiations.

Some urgency was lent to this movement by the mounting
tide of United States protectionism in 1984-5. This was reflected
in an increase in the number of investigations of Canadian
export practices under the American countervailing duty process as well as in the introduction of specific congressional legislation that would limit Canadian imports. Not surprisingly,
problems related to trade were at the top of the agenda when
Prime Minister Mulroney and President Reagan arrived in Que-
bec City for their first summit meeting in March 1985. Although
that meeting did not produce an explicit statement of policy by
either government, the leaders did call for an examination of
means for liberalizing trade and directed their respective cabinet officers to explore ways to reduce and eliminate existing
barriers to trade.

Following this joint declaration, the External Affairs task
force proceeded to flesh out the free trade option in preparation
for the presentation of a recommendation to cabinet. In so
doing, it encountered considerable opposition to the initiative
both within its own department and from other departments.
At the same time, Canadian officials were meeting with their
United States counterparts to determine whether there was a
basis for negotiation, and these preliminary soundings suggested that an agenda could be shaped to satisfy the interests
of both countries.

Another step in Canada's incremental movement towards a
commitment to negotiate was played out in the release of the

25 David Leyton-Brown, 'Canada-U.S. relations: towards a closer relationship,' in
   Maureen Appel Molot and Brian W. Tomlin, eds, Canada Among Nations, 1985:
   The Conservative Agenda (Toronto: Lorimer 1986), 182.

government's green paper on foreign policy in May 1985.[26] The paper reaffirmed the goal of enhanced and secure access to the United States market, set out the same options that had been presented in the January discussion paper, and again made the case for a comprehensive agreement by raising doubts about the other options. Green papers are intended to stimulate discussion of new directions in policy, and to achieve this end, Mr Clark chose to have the paper serve as a basis for a review of foreign policy by a special joint committee of the House of Commons and the Senate. In so doing, the minister provided opponents of comprehensive free trade negotiations with a very public forum in which to mount their challenge to the emerging free trade policy.

Opposition members on the special joint committee began their campaign by forcing separate hearings on this issue (along with that of Canadian participation in the United States Strategic Defense Initiative) so that the committee's review could be completed before a decision on negotiation was taken by the government. In its interim report of August 1985,[27] the committee recommended a cautious approach to the trade issue, suggesting that the government begin preliminary discussions with the United States but not move immediately to bilateral negotiations. Instead, the report urged the government to centre these discussions on the resolution of existing trade irritants in order to determine whether a basis for more comprehensive negotiations existed.

The committee's recommendations on trade were overshadowed by the second, more controversial section of the interim report dealing with the Strategic Defense Initiative. In addition, its call for caution was offset a few days later when

26 *Competitiveness and Security: Directions for Canada's International Relations* (Ottawa: Department of External Affairs/Supply and Services Canada 1985).

27 Canada, Parliament, *Minutes of Proceedings and Evidence of the Special Joint Committee of the Senate and of the House of Commons on Canada's International Relations*, 33rd Parl, 1st sess, no 18, 19 August 1985. The final report of the committee was submitted in June 1986: *Independence and Internationalism* (Ottawa: Queen's Printer/Supply and Services Canada 1986).

the report of the Macdonald Commission was released with its recommendation of free trade with the United States.[28] The report of the royal commission had been in the hands of the prime minister earlier in the summer, and shortly after its release, in reply to a question in the House of Commons on 9 September 1985, Mr Mulroney indicated that the government had decided to pursue 'freer' trade with the United States. On 26 September, the prime minister told the Commons that he had telephoned President Reagan to ask him to explore with Congress Canada's interest in pursuing negotiations to reduce tariffs and non-tariff barriers between the two countries.[29] This call, and the formal written proposal that followed on 1 October, finally signalled Canada's commitment to negotiation, the turning point to the next stage in the prenegotiation phase.

Stage four
The Canadian commitment to negotiation on free trade led the prenegotiation phase into its fourth stage as the two parties sought the basis for an *agreement to negotiate*. This stage lasted more than six months and centred largely on events in the United States as various elements in the American system of divided powers took up the issue. Although the formal response to the prime minister's proposal from President Reagan was favourable, some administration officials viewed the Canadian initiative as inopportune in light of the protectionist mood in Congress and a new offensive against unfair trade practices just announced by the administration. As a result of the ensuing internal United States debate over proper timing, movement on the initiative was postponed, and it was not until 10 Decem-

28 Royal Commission on the Economic Union and Development Prospects for Canada (Macdonald Commission), *Report* (3 vols; Ottawa: Supply and Services Canada 1985).
29 On this day as well, Mr Kelleher presented yet another report on trade relations, prepared in the aftermath of the March summit. The report recommended exploratory bilateral negotiations on the scope and prospects for a new trade agreement.

ber 1985 that President Reagan notified Congress of his administration's desire to begin the negotiations.[30]

No objection was raised by the Ways and Means Committee of the House of Representatives, but the prospects for an agreement to negotiate faced a serious challenge in the Senate Finance Committee. On 11 April 1986 a majority of the members of that committee announced their readiness to veto the start of the negotiations. This opposition was partly a result of congressional frustration with the overall trade policies of the Reagan administration, but it stemmed as well from the spate of unresolved complaints about unfair trading practices on the part of Canadians, especially with respect to softwood lumber. Two of the leading opponents of the negotiations on the committee were Senators Packwood (the chairman) and Baucus from Oregon and Montana, respectively, two of the largest lumber-producing states. Only intense pressure from the administration, prompted by Canadian insistence that the initiative could not be delayed or allowed to die, and a letter from Reagan to Packwood setting out the specific goals for the negotiation headed off the veto.[31] On 23 April, a motion requiring the resubmission at a later date of the request for authorization of the negotiation failed by a 10-10 vote. The threat to the talks passed, marking a turning point to the next and final stage of prenegotiation.

Stage five
Executive approval and congressional authorization in the United States led the prenegotiation phase into its fifth stage as the two parties focussed their attention on *setting the parameters* for the forthcoming negotiation. The line of demarcation between the last two stages of the prenegotiation process is not as clear-cut

30 Notification of Congress was required in order for the negotiations to be handled under the so-called 'fast track' of accelerated implementing authority.
31 See David Leyton-Brown, 'The political economy of Canada-U.S. relations,' in Brian W. Tomlin and Maureen Appel Molot, eds, *Canada Among Nations, 1986: Talking Trade* (Toronto: Lorimer 1987), 153.

as with previous stages, however. The prospect of an agreement to negotiate is likely to touch off structuring activities in anticipation of such agreement.

For Canada, this prospect emerged after the government's decision in late summer 1985 to pursue negotiations and led to Canadian efforts to reserve certain issues as exclusions from the negotiating agenda. Thus, in an interview on 14 September, Brian Mulroney began the Canadian campaign to limit the scope of the negotiations, indicating that issues such as the Strategic Defense Initiative and Arctic sovereignty would not be on the table. Although the prime minister's aim may have been to reassure his domestic constituency, the statement marked the beginning of the Canadian transition to the structuring activity that predominates in stage five of the prenegotiation process. At the end of September 1985, Joe Clark announced Canada's intention to exclude the 1965 Automotive Agreement (auto pact) from the negotiations. Subsequently, he indicated that Canada would not negotiate its subsidies to cultural industries, a position that was reiterated by the prime minister before an American audience in December.

Following President Reagan's notification of Congress in December 1985, American structuring activity began in earnest as well and concentrated on refuting the exclusions stipulated by Canada. The United States trade representative, Clayton Yeutter, indicated that everything should be subject to negotiation in the talks requested by the president including the auto pact and cultural industries. To do otherwise, he claimed, would threaten the success of the negotiations. The same argument was presented subsequently by the United States ambassador to Canada, Thomas Niles, as well as by the chief negotiator, Peter Murphy, the latter adding social programmes to the list of items that had to be on the table.

Congressional approval of the negotiations in April 1986 produced more detailed statements of appropriate parameters from both parties. In his letter to the Senate Finance Committee, President Reagan identified clearly the goals that the United

States would pursue in the negotiations with Canada. Principal among these was the reduction by Canada of government subsidies and support to industry. In addition, Reagan indicated that the United States would retain 'full access to multilaterally sanctioned trade remedies,' that is, the contingency protection provisions of United States trade law that threatened the security of Canadian access to the United States market.

Canada's minister for international trade, in announcing the date for the first round of negotiations a few days later, set out Canadian priorities. These would include a reduction in American tariffs as well as greater access to government procurement markets in the United States. Mr Kelleher indicated that Canada would also be seeking relief from trade penalties imposed under the contingency protection provisions of United States trade law. In return, he speculated that the Americans would be seeking concessions on trade in services and on protection for intellectual property.

Services and intellectual property had indeed been items on the United States agenda as early as the previous summer when Canadian officials took preliminary soundings in Washington to determine whether an agenda could be shaped to satisfy the interests of both countries. However, national treatment and right of establishment for investment were also American priorities although the minister chose not 'to include them in his speculations. Those same Washington consultations in the summer of 1985 had offered a potential link between American movement on United States contingency protection measures and Canadian subsidy practices, a link apparently precluded in the Reagan letter to Packwood.

The differences in the perceptions of the two parties of what would constitute appropriate parameters for the negotiation were not resolved prior to the conclusion of the prenegotiation phase on 21 May 1986, when the formal negotiation began in Ottawa. However, the important differences in the agendas of the two countries that were revealed in their efforts to influence negotiating parameters would subsequently emerge as significant impediments in the negotiation process itself. For the United States, the focus of the negotiations would be agreement on the need to eliminate Canadian industrial and regional subsidy practices. For Canada, the negotiations centred on the need for a new régime on American contingency protection, one that would remove the threat to Canadian exports resulting from existing United States trade remedy laws. Because the two parties were unable to resolve these fundamentally different views of the nature of the problem to be addressed, their efforts to influence the definition of the initial scope of the negotiation simply merged into the formal talks, bringing the prenegotiation phase to an end.

DISCUSSION AND CONCLUSION

The fundamental shift in the Canada-United States relationship that originated in the acute bilateral conflict of 1981 and was shaped by the severe recession in 1982 marked the beginning of a process that would lead ultimately to the conclusion of the free trade agreement of October 1987. The process that led up to the opening of formal negotiation in May 1986 went through several distinct stages. The passage of the two countries through and between the stages was marked by a series of crises and stalemates that, once resolved, became turning points in the prenegotiation phase.

In the problem identification stage, the crisis generated for Canada by the severe recession had a major impact on the identification of secure access to the American market as the central problem of trade policy as well as on the definition of alternative approaches to the problem. Similarly, the recession produced a major problem for American trade policy, but one identified with the export practices of others.

When the option of sectoral free trade was put to the Canadian government in stage two, the reaction of business to the economic crisis was significant in the decision to explore the prospects for sectoral negotiations. For the United States, it was the dim prospects for multilateral solutions that made a bilateral agreement attractive. The subsequent impasse in the sectoral discussions resulted in a shift to a consideration of more comprehensive arrangements, a shift promoted in Canada by a strong business lobby and moved along incrementally by a steady stream of reports prepared for the government suggesting that few other options were available.

While this third stage of the prenegotiation process was characterized by incremental movement towards negotiation, the turning point occurred when the report of an independent royal commission provided a way out of incrementalism for the Canadian government by putting its stamp of approval on free trade. There was no easy passage to an agreement to negotiate, however, as delay on the part of the United States administration and the prospect of a Senate committee veto threatened the talks. The resolution of this threat to the achievement of an agreement to negotiate marked the passage of the prenegotiation process to a final turning point. In this last stage, the two parties shifted their attention to the scope of the prospective negotiation.

The onset of the prenegotiation phase of the Canada-United States negotiating process was triggered by a bilateral conflict and shaped fundamentally by a severe economic recession. These common origins gave rise to the identification of quite different definitions of the central trade policy problem facing each country, however, and these differences in perspective would subsequently be reflected in the negotiations. For Canada, the central problem was the use of the contingency protection measures available to American companies under United States trade remedy law to harass Canadian exporters. For the United States the problems confronting American trade resulted from the unfair trading practices of other countries, including Canada.

From these different formulations of the problem flowed sharply divergent agendas for the negotiations. For the United States, the problem of unfair trading practices could be addressed in a negotiation focussing on the elimination of (Canadian) subsidies. For Canada, however, subsidy practices were not so much trade-related as aspects of cultural and regional development policies. The Canadian agenda focussed instead on the elimination of the means of harassment through the amendment of United States contingency protectionist measures as these applied to Canadians. United States trade law, however, was increasingly the preserve of a protectionist Congress that would resist such amendments to domestic legislation. These important differences in the agendas of the two countries were revealed in their efforts to influence the parameters of the forthcoming negotiations. Their inability to resolve the differences would subsequently lead to a lengthy impasse in the negotiation process itself, one that would only be resolved at the eleventh hour through the intervention of senior policy-makers in each country.

This divergence in agendas is attributable not only to the different ways in which the two countries defined the trade problem confronting them, but also to the way in which the prenegotiation process itself evolved. On the Canadian side, the decision to negotiate a comprehensive free trade agreement emerged incrementally as a trade policy response to ascendant United States protectionism. Given the political sensitivity of the issue, this movement had to be incremental and could only be sustained by emphasizing the goal of securing market access for Canadian exports. This emphasis was directed to the domestic decision-making process, however. It was only following the achievement of an agreement to negotiate in stage four of the prenegotiation phase that Canadian efforts were directed to narrowing the agenda for the forthcoming negotiations.

For their part, the Americans were content to follow the Canadian lead for much of the prenegotiation process, emphasizing only their general commitment to trade liberalization. As the prenegotiation stages were passed, however, congressional imperatives dictated that a greater role be assigned to fair – as opposed to free – trade in the formulation of the American agenda. In the final stage before the start of negotiations, United States officials insisted that everything be on the negotiating agenda, especially domestic subsidies.

These efforts at agenda setting were too little and too late to avoid the deadlock that would impede the negotiations. Preoccupied as they were with the internal decision-making process, Canadian officials turned their attention only late in the prenegotiation phase to the need to define a common negotiating agenda. Preoccupied with other issues entirely, the Americans apparently had little in the way of an agenda in mind, beyond the specific trade irritants that raised congressional ire and a determination to deny the Canadian exclusions. Ironically, it may well have been the failure of the two countries to address a prospective negotiating agenda in detail until late in the stages of prenegotiation that enabled them to begin formal negotiation. Earlier discovery of the degree of divergence in their respective agendas might have been sufficient to prevent the achievement of important turning points in the prenegotiation process.

In his analysis of the free trade initiative, William Watson argues that it 'does not make sense as a rational act of policy, and that the government has simply stumbled into it, more or less unwittingly.'[32] The present reconstruction of the prenegotiation process makes it clear that, while passage through the stages was not foreordained, neither was it haphazard, for either country. Movement towards negotiation could have come to a halt at a number of points along the way, but specific events and conditions resulted in the turning points being reached for movement to the next stage. Prenegotiation was a distinct phase in the relations leading up to the negotiation between these two countries to restructure their relationship, one which carried important consequences for the negotiation that followed.

32 William Watson, 'Canada-US free trade: why now?' *Canadian Public Policy* 13(September 1987), 346.

3. *The Prenegotiation Phase of the Uruguay Round*

GILBERT R. WINHAM

On 20 September 1986, at a special session held in Punta del Este, Uruguay, the contracting parties of the General Agreement on Tariffs and Trade (GATT) adopted a declaration that launched the eighth round of multilateral trade negotiations since the organization was formed in 1947. Known as the Uruguay Round, this undertaking promises to be the most complex and ambitious negotiation yet attempted by the ninety-two members of the GATT.

The path to the Uruguay Declaration was tortuous. The previous GATT multilateral negotiation (the Tokyo Round), concluded in 1979, had made considerable progress in reducing protectionism from non-tariff barriers. Pressure began to build shortly after 1979 to expand the GATT régime to include 'new' issues like services and investment in addition to the 'old' issues which dealt with trade in goods. The United States was particularly insistent on a new negotiation, and in 1982 a GATT ministerial meeting was convened to consider this possibility. The idea met sharp resistance, particularly from developing countries. The 1982 ministerial meeting was a failure for the pro-

Professor of Political Science, Dalhousie University, Halifax, Nova Scotia; author of, inter alia, *International Trade and the Tokyo Round Negotiation* (1986) and *Trading with Canada: the Canada-U.S. Free Trade Agreement* (1988).

Data for this paper were taken from about 15 personal interviews with GATT officials and national delegates, and from the working documents of the GATT Senior Officials Group and the Uruguay Round Preparatory Committee. The documents are restricted and cannot be cited, and interviewees were guaranteed anonymity. I have made every attempt to represent accurately the information obtained from these sources.

ponents of a new negotiation, although it did establish important (and controversial) work programmes within the GATT bureaucracy on services and on agriculture.

Pressure for a new negotiation continued to mount after 1982 as the United States gained the support of other developed countries as well as some key developing countries. The prospects for a new negotiation were debated in regularly scheduled meetings of the GATT Council. In October 1985, a Senior Officials Group (SOG) was established with the purpose of reconciling the conflicting views of members towards a new negotiation. A Preparatory Committee (PREPCOM) was constituted in January 1986 and continued its work through to August 1986. At every step during the long process from 1980 to 1986, the movement towards a new negotiation was organizationally complex, technically difficult, and politically controversial. The agreement at Punta del Este to begin a new negotiation was reached at the eleventh hour, and most observers (including seasoned GATT officials) were surprised that the effort did not end in collapse.

The entire movement towards the Uruguay Declaration falls within the definition of a 'prenegotiation' process; that is, everything from the conclusion of the Tokyo Round in 1979 to the Uruguay Declaration constitutes 'prenegotiation.' For the purposes of this volume, the prenegotiation process is defined as beginning when one or more parties considers negotiation as a policy option and communicates this intention to other parties. It ends when the parties agree to formal negotiations or when one party abandons the consideration of negotiation as a policy option. Prenegotiation consists largely in identifying common interests that parties might share and in removing political obstacles that prevent the parties from taking action on those common interests through negotiation.[1]

Much of the thought about prenegotiation has arisen in the

---

1 Harold H. Saunders, 'We need a larger theory of negotiation: the importance of pre-negotiating phases,' *Negotiation Journal* 1 (July 1985), 249-62.

context of the Middle East, where the main problem has been to get the parties to talk to each other and to resolve problems through negotiation rather than through warfare. In theoretical terms, if negotiation can be seen to be a mixture of conflictual and co-operative behaviours, the task has been to expand the co-operative as opposed to the conflictual elements of the relationship sufficiently to begin a more formal exchange of proposals on how to manage that relationship in the future. Negotiations in the Middle East deal largely with security issues, and they are more or less bilateral.

The negotiation dealt with in this article is multilateral and economic. One major difference between these two cases is that the subject matter of the Uruguay Round is less important to the national interests of the parties, and there are more points of view represented at the negotiating table. A second difference (especially regarding the prenegotiation phase) is that the parties to the Uruguay Round conduct economic negotiations frequently and hence there was little psychological resistance to starting a new negotiation. The main issues that characterized the difficult prenegotiation phase of the Uruguay Round were: which subjects would be negotiated, and in what order; which parties would be called upon to negotiate those subjects; how the negotiations would be structured, and with what implications for probable later trade-offs; and within which forum (for example, the GATT versus the United Nations Conference on Trade and Development) certain subjects would be negotiated.

At first glance, the negotiating situation in the Middle East could not appear to be more different from that of the Uruguay Round. The former seems unstructured, psychological, and politicized, while the latter is institutional, businesslike, and technical. What is interesting, however, is that some elements of the prenegotiation process appear to be quite similar in both situations. For example, in both instances parties are concerned with how the negotiating situation will be defined and about what values, or assumptions, will be built into the negotiation process. These similarities make it possible to talk generally about a prenegotiation phase in otherwise dissimilar negotiations.

WHY DID PRENEGOTIATION BEGIN
IN THE URUGUAY ROUND?

A first important question about the prenegotiation phase in the Uruguay Round is why it occurred at all, and what the factors were that brought it about. Because negotiation is usually thought of as a specialized form of behaviour designed to resolve a particular problem, rather than an ordinary form of constant behaviour, it seems plausible to assume that prenegotiation will occur in response to a fundamental shift in the relationship between the parties seeking the negotiation, or to some change in the political environment.[2] Furthermore, it seems likely this shift or change may have been sufficiently dramatic for the parties so as to cause a crisis, for which a negotiation could then been seen as a preferred alternative to other more harmful responses that the parties might undertake.

In examining prenegotiation in the Uruguay Round, it should be noted that the Uruguay Round is a GATT negotiation and that negotiation is a continuous process in that organization. GATT negotiation is not unlike legislative behaviour, and the results can be viewed as a type of 'international legislation.' The GATT is thus a specialized form of international negotiation, and in comparison to some security negotiations or to negotiations in the Middle East, GATT negotiations would appear to be a modal rather than an exceptional form of behaviour. As a result, it is less likely that negotiations would occur as a result of great changes or crises in the parties' relationships.

The answer to why prenegotiation began in the Uruguay Round is to be found at different levels. At the most general level, it is frequently argued that any negotiation in the GATT is an attempt to forestall, and then to reduce, protectionist measures in the member-countries. From this perspective, the Uruguay Round would be no different from any other GATT negotiation; nor in fact would the reason behind the Uruguay Round negotiation be any different from that behind the *pre-*

---

2 I. William Zartman and Maureen R. Berman, *The Practical Negotiator* (New Haven CT: Yale University Press 1982), 50-7.

negotiation to the Uruguay Round. The argument is often expressed in terms of the so-called bicycle theory: unless the GATT
sustains the momentum in the fight to maintain a liberal trade
régime, this régime will collapse as nations take unilateral actions to protect their producers from foreign competition. Negotiation is therefore perceived as an antidote to protectionism,
and by and large the history of trade relations has supported
this perception. However, in case it is assumed that the connection between negotiation and liberal (or internationalist) outcomes is an obvious one, an interesting comparison can be made
between GATT negotiations and recent strategic arms control
negotiations.[3] Whereas the former have generally promoted a
reduction of nationalistic behaviour in the economic sphere,
the latter have been consistent with nationalistic competition in
strategic arms and, indeed, may have even promoted certain
aspects of the arms race. One reason then for the Uruguay
Round is that nations felt it necessary to mount a major effort
to promote trade liberalization in the 1980s, just as had been
done at regular intervals over the past four decades.

A more immediate reason for the Uruguay Round prenegotiation was the pressure exerted by the United States administration. Since the conclusion of the Tokyo Round in 1979, the
United States had pressed for a new negotiation to make progress on old issues left from the Tokyo Round, such as protection
in agricultural products, and to begin the process of bringing
new areas like trade in services within GATT's discipline. On
both these issues the United States initiative was an exercise in
economic national interest. The United States is a major agricultural exporter, and recently its economy has become more
dependent on the production of services than of goods. The
pressure from the United States led to the GATT ministerial
meeting of 1982 which fell far short of achieving general political agreement, but which nevertheless succeeded in taking

3 Thomas C. Schelling, 'What went wrong with arms control?' *Foreign Affairs*
64(winter 1985/6).

bureaucratic action by establishing work programmes for services and agriculture in the GATT secretariat. Continued pressure after 1982 gradually secured the support of the European Community (EC) for a new negotiation. Again, this occurred through a process whereby the Europeans recognized that services were important to their own economies and that a need existed for reform in the agricultural régime of the EC to which a new negotiation might be able to contribute.

Another motivation for the pressure from the United States administration for a new negotiation was a concern over potential actions in Congress. Since the Tokyo Round, the United States has run a trade deficit of historic proportions which has led to a sharpening of protectionist sentiment throughout the country. This mood is reflected in Congress, and there has been a growing fear that Congress would force unilateral protectionist action on the administration through strongly worded and uncompromising trade legislation. The Reagan administration sought to forestall congressional action, and as other administrations have done in the past, it used the promise of a new multilateral negotiation to buy time.

One factor which appeared to motivate all countries during the prenegotiation phase of the Uruguay Round was a concern over the role of the GATT in international trade. The GATT is a legal contract and around this contract has been established a commercial régime based on non-discrimination and liberalized trade. All GATT members share some interest in maintaining this régime, but the régime has been threatened in recent years by a series of extra-legal actions (such as 'voluntary' restraint agreements) taken by member-governments. Today it is estimated that upwards of 40 to 50 per cent of total world trade probably occurs outside GATT disciplines, and if this erosion is not stemmed, the GATT will cease to be a meaningful régime in the international economy. In any GATT negotiation, it is always possible to hear pious references to the need to support the régime, but in the prenegotiation phase of the Uruguay Round these statements were especially frequent in meetings of the SOG and the PREPCOM. Taken together, they appeared to represent a genuine desire on the part of member-nations to embark on a new negotiation to revitalize a threatened trade régime in which all countries had an interest.

In any GATT prenegotiation period, it can be assumed that not all countries will support a new negotiation. Movement towards negotiation necessarily involves the exercise of persuasion, particularly in motivating the uncommitted or those opposed to the decision to begin the negotiation. Such an exercise is a delicate affair in the GATT because the organization traditionally moves on consensus (which theoretically gives veto power to any member or small group of members), and only in extreme situations will it call for a vote. In the Uruguay Round prenegotiation, the call for a new negotiation was strongly resisted by a group of developing countries led by India and Brazil, two of the most influential such countries in the GATT. The developing countries took the position that they were not sufficiently developed to negotiate the new issues like services on an equal footing with the developed countries, and they therefore insisted that the services issue not be included on any negotiating agenda. Additionally, the developing countries held that the developed countries had evaded their obligations in some areas of traditional goods such as textiles or agricultural products, which were of particular interest to developing countries, and they demanded (through the principles of 'standstill' and 'rollback') further liberalization in these areas as a precondition to any new negotiation. This debate occupied about four years, during which India and Brazil gradually lost the support of all but a handful of developing countries. In the end the Uruguay Round prenegotiation concluded with a consensus decision to start a new negotiation, which was a convincing demonstration that the power of the majority would be served. Throughout this long debate some argued in favour of forcing the issue through a vote in the Council, although this action undoubtedly would have had serious consequences for relations between developing and developed countries and for the GATT as an international organization.

The issues which had been simmering for four years were played out again in a six-day special session of the GATT contracting parties at Punta del Este, Uruguay, in 1986. Despite the enormous amount of preparatory work, it was wholly unclear whether sufficient agreement existed for the parties to draft a declaration that would be both widely acceptable and yet concrete enough to underpin a new negotiation. Strong although not widespread opposition continued to come from the developing countries, and the French complicated the EC position by entering reservations on the negotiation of agriculture. The factors that salvaged the new negotiation were strong leadership and organization of the Punta del Este meeting, and the knowledge that a failure to negotiate would have left the GATT without any programme for the immediate future. Delegates to the Punta del Este meeting commented that the fear of renewed protectionism (especially in the United States) finally seemed to have had an impact on all national delegations, and a certain fear of the 'long shadow of the future' promoted a willingness to seize on negotiation as a way of avoiding that future.

To sum up, the explanation of the Uruguay Round prenegotiation is a mixture of business as usual, opportunity, and crisis avoidance. First, the decision to negotiate the Uruguay Round was taken in an organization in which formal multilateral negotiation is a normal, but not exclusive, means of conducting business. There is a natural proclivity towards negotiation in this régime which tends to ensure that any major problems facing the organization will sooner or later produce a call for negotiation. Second, many countries saw a new negotiation as an opportunity to address issues that are inadequately covered under existing international trade rules. While these nations tended to be the developed countries, even many of the developing countries which initially resisted the negotiation came to use the new negotiation as a means to force their own concerns onto the GATT agenda. Finally, a pervasive sense of impending disaster and lack of alternatives pushed even those countries whose interests opposed the negotiation into the ranks of its supporters. While this final reason may not have been the most important cause, it was nevertheless the most proximate cause, and it help to ensure that a negotiation would be conducted immediately rather than further delayed.

WHAT ARE THE CHARACTERISTICS OF THE PRENEGOTIATION PHASE?

There is reason to believe that prenegotiation has different characteristics from negotiation. Prenegotiation is a preparatory process, and it is expected to generate wide-ranging discussion as parties attempt to single out those issues to be included in the negotiation. One expects a narrowing of focus as the negotiation begins, especially as the parties move towards the basic trade-offs from which they will construct an agreement. The negotiation phase is therefore expected to be more focussed and concrete; by comparison, the prenegotiation phase is seen as more uncertain and diffuse.

In GATT negotiations, the evidence both supports and contradicts this description of prenegotiation. In the Tokyo Round, for example, nations began the negotiation without much understanding of non-tariff measures (NTMs), which were to be its main focus. To get a handle on these measures, the parties adopted a notification process during the prenegotiation phase in which any party feeling itself injured by another country's measures could identify those measures and have them included in a GATT NTM inventory.[4] This process produced an enormous amount of information, which was then gradually structured into negotiable categories, from which the Tokyo Round codes eventually evolved. This entire process would seem to reflect the description of prenegotiation. Once the Tokyo Round was engaged, however, a negotiating momentum was achieved which tended to broaden debate between the parties, and even to sweep up new issues late in the negotiation, such as government procurement or trade in civil aircraft. This ten-

4 Gilbert R. Winham, *International Trade and the Tokyo Round Negotiation* (Princeton NJ: Princeton University Press 1986), 2.

dency of the Tokyo Round to 'snowball' is contrary to the view that negotiations become more focussed as they pass from the prenegotiation phase to the formal negotiation; and it suggests instead that in some cases the negotiation process may have a capacity to generate broader discussion rather than the reverse.

The Uruguay Round (with some exceptions) seems to be less a discovery of new problems than a renewed willingness to tackle old ones like agricultural barriers which have been around for a long time. New ground is admittedly being broken in the areas of intellectual property, investment, and, especially, services which are the subject of a major work programme in the secretariat. But the remaining issues before the Uruguay Round are not really new; if there is anything different now, it is more in the attitudes of the parties than in the issues themselves, and particularly the importance the developing countries have assumed in the negotiation of traditional GATT concerns. As a result of the stability of issues the prenegotiation phase in the Uruguay Round tended to resemble very much the negotiation itself. The current negotiation (since 1986) is more organized in bureaucratic terms than was the prenegotiation (1979-86), but other than that there has been relatively little change in the issues or in the positions nations take on those issues.

In any large multilateral negotiation the problem in establishing co-operation tends to come from two sources: one is the number of parties to the negotiation and the other is the number and complexity of issues that those parties manage to bring forward. Regarding the first, the problem of numbers of parties can be expressed in terms of the negotiating relationships that occur with multiple parties. In a bilateral negotiation there is one relationship; but in a multilateral negotiation the number of relationships expands rapidly. If a multilateral negotiation is to achieve any direction at all, it has to be structured through some mechanism, and the most likely mechanism for this is political power. The more uncertain the situation, as in the prenegotiation phase, the more likely political power is to be a factor.

In the Tokyo Round, power came to be exercised in the

negotiation through a pyramidal structure whereby issues tended to be first negotiated between the United States and the EC; and once a tentative trade-off was established the negotiation process was progressively expanded to include other countries. In this way co-operation between the United States and the EC served to direct the negotiation. Where co-operation was not forthcoming between these economic 'superpowers,' the negotiation went nowhere because they had effective veto power; and when the two did agree, only the combined efforts of other parties (usually the developing countries) had any real prospect of altering the outcome.

In the Uruguay Round prenegotiation, a similar kind of power was exercised by these superpowers in defining the agenda for a new negotiation. This brought forth an extraordinary effort on the part of the developing countries to maintain their cohesion on issues like the consideration of services, which they resisted, and issues like textiles quotas, which they sought to include. However, because power is persuasive (which is one definition of power), the resistance to the negotiation gradually crumbled, and in the end the main surprise was that the resistance had been as effective and as long-lasting as it turned out to be. In summing up the prenegotiation period, one official described it as a 'brutal but salutary demonstration that power would be served, in that nations comprising 5 per cent of world trade were not able to stop a negotiation sought by nations comprising 95 per cent of world trade.'[5]

A second source of complexity in multilateral negotiation comes from the issues. The process of structuring issues in the Tokyo Round was done through the inventory of non-tariff measures already described. In the Uruguay Round the process was not as formal, but there nevertheless was an exhaustive enumeration and discussion of the different potential agenda items in the meetings of the SOG and the PREPCOM. The culmination of this process was the Uruguay Declaration itself, which identified the issues and negotiating structures (that is,

5 Personal interview.

negotiating committees, work programmes, etc) for the subsequent negotiation.

One important question about the definition of agenda items
is whether the definition is technical or political. In a technical
organization like the GATT, the answer to this question is that
negotiating issues (that is, sundry trade restrictions) are nor-
mally defined in technical terms, which deal with matters like
the nature and types of trade restrictions, their effects on world
trade, and the manner of their application. However, it is well
known that defining even technical issues can be a political
action, particularly if that definition implies obligations on the
part of one party to another. For example, countervailing duties
can be viewed as contingency protectionism or responses to
foreign unfair trading practices, depending on the viewpoint
of the observer. In the Uruguay Round prenegotiation most
issues were handled in a technical manner, although this was
not at all the case with services. As noted earlier, certain developing countries did not want services negotiated, and one
of the tactics they pursued was to define services as outside the
competence of the GATT. This position was pursued so force-
fully that for a period of about one year the secretariat was
prohibited from holding meetings on services or from otherwise
gathering information that could be used to promote negotiation in this area. The controversy on services continued right
into the drafting of the Uruguay Declaration, and the special
session at Punta del Este set up an entirely separate negotiating
structure for services independent of the negotiation on goods.
The separate structure allows developing countries to make the
argument that services have not been defined as part of the
GATT; and it may reduce the prospects that developed countries
will ask developing countries for concessions in services in return for concessions on goods, a trade-off that the developing
countries were particularly anxious to avoid. In any event, the
separate services negotiation stands as a testimonial to the poli-
ticization of the GATT agenda in the context of an otherwise
businesslike and technical negotiation.

Another aspect to be examined in the prenegotiation phase

of the negotiation process is constituency involvement, or the impact of domestic coalitions on the external negotiation. In most negotiations, constituency involvement becomes particularly intense at the end of the process when major decisions are made about whether to accept or reject the terms available to the parties. Constituents are also engaged heavily at the beginning of a negotiation because it is usually necessary for parties to get their opening offers approved through some domestic process that can marshal constituency opinion and even provide approval. The exact amount of constituency influence probably varies a great deal in negotiation and will depend on the nature of the parties, on the issues themselves, and even on the strategies pursued by the parties. For example, it is well understood that parties with democratic governments will have more constituency involvement in external negotiations than those with authoritarian régimes; and one can expect some issues like monetary relations to involve constituents much less than do other issues like trade relations. As for the effect of strategy on constituency involvement, one can compare the strategies pursued by the United States and the European Community in the negotiations over tariff reductions in the Tokyo Round. The United States chose to make a high initial offer, which necessitated taking the heat from constituents early in the negotiation, but then left the United States delegation with a relatively free hand to conclude an agreement. The EC however made a lower initial offer, which made for easier constituency relations at the outset, but then produced more difficult relations at the end of the negotiation when the Community sought to improve its concessions to its trading partners.

In keeping with this analysis, one would expect constituency involvement to occur during the prenegotiation phase. The intensity of this involvement would likely depend on the extent to which real commitments were made in the prenegotiation phase and on how much of a change in the status quo the negotiation represented for the parties. In the Uruguay Round prenegotiation one might have expected considerable constituency influence on the more controversial issues, which would have included services, investment, and agricultural restrictions. In fact, there was relatively little such involvement in the United States, the nation most insistent on a new negotiation, and there was correspondingly little involvement by constituency groups in other countries as well.

The prenegotiation phase of the Uruguay Round was very much an external exercise; indeed, one of the main problems on the United States side was to motivate an internal constituency in the services area in order to give its demand that services be included in a new negotiation greater credibility. One indication of this lack of involvement of the services sector in the Uruguay Round prenegotiation is that when services were later discussed in the Canada-United States bilateral free trade negotiation, it became obvious that the services industries in the United States did not all speak with the same voice with respect to the liberalization of this trade sector. Nor is the United States experience an isolated one, for there is also evidence that the government of Brazil (which did not want negotiation on services) was out of touch with certain industries in its own informatics sector which were far more supportive of such a negotiation. Thus, domestic constituencies and coalitions did not seem to play as large a role in the Uruguay Round prenegotiation as they did throughout the negotiation phase in the Tokyo Round. Furthermore, in keeping with this observation, there also seemed to be few attempts by parties to the Uruguay Round prenegotiation to influence directly the domestic constituencies of other parties.

To sum up, it is clear that the prenegotiation phase in the Uruguay Round generally resembled the process of negotiation that followed from it. In terms of process alone, it is doubtful that an uninformed observer could have distinguished one phase from the other, although it is possible that the absence of constituency involvement in the prenegotiation phase might have constituted an important procedural difference. In terms of substance, however, there do appear to be some important differences, mainly that prenegotiation appears to be a more generalized and less bureaucratized discussion than negotiation itself. Furthermore, prenegotiation does seem to set parameters and a framework for subsequent interaction. The Uruguay Round prenegotiation defined the substance for the negotiation, and parties now at the Uruguay Round are taking up in an orderly fashion the subjects defined and organized by the Uruguay Declaration. While new substance may well be added as the negotiation goes along, it is certain that the prenegotiation defined almost completely the tasks for the first two years of negotiation.

EXPLANATION OF THE OUTCOME OF PRENEGOTIATION

The most dramatic part of the Uruguay Round prenegotiation came in the week-long special session at Punta del Este in September 1986. This meeting, which produced the Uruguay Declaration, was a make-or-break session for the overall negotiation. It was a microcosm of the prenegotiation process, for in a space of less than seven days the meeting accurately reflected the problems that had dogged the prenegotiation for seven years. The meeting was conflictual, and the pressure was intense. There was no assurance of agreement. As one GATT interviewee, who obviously supported a new negotiation, put it: 'Anyone who thought that this was not a real victory just doesn't know what could have happened.'[6]

Multilateral meetings like the Punta del Este session usually begin with an agreed negotiating text which, in turn, is a result of previous negotiation. As an indicator of the discord in the process of prenegotiation of the Uruguay Round, the special session began with three texts, which left the session's chairman – Enrique Iglesias, the minister of foreign affairs of Uruguay – in some uncertainty as to how to proceed. The main text (known in GATT classification terminology as w/40/rev.1) came forward from the preparatory committee and was spon-

6 Personal interview.

sored by a group of 40 developed and developing countries chaired by Colombia and Switzerland (G-40).[7] The second text represented the views of a group of 10 developing countries (G-10) which followed the lead of India and Brazil in opposing the negotiation. A third text was submitted by Argentina.

The main contention was between the first two texts and resulted from the resistance of some developing countries to expanding the GATT agenda to include new issues like services, investment, and intellectual property. The United States was absolutely insistent that any future negotiation should include these issues and declared it was ready to withdraw entirely over this matter. The United States was strengthened by a growing consensus behind its position and a corresponding erosion of support for the Brazilian/Indian position. However, the United States position was seriously weakened by the refusal of the European Community fully to accept the G-40 text on an un-related point, namely, agriculture. The French were unwilling to back the agricultural provision of the w/40/rev.1, which left the EC representative in an ambiguous and exposed position. Thus at the outset there were two major problems of substance: the first was services, which was largely a dispute between the developed and some developing countries; and the second was agriculture, which divided the developed countries and especially the United States and the European Community.

The meeting began on 15 September, a Monday. The chairman sought to assemble the delegations as quickly as possible, but some nations resisted – a strategy designed to increase pressure at the meeting. The session began with a plenary meeting at which each delegation was to read a speech of about ten minutes. With some ninety nations at the session this would take two days, and it demonstrated beyond any reasonable doubt the need to restructure the meeting. The interaction had to be narrowed and made more efficient, while continuing to rep-

7 The text designation (w/40/rev.1) refers to the 40th draft and bears no relation to the Group of 40. The latter was also known as the *café au lait* group, a tongue-in-cheek reference to Colombian coffee and Swiss dairy products.

resent the main lines of cleavage at the meeting.[8] Furthermore, the discussion had to be focussed on a single negotiating text as soon as possible, and the problems with services and agriculture had to be reconciled. The text was the more urgent problem; even with one text there was no assurance of a final agreement, but with multiple texts the prospect was hopeless.

On Tuesday the chairman moved to restructure the meeting. First, he turned the plenary session over to the vice-chairman, who continued hearing opening statements until all delegations had spoken. This did not conclude until late morning on Thursday, at which time the plenary was suspended until the final hours of the session. The assignment of the plenary to the vice-chairman freed the chairman to direct the overall meeting, and it carried an additional advantage in that the vice-chairman was the representative from Egypt, which was one of the G-10 nations. The move thus marginally weakened the faction that was most opposed to the establishment of a new negotiation.

Second, the chairman created a 'little plenary' which consisted of the leading minister from each country plus one deputy, about 180 people in all. The little plenary was able to settle a number of problems that could have proved difficult. For example, this forum headed off the politically contentious matter of the participation of the USSR in the negotiation, and it resolved an allegation by the EC against Japan that the latter had not provided the EC with a 'balance of benefits' in bilateral trade. Essentially the little plenary functioned as a heads-of-delegation meeting, which is a common stratagem used in multilateral negotiations to steer the discussion and to resolve difficult issues.

The little plenary proved inadequate for managing the

8 Efficiency (or more precisely, inefficiency) is a common but infrequently analysed problem in negotiation. For an analysis from simulation data, see Gilbert R. Winham and H. Eugene Bovis, 'Agreement and breakdown in negotiations: report on a State Department training simulation,' *Journal of Peace Research* 15(November 1978), 285-303.

meeting as whole, however, and by Thursday no agreements had been reached on any subject. Therefore, the chairman undertook a third initiative, supported by advice from the GATT secretariat, and set up a small consultation committee of twenty nations representing the main factions at the meeting. Membership in this committee was by invitation only, and it met about five miles outside Punta del Este in order to operate in confidence. Its existence became known to other delegations, but the fact that the little plenary had been established appeared to head off any protest from other countries about being excluded. A final initiative, which did not occur until late Thursday night, was to establish two substantive groups on services and agriculture which would run parallel to the meetings of the consultation committee. The services group was chaired by Iglesias himself, while the task of chairing the agricultural group was given to the ambassador from Austria, a nation well positioned to mediate between the United States and the European Community. The groups worked feverishly throughout Friday, and in the case of the agricultural group an agreement was not reached until early Saturday morning.

The various negotiating forums established at the Punta del Este conference structured the discussion and made agreement possible. They were set up in response to the main problems faced by the chairman. One such problem was the need to maximize the interaction between the most important nations at the meeting; that is, nations whose economic size was large enough virtually to ensure that they would have to be included in an agreement and nations which possessed political importance deriving from their positions of leadership in GATT affairs. Another problem was the need to maximize discussion on the most important issues before the special session, particularly agriculture and services. It can be expected that prenegotiation itself will narrow the parameters of the issues facing the negotiating parties, but in a large and complex meeting, this narrowing probably cannot be achieved without creating appropriate machinery.

The chairman's actions created a more effective process, but he still had to address problems of substance and especially the lack of a single negotiating text. There was no institutional procedure for deciding which text to use, and so the chairman simply decided to accept the G-40 text (that is, w/40/rev.1) as representing majority opinion and use it as a basis for subsequent negotiation. This action dismayed the developing countries which supported the G-10 text; to compensate, the chairman accepted amendments to the G-40 text, which in turn drew protests from some developed countries. Some thirty-three amendments were put forward, quickly reduced to fourteen in subsequent debate. All fourteen were circulated as formal proposals at the session. Meanwhile, the two major issues of substance – agriculture and services – were thrashed out in the parallel meetings. In agriculture, the main issue was subsidies, and the French continued to oppose giving the Uruguay Round a mandate to negotiate in this area. Similarly on services, the Indians and Brazilians continued to argue that the discussion of services should not be incorporated into the GATT, which they saw as limited to dealing with international trade exclusively in goods.

The last meeting of the consultation committee started about 6:00 PM on Friday. To this point nothing substantial had been decided. The United States delegation ostentatiously scheduled its departure for Saturday morning and insisted it would leave with or without an agreed declaration. A further United States stratagem was to threaten to call for a vote, which would have isolated the developing countries still opposed to the majority text. It is doubtful how effective this threat was, however, because the EC had promised the Indian and Brazilian delegations it would not support a vote. The EC had its own reasons for this position: because the EC itself is not a member of the GATT, voting by nation-states could expose a serious division of opinion within the Community. If the United States had pressed for a vote, it likely would have been a destructive action that could have damaged far more than simply the chance to establish a new multilateral trade negotiation. Such are the problems of conducting policy in an organization based on consensus.

The consultation committee went point by point over the G-40 text. As disputes arose over wording, the main protagonists in each case left the room to settle differences while the meeting continued. By midnight the way out of the impasse over services was reached; it was agreed between the Americans and the Indians that the session would launch a negotiation on services, but that it would be undertaken in a separate structure from that on goods, which presumably would lessen the prospect for trade-offs between these two areas.[9] Once the breakthrough on services occurred, it was obvious the remaining issues were not worth risking the agreement to achieve, and settlement followed quickly on investment and intellectual property which had also been major sticking points between the developed and developing countries. With regard to agriculture, an agreement was reached in the parallel meeting around 2:00 AM and was quickly transmitted back to the chairman and the consultation committee. The agreed wording authorized the subsequent negotiation to consider increasing disciplines on all direct and indirect subsidies affecting trade in agricultural products. Again, this represented a victory for those delegations which sought a wider negotiation, and indeed the wording of the agricultural section seemed stronger than the w/40/rev.1 text which the French had earlier rejected. However, the final text produced 'something different' which is all the French had previously demanded, and it is likely this imprecision of language (whether calculated or not) was sufficient to allow the French to accede to the majority.

At 3:30 AM the consultation committee got around to the fourteen amendments to the G-40 text. Several represented potential torpedoes to an agreement. By this point, however, momentum had gathered behind an agreement and by 4:30 AM

9 This agreement is reflected in the Ministerial Declaration on the Uruguay Round, in which provisions on goods and services are contained in part I and part II, respectively. *GATT Focus* (October 1986), 2-5.

all amendments were withdrawn except a statement calling on nations to link actions on trade liberalization with efforts to improve the functioning of the international monetary system. This statement was incorporated without undue difficulty into the objectives section of the final text.

An agreement in principle on the entire text was reached by morning. Immediately the task became one of swiftly writing a draft declaration which incorporated the bargains reached a few hours earlier. The schedule called for the draft to be presented to the little plenary by 10:30 AM and to the full plenary by noon. The schedule was met, but it occasioned frantic side consultations with delegates who had not been included in the restricted forum of the consultation committee. The draft was approved by the plenary in its turn, and in the afternoon of 20 September 1986, the Uruguay Declaration was announced to the press.

The Punta del Este session, and indeed the entire Uruguay Round prenegotiation, succeeded in the end because of the widely held perception that failure to begin a new negotiation would have harmful consequences for the GATT régime and for the prospects for continued liberalization of international trade. Thus, crisis avoidance was an important motivation during both the early prenegotiation period and the Punta del Este session. However, once the momentum in favour of a new negotiation had developed, the main motivation behind each delegation's activities became even more sharply focussed as a fear of being isolated and blamed for the failure of the special session. For example, most of the G-10 developing countries abandoned their hard-line opposition to a services negotiation during the Punta del Este session, until only India and an increasingly uncertain Brazil were left. In the end, India found it impolitic to be isolated and it acquiesced. The same explanation accounts for the eleventh hour acceptance by the French of a negotiation on agriculture. The actions of these countries, as well as others that withdrew amendments to the draft declaration, point up that even in a consensual régime majority rule still exercises a profound influence over political behaviour. What is avoided in consensual régimes are narrow votes to break deadlocks, which means that action is more difficult to achieve than in democratic régimes which operate on the basis of formal majority rule. However, the special session demonstrated that the will of a large majority can be ultimately persuasive in a consensual organization even in the face of a powerful and determined minority.

DID PRENEGOTIATION MATTER?

In evaluating the prenegotiation process in the Uruguay Round, it is first necessary to take context into account. Prenegotiation in the GATT takes place within an institutionalized régime; indeed, the GATT is one of the most enduring examples of a régime in the contemporary international system.[10] As a result, the régime itself is a factor in prenegotiation. Prenegotiation in the GATT tends to involve a mixture of substantive and organizational demands, with no clear dividing line between the two. Issues appear to be formed in terms of their importance to the régime. For example, the demand for a negotiation on services was couched partly in terms of the need to adapt the GATT to modern trade realities. Furthermore, in any régime much of the dialogue between the participants is likely to be over the issue of whether the participants are fulfilling their obligations to each other, and to the régime itself. This phenomenon manifested itself in the prenegotiation with demands by the developing countries for 'standstill' and 'rollback,' which were driven by the perception that some developed countries were not meeting their GATT obligations to other members. Both these examples illustrate the self-evident point that régimes influence behaviour and that that influence is no less apparent in prenegotiation than in other forms of interaction.

10 Régimes are understood as a set of principles, norms, rules, and decision-making procedures around which actors' expectations converge in international relations. See Stephen D. Krasner, ed, *International Regimes* (Ithaca NY: Cornell University Press 1983), 2.

Régimes have other influences on prenegotiation as well.
The Uruguay Round prenegotiation was motivated to some
extent by crisis avoidance, and this motivation was stimulated
by the perception of the effects renewed protectionism would
have on the GATT. Prenegotiation helped to identify threats to
the régime that needed to be managed before they produced
a crisis, and thus prenegotiation served a function of régime
preservation. Régimes also tend to reduce the distinctiveness
of prenegotiation. Régimes usually require some form of interaction for self-maintenance, and in international relations
this interaction is usually international negotiation. Negotiation
is thus commonplace in régimes (and certainly in the GATT),
with the result that the distinction between prenegotiation and
negotiation may be less clear-cut than in environments such as
the Middle East where negotiation is an exceptional form of
behaviour. The Uruguay Round prenegotiation was conducted
rather like the Uruguay Round negotiation that has followed
it. What differed was the nature of tasks rather than the nature
of behaviour itself.

Prenegotiation did matter in the Uruguay Round. In legal
terms, it created an agenda for the negotiation that followed
it. That agenda is set out in the Uruguay Declaration which
organized the work for the Uruguay Round. In broader and
more behavioural terms, prenegotiation structured the situation, created boundaries and identified issues, and generally
provided a framework for future bargaining and trade-offs. As
well, prenegotiation stimulated new learning by the participants, which is especially important in complex and technical
fields where the data are continually changing and are difficult
to master. The Uruguay Round prenegotiation exposed delegations to the new trade issues of the 1980s and particularly
through the GATT work programme begun in 1982, it generated data on trade in services which were hitherto unavailable
to the international community. Perhaps an even better example of the structuring and learning promoted by prenegotiation was the inventory of non-tariff measures established in

the period leading up to the Tokyo Round negotiation in the 1970s. Prior to the Tokyo Round, the task of negotiating a reduction of NTMs was problematic because they were largely unidentified, numerous, and often concealed in government policies designed to achieve purposes unrelated to trade. The inventory helped to define these practices for the purpose of trade negotiations and therefore rendered it possible to act in this area where previously nations had been uncertain about how to proceed. The NTM inventory is a particularly dramatic example of the function prenegotiation has in increasing the capacity (and possibly also the will) of the parties to undertake negotiation.

A final conclusion from the Uruguay Round is that process (that is, what issues will be raised and how they will be dealt with) appeared to be elevated over substance (that is, how the issues would be resolved) in prenegotiation. Process concerns are often played down in relation to substance in government policy-making because in established democratic governments the procedures for making policy are usually well understood and accepted by the participants. But international negotiation is a less stable form of policy-making than democratic government, and a process has to be worked out between the parties for each negotiation. How this process is established, and whether or not it will facilitate any negotiation that might follow, is what the prenegotiation is all about. It is of considerable importance to the overall endeavour.

4. *The Soviet Experience of Arms Control*
FRANKLYN GRIFFITHS

Westerners tend to view negotiation for arms control and disarmament as a tabular exercise, one in which governments seek agreement through formal discourse among representatives seated around a piece of wood. Yet it is generally recognized that the locus of decision in achieving international agreement on the management and reduction of nuclear weapons lies not so much at the table as in national policy processes which serve both to enable and to constrain the negotiator. We nevertheless continue to focus on the figure of formal arms bargaining at the expense of political processes and events in the extra-negotiatory context, or the ground on which agreements are sought.[1] The approach of the Soviet Union has been rather different. 'Extra-negotiatory' considerations loom sufficiently large in Soviet practice to oblige us to consider what 'negotiation' and therefore prenegotiation' for nuclear arms control are all about.

This paper considers four cases of Soviet arms bargaining behaviour since 1917. Each was a turning point in the readiness of the régime to come to terms with a world it was sworn to transform. The first, represented by Soviet preparations for the

Professor of Political Science, University of Toronto, Toronto, Ontario.
I wish to acknowledge the support of the Center for Russian and East European Studies at Stanford University, where I was a visiting scholar in 1987-8, in the preparation of this paper.

1 Franklyn Griffiths, 'Limits of the tabular view of negotiation,' *International Journal* 35(winter 1979-80), 33-46, and 'The political side of "disarmament",' *ibid*, 22(spring 1967), 293-305.

Genoa Economic Conference of 1922, established certain conceptions and procedures which figure in Soviet policy to this day. It saw the Bolsheviks commit themselves to negotiations for disarmament and what we now call arms control despite a belief within the party that arms talks were not only futile but counter-revolutionary. It took Moscow some forty years to reach the next turning point, a peripheral nuclear arms control agreement with the United States and Britain in the form of the Limited Nuclear Test Ban Treaty of 1963. Slightly less than a decade later, the Soviet régime made the transition from peripheral to central nuclear arms control in entering the Strategic Arms Limitation (SALT I) agreements with the United States. And then, after another decade and a half, asymmetrical Soviet concessions eased the way to agreement on the first measure of limited nuclear disarmament – the American-Soviet treaty of December 1987 on the elimination of intermediate- and shorter-range nuclear weapons.

In each nuclear arms bargaining exercise the Soviet Union engaged in protracted on-again, off-again negotiations with the United States. Rather than consider the entire record in each instance, I will focus on the ultimate prenegotiation – on the process that brought the Soviet Union to the table for what in retrospect proved to be the final sequence of formal negotiation. Soviet data set large limits on what can be said with assurance about the régime's behaviour and the forces that give rise to it. Nevertheless, it is clear that prenegotiation for nuclear arms control has repeatedly obliged the leadership to clarify its underlying predispositions in dealing with international security issues that bear on the whole range of its foreign and domestic operations. Soviet predispositions, the influences that shaped them, and the implications of Soviet prenegotiatory practice for the understanding of strategic arms negotiations as such are the principal concerns of this study. Not surprisingly, Soviet predispositions in nuclear arms bargaining owe something to the founder of the Soviet state.

PREPARATIONS FOR GENOA

The Bolsheviks came to power with the firm belief that negotiations for disarmament and arms limitation were illusory and
indeed injurious to the cause of socialism.[2] War being inevitable
under conditions of capitalism, the very thought of negotiations
for disarmament by governments-in-being was rejected on
the grounds that it got in the way of revolutionary socialist
governments-in-waiting. It got in the way by encouraging the
popular belief that lasting peace could be had without revolutionary transformations, and by lending support to reformist
socialists who in some ways were more the enemy than the
capitalists themselves. Nevertheless, in his opening statement
to the Genoa Economic Conference on 10 April 1922, the com-
missar for foreign affairs, G.V. Chicherin, formally announced
Soviet support for international negotiations aimed at a general
limitation of armaments. As well, he offered Soviet support for
efforts to reduce the economic burden of defence provided
that all countries accepted any ensuing constraints and provided
that the rules of war were supplemented by prohibitions on the
use of chemical weapons and attacks on civilian populations.[3]
The Soviet proposals attracted considerable attention at the
time, but came to naught in terms of formal negotiation. The
secret preparations in Moscow that led up to them were to have
a lasting effect on Soviet arms bargaining behaviour.

Remembered most for what transpired at nearby Rapallo,
the Genoa Conference was the first multilateral gathering to
which a hitherto isolated Soviet Russia had been invited. In-

2 For pre-revolutionary Bolshevik approaches to the disarmament question, see
  Walter C. Clemens Jr, 'Lenin on disarmament,' *Slavic Review* 23(no 3, 1964),
  505-6.
3 'Statement by Chicherin at the First Plenary Session of the Genoa Conference,'
  in Jane Degras, ed, *Soviet Documents on Foreign Policy* (London: Oxford University Press 1951), I, 299-300. Discussions of Soviet preparations for Genoa are to
  be found in A.O. Chubaryan, *V.I. Lenin i formirovanie sovetskoi vneshnei politiki*
  (Moscow: Nauka 1972), and Franklyn Griffiths, *Genoa plus 51: changing Soviet
  objectives in Europe*, Wellesley Papers 4 (Toronto: Canadian Institute of International Affairs 1973).

ternational stability and internal reconstruction being the order of the day following the introduction of the New Economic Policy in 1921, V.I. Lenin was determined to pursue trade and improved political relations as priorities in Soviet policy towards the West. Because all the Western powers were to be at Genoa (the United States with observer status), the occasion called for a review of the international situation and an effort to generalize on the basis of practices that had thus far stood a beleaguered Soviet régime in good stead. The result was a set of perceptions and operational procedures consistent with what today would be termed a posture of détente.

Surveying Western foreign and military policies in a speech delivered in March 1922, Lenin discerned three main tendencies: to resume military operations against Russia and to frustrate the conference, to expand trade and thus to make a success of the Genoa gathering, and to pursue pathetic pacifist solutions to the world's problems. Going to Genoa 'as a merchant,' would allow the Soviet government to exploit the difference between pacifism and the preference for military solutions in order to strengthen Western tendencies to trade and to stabilize relations with Russia.[4] As had already been worked out behind the scenes in Moscow, this meant a Soviet effort to enhance the influence of the 'pacifist wing of the bourgeoisie' and to weaken the influence of the 'war party.'

Pacifist and liberal opinion, as represented by the British socialist Arthur Henderson and the economist J.M. Keynes, was to be 'flattered' and persuaded that Soviet Russia sought to deal with it in particular on trade and political matters. 'Everything possible and even the impossible' was to be done not only to strengthen the influence of the 'pacifist' tendency, but to increase its electoral power so as to face Moscow with reformist Western governments more ready to come to acceptable terms.

4 'Politicheskii otchet Tsentralnogo Komiteta RKP(b) 27 marta' (27 March 1922), in V.I. Lenin, *Sochineniya* (Moscow: Gospolitizdat 1950), xxxiii, 235-6.

To this end, the Soviet delegation at Genoa was to put forward 'a very broad pacifist programme,' to refrain from presenting 'frightening' communist views, and to gain a first-rate knowledge of the 'bourgeois-pacifist' literature so as to be able to appeal effectively to relatively well disposed Westerners.[5]

Lenin was delighted when he received from Chicherin the outline of a 'pacifist programme' that included the call for disarmament and arms limitation, offers of lucrative trade opportunities, and a variety of other measures calculated to appeal to reformist governments-in-waiting and to stop short of what Western governments as then constituted could accept. The programme, he noted, was 'both nasty and "nice," ' 'both nice and unacceptable.' It would have to be rejected. It would 'divide and humiliate' (*oplyuem*, literally, we will cover with spit) the bourgeoisie in a 'nice' way.[6] Clearly, the man was not too keen on the people he was proposing to do business with.

In no way were Lenin and his associates prepared simply to go to the negotiating table and to deal with the agenda there. Quite the opposite. Soviet behaviour was calculated to manipulate the politics of Western policy so as to make opponents not only more forthcoming in formal talks, but more benign in all their dealings with Russia. Reassurance was to be offered to certain groupings in Western society through 'nice' moves designed to reduce the perception of Soviet threat and to evoke greater willingness to deal. At the same time, the rejection of appealing but non-negotiable Soviet proposals would expose Western reactionaries to their own peoples. The interplay of political forces in the Western countries could thus be altered to Soviet advantage, possibly even to the point of assisting the

5 'Proekt postanovleniya TsK RKP(b) o zadachakh Sovetskoi delegatsii v Genue' (24 February 1922), in V.I. Lenin, *Polnye sobrannye sochineniya* (Moscow: Politizdat 1964), XLIV, 407-8; and 'Proekt direktivy TsK RKP(b) dlya Sovetskoi delegatsii na Genuezskoi konferentsii' (6 February 1922), in Lenin, *Polnye*, XLIV, 382-4.

6 'Pometki na pisme G.V. Chicherina' (14 March 1922), in V.I. Lenin, *Leninskii sbornik* (Moscow: Gospolitizdat 1959), 454-5.

election of reformist governments. Meanwhile, the Communist International was to describe the positions taken by Soviet Russia at Genoa as 'not harmful but almost useless, *for revolution is necessary.*'[7] Thus did Soviet Russia formally commit itself to arms negotiation and prenegotiation under conditions of capitalism.

Explanation
A host of considerations shaped the Soviet decision to endorse the proposition of international negotiation for disarmament and arms control. Whereas prior to 1917 the situation faced by the Bolsheviks had encouraged them to deny the very thought of arms talks, reasons of state had served to alter the picture for a ruling party some four years later. New external and domestic variables militated for a revision of the Bolshevik position on arms bargaining. The effect of these variables was mediated by ideology and politics within the Soviet régime. The result was a highly politicized conception of negotiation for disarmament and arms control, one that bore the marks of the revolutionary urge to bring about extra-negotiatory social transformations.

Of prime significance was the failure of socialist revolutions to occur in the West as anticipated in 1917. Soviet Russia was on its own for the time being. But if capitalism had achieved a temporary stabilization by 1921, so also had the Soviet position in world affairs following the termination of foreign military intervention and the civil war, and the achievement of a trade agreement with the principal adversary, Britain. In these circumstances, the strength of revolutionary imperatives diminished in Soviet policy relative to the need for further improvement of the régime's international position through trade, diplomatic recognition, and, if need be, agreement with the other outcast state, Germany.

Because the working classes in the West had failed to gain

7 Lenin, 'Proekt direktivy,' 384.

state power, they were unable themselves to ensure the adoption of the co-operative stance that Moscow required of the major powers and above all of Britain. The makers of Soviet foreign policy were thus obliged to look to the Western countries for additional sources of support. In so doing, they could not but notice the widespread pacifist reaction to the World War I amongst the bourgeoisie. Russian policy-makers having committed themselves to what in the West was termed a 'peace offensive' as early as 1919-20, this evolution in Western opinion on disarmament favoured a broadening of the Soviet peace position. In fact, Soviet Russia had expressed an interest in attending the Washington Naval Conference in 1921,[8] but found itself excluded on the grounds that it constituted a threat to peace. The Washington Conference was in progress as Moscow prepared for Genoa.

If the international setting favoured a deferral of revolutionary objectives and the assumption of an increasingly conciliatory position on questions of war and peace, internal economic needs demanded an increasingly vigorous effort to improve relations with the West. Moscow now required not only trade and joint ventures but also loans.[9] Though France remained resolute in its determination to recover tsarist debts, Britain had already evinced an interest in trade expansion and was the prime mover for the Genoa Conference, notwithstanding the views of Winston Churchill and others who believed Bolshevism ought to be strangled in its cradle. Again, a reduction of the perceived Red menace was called for as economic opportunity moved Moscow to adopt a stance that made Soviet Russia more appealing to the principal adversary, that subverted the arguments of diehard anti-Bolsheviks, and that enhanced the outlook for expanded commercial relations until Soviet requirements altered.

8 'Protest from Chicherin ... against the Exclusion of the RSFSR from the Proposed Washington Conference' (19 July 1921), in Degras, ed, *Soviet Documents*, 249-51.

9 Chubaryan, *V.I. Lenin i formirovanie*, 224-5.

But for foreign political and domestic economic variables to make for a more forthcoming arms bargaining position, they had to be perceived as such by a party-state that could not forswear its revolutionary mission. Ideology, domestic politics, and above all leadership were critical variables in mediating the relationship between independent situational constraints and opportunities, on the one hand, and a new arms negotiating policy, on the other.

In those years, and since, ideology was by no means a uni-directional force. On the contrary, it lent itself to contrasting interpretations of the situation and of the requirements for action. Nevertheless it did mandate that all Soviet acts somehow serve the cause of world socialist revolution. A new position in favour of negotiated disarmament had therefore to be recon-ciled with the commitment to revolutionary transformation of the capitalist order. Hence the need to view arms bargaining by the Soviet state not as an exercise in quiet diplomacy but as an endeavour to promote political change within capitalist society.

The Leninist variant of Marxian ideology also caused Soviet policy-makers to view opposing states not as undifferentiated wholes, but as internally heterogeneous entities whose behav-iour could be influenced by the splitting tactics that had served Bolshevism so well since its very inception. The impulse to di-vide and to manipulate was reinforced by the reality that after 1917 Bolshevism was operating from a position of international weakness and needed all the foreign political assistance it could rightly muster. Hence the powerful incentives to emphasize the extra-negotiatory utility of arms negotiation in shaping the com-position as well as the immediate preferences of Western governments.

The mediating effects of ideology were compounded by intra-party debate over the Genoa policy. Though only a little is known about the interests and perspectives that came into play, it is clear that the Soviet leader was obliged to shape an internal as well as an external bargaining position in preparing for Genoa. Just as he saw three tendencies in Western policy towards Soviet Russia, three tendencies appear to have surfaced among Soviet decision-makers.[10] The first favoured the use of Genoa as a platform for revolutionary propaganda, presumably by endeavouring among other things to explode pacifist illusions as to the possibility of negotiated disarmament under conditions of capitalism. A second tendency seemed to prefer the exploitation of conflicts between capitalist states by dealing primarily with isolated Germany and avoiding the ideological compromises entailed in the attempt to strengthen reformist tendencies in the conduct of the principal adversary. Still others stressed the foreign economic objectives of the Soviet state, urging a businesslike approach to the conference and attaching priority to the Anglo-Soviet relationship.

Lenin's response to these contrasting positions was to reject the first, to treat the second as a secondary but feasible objective, and to stress the long-term improvement of relations with the principal adversary.[11] But to counter orthodox criticism and to build a supporting coalition for the Genoa policy, he chose to emphasize what was no doubt a personal predisposition to view co-operation as a form of conflict. In being 'nice,' Moscow could weaken the most reactionary elements of the imperialist bourgeoisie and their ability to resist the advance of socialism in the future. Meanwhile, the Comintern would explain the real state of affairs on disarmament, and Soviet state interests in trade and international stability would be served by an appealing but anti-imperialist stance on disarmament and arms regulation.

From the foregoing it should be apparent that strong political leadership was required for Moscow to engage in the unnatural act of apparent collaboration with imperialist adversaries in arms negotiations. Lenin was able to provide it, but

10 *Ibid*, 228, 238-43, and A.O. Chubaryan, 'V.I. Lenin i Genuya,' *Istoria SSSR*, no 2(1970), 37-48. In Chubaryan's words, the debate of 1922 centred on 'the old sacramental questions: the character and limits of concessions and compromises with the bourgeoisie, the connection of these concessions with the task of supporting world revolution' ('Lenin i Genuya,' 39).

11 Lenin, 'Proekt postanovleniya,' 407-8.

soon after Genoa he suffered the first of a series of strokes and was effectively taken out of play. The unorthodox concepts which had guided Soviet arms bargaining policy early in 1922 remained a closely held secret, as did the analysis of Western policy-making on which they were based. Though Soviet diplomacy was to pursue the disarmament issue with increasing vigour throughout the 'era of bourgeois pacifism,' as the Soviet foreign minister called it at its end in 1933,[12] the Genoa policy failed to receive sanction beyond a few cryptic public comments made by Lenin in 1922. The task of later Soviet leaders who sought the benefits not only of negotiation but of arms agreements with the principal adversary would therefore be a difficult one.

A final comment is in order before we move to Soviet pre-negotiatory behaviour in the early 1960s. To the Western observer, much in this account of the Soviet decisions of 1922 may seem contorted. Mightn't the better judgment be that Lenin was engaged in an elaborate effort to justify the simple Soviet need to participate in international negotiation? I think not. The concepts and procedures he settled upon were sufficiently problematic and contentious − for example, threat-reducing activity to strengthen the electoral appeal of British pacifist, liberal, and socialist opinion − to be counterproductive in terms of policy legitimation. They could have been advanced only in the belief that negotiated disarmament and arms regulation were inherently dependent upon inner transformations of the leading capitalist societies and had only a little to do with the give-and-take of the bargaining table. By the same token, Lenin seemed to attach real significance to the political use of arms proposals in pursuit of Soviet goals that extended well beyond the direct objectives of formal negotiation as such. In short, not only was formal arms bargaining thought to be heavily context-dependent, but Soviet arms bargaining moves could best be employed to obtain favourable change in the context faced by the régime.

12 M. Litvinov, *Vneshnyaya politika SSSR* (2nd ed; Moscow: Sotsekgiz 1937), 74.

LIMITED NUCLEAR TEST BAN TREATY

The Limited Nuclear Test Ban Treaty was ultimately negotiated by American, British, and Soviet representatives meeting in Moscow from 15 to 27 July 1963.[13] The preliminaries, including multiple prenegotiations and negotiations, reached back to India's original proposal for a nuclear test ban in 1954. The ultimate prenegotiation that brought about the tripartite Moscow talks may be said to have begun with the resolution of the Cuban missiles crisis of October 1962.

Prenegotiation is quite simple in practice. Other requirements may be raised, but basically what is needed is agreement on agenda, participation, place, and date for formal negotiation. Nikita Khrushchev committed the Soviet Union first on participation and place in a letter of 8 May 1963 to President Kennedy. This was in response to an Anglo-American proposal to send senior emissaries to discuss a comprehensive test ban agreement either in Moscow and directly with Khrushchev, or in Geneva. In opting for Moscow, Khrushchev guaranteed that the talks would be confined to the three powers. A date was set by Khrushchev in a letter received in Washington on 8 June. Prenegotiatory exchanges had not however produced an agreed agenda when the talks began in Moscow.

Through tacit bargaining or the informal exchange of signals, it seemed increasingly likely by early July that if there was to be an agreement, it would be for a limited test ban that permitted the continuance of underground detonations. The United States Senate had made clear its preference for a limited ban in a resolution passed on 27 May, and Khrushchev had come out in favour of a limited test ban in a speech given in East Berlin on 2 July, where he linked the measure to agreement on an East-West non-aggression pact. As of 14 July, however,

13 The following discussion draws on Lincoln P. Bloomfield, Walter C. Clemens Jr, and Franklyn Griffiths, *Khrushchev and the Arms Race* (Cambridge MA: M.I.T. Press 1966); Christer Jönsson, *Soviet Bargaining Behavior: The Nuclear Test Ban Case* (New York: Columbia University Press 1979); and Glenn T. Seaborg, *Kennedy, Khrushchev, and the Test Ban* (Berkeley: University of California Press 1981).

there was no assurance that any agreement would be reached despite the favourable auguries. Moscow could have reverted to its demand for a comprehensive test ban without on-site inspection to guard against underground testing; it could have called for a limited ban linked to a moratorium on underground testing; or it could have insisted on the linkage to a non-aggression pact or other items.

As it happened, Khrushchev, in a personal appearance at the first day's formal negotiation, tabled a draft limited test ban treaty and non-aggression pact, thereby indicating that the Soviet side had indeed ruled out a comprehensive ban. Further, the relative ease of the negotiations and Soviet willingness to set aside the matter of a non-aggression pact suggested that the leadership had indeed come to the talks with its mind made up to have a limited test ban. Moscow had, however, been offered a limited ban as recently as 27 August 1962, only to reject it on the grounds that such a measure would allow continued underground nuclear testing.[14] Evidently something happened to Soviet negotiating preferences between early September 1962 and mid-July 1963. And there is something else that needs explaining.

In 1959 the first of a series of documents pertaining to Soviet decision-making for Genoa had been published.[15] At about the same time, official and expert commentary began to distinguish between 'sober-moderate' and 'militaristic-aggressive' tendencies in Western and particularly United States policy-making. (This was some years before Americans began to speak of 'hawks' and 'doves' in the Soviet Union following the Cuban missiles crisis.[16]) References to Genoa, and to a differentiated view of American influentials, appeared with notably greater frequency after October 1962.[17] Was Leninist practice in 1922 cited primarily to legitimize the entry of the Soviet Union into détente

---

14 Seaborg, *Kennedy, Khrushchev, and the Test Ban*, 168.
15 Lenin, 'Pometki.' Additional documents, including photocopies of the originals, were released from time to time until April 1964, when the process ceased.
16 Bloomfield et al, *Khrushchev and the Arms Race*, 119-22, 210-14.
17 Jönsson, *Soviet Bargaining Behavior*, 59-60, 200-2.

and arms agreements with the principal adversary? Or had the Genoa precedent also become a guide to practice under Khrushchev? Was the Soviet leader endeavouring to do 'everything possible and even the impossible' to strengthen the influence of liberal and anti-nuclear opinion against 'militaristic-aggressive' preferences in the United States? Was he looking to bolster the electoral prospects of the Kennedy administration? Was he seeking to use the Kennedy administration to constrain the most reactionary elements of the American ruling class by means of negotiated arms control and détente? In brief, what did the Soviet leadership think it was doing in moving towards acceptance of a test ban treaty after 27 August and more particularly after October 1962?

Explanation

In Moscow, the principal prenegotiatory issue seems to have been not so much what kind of test ban agreement as whether there should be any agreement at all. To insist on a comprehensive test ban without on-site inspection, as Soviet negotiators had done for years, was broadly consistent with evading a test ban while continuing to test and maintaining the foreign political advantages of apparent active Soviet interest as against American footdragging over agreement. But Khrushchev became increasingly interested in agreement as well as appearances in dealing with the United States after October 1962.

In December he secured his colleagues' acceptance of 2 or 3 on-site inspections for a comprehensive test ban and then claimed acute personal embarrassment when the proposal was turned down by the Kennedy administration, whose actions might readily have been interpreted in Moscow as a policy of appearances.[18] The two sides seemed no more able than in previous years to bridge the gap on a comprehensive test ban and descended into wrangling and grandstanding at the Eighteen-Nation Disarmament Committee in February and

18 Seaborg, *Kennedy, Khrushchev, and the Test Ban*, 177-9.

March 1963. But all along there remained the option of a limited test ban, which posed considerably fewer political and technical problems for the Soviet Union.

If a limited ban was not pursued by Khrushchev late in 1962 and early the following year, was it because he favoured a comprehensive ban, as his personal behaviour suggested, or because within the Soviet hierarchy there was opposition in principle to an arms agreement with the United States? I believe that both considerations applied. As in 1922, but now much more so, the leader found himself engaged in simultaneous external and internal bargaining in dealing with the principal adversary.[19]

Externally, Khrushchev's hopes for rapid advances on all fronts without war, which had governed Soviet foreign political strategy since the Twentieth Congress in 1956, had proven illusory.[20] Advances had been made amongst the developing countries, but the Western powers had held firm through two Berlin crises and then the confrontation in the Caribbean. The Cuban crisis in particular served to underline Khrushchev's inability to achieve a breakthrough in improving the Soviet capacity to negotiate from acknowledged strength. Meanwhile, peace movements in the West had not lived up to the expectations of 1956. Moreover the unity of the international communist movement had been shattered by the dispute with the Chinese party. This conflict, which broke out into the open after October 1962, saw Beijing insist, inter alia, on the continued validity of Lenin's pre-revolutionary rejection of negotiated arms agreements under conditions of capitalism.[21] Most important, the socialist camp – the prime factor in the world correlation of forces between opposing social systems – had been gravely weakened by the Sino-Soviet conflict. The bipolar in-

19 The interrelation between internal and external bargaining is emphasized in Jönsson, *Soviet Bargaining Behavior*, esp. 143-207.
20 Richard Lowenthal, 'The end of an illusion,' *Problems of Communism* 12(January-February 1963), 1-10.
21 Jönsson, *Soviet Bargaining Behavior*, 94-121, provides a discussion of the Chinese view.

ternational system had begun to yield to multipolarity. To offset new vulnerability in the east, Moscow required a more supple and differentiated approach to the West. At the same time, the venture to the brink in the missiles crisis had surely drawn attention to the need for greater stability in Soviet-American relations.

In these circumstances, Khrushchev would seem to have attached new value to collaboration with the principal adversary. Co-operation promised a respite in a political-military competition that had become increasingly difficult for Moscow to sustain at acceptable levels of risk and cost, including cost to the leader's domestic programme. Of the significant measures that might have been agreed upon with the United States late in 1962 and early the following year, the test ban was clearly the furthest advanced. The experience of the October 1962 crisis should not be underestimated among the factors that moved Khrushchev to seek a test ban treaty. Nor in my view should the fact of that crisis be allowed to obscure the larger failure of the foreign political strategy that had been pursued under Khrushchev's leadership since 1956.

More broadly, co-operation was increasingly necessary in adapting to the emergent requirements of multipolarity. A special premium would be placed on agreements with the United States that imposed constraint both on the Chinese programme to acquire an independent nuclear deterrent and on possible West German access to nuclear weapons either on its own or through a multilateral nuclear force within the North Atlantic Treaty Organization (NATO).[22] For its part, the United States far outdistanced the USSR in strategic nuclear weaponry and conventional power projection capabilities. At the same time, indications of 'moderation' and 'sobriety' in American opinion on international security affairs, and on relations with the Soviet Union, offered some prospect of a co-operation that would stabilize the international situation as Khrushchev sought to

22 Bloomfield et al, *Khrushchev and the Arms Race*, 204-5; Jönsson, *Soviet Bargaining Behavior*, 117, 125.

regroup his own and Soviet forces so as to regain the initiative in domestic and foreign affairs.

Internally, Khrushchev's position was paradoxical. On the one hand, as first secretary of the party and chairman of the Council of Ministers, he had an extraordinary range of powers. As of late 1962 he had recently bisected large parts of the party apparatus into agricultural and industrial wings, launched a renewed campaign of de-Stalinization, authorized wide-ranging debate on economic reform, and emplaced intermediate-range nuclear weapons in Cuba. On the other hand, he seemed to have lost effective control over large areas of policy, including weapons acquisition. Having preferred to rely upon minimum nuclear deterrence bolstered by bluff, he was faced with a massive Soviet nuclear and conventional force build-up whose effects would be seen only as the USSR achieved essential strategic equivalence with the United States towards the end of the decade. As well, his spending priorities on agriculture and the civilian economy were consistently inhibited by colleagues in the leadership who favoured heavy industry, defence, and conservative solutions in internal and foreign affairs.[23]

By March 1963, Khrushchev's personal political fortunes had reached a low point. With this went his ability to move the test ban negotiations forward. Led, it would appear, by Frol Kozlov, a Presidium member, Khrushchev's opponents succeeded in reimposing much of their policy and institutional agenda.[24] They also cleared the way for a Central Committee plenum on ideology, intended no doubt to set the leader on the straight and narrow.

Early in April 1963, Kozlov was disabled by a heart attack and Khrushchev's internal and external bargaining situations improved.[25] On 5 April Moscow informed Washington of its willingness to discuss a direct communications link or 'hotline' with Washington, which was eventually agreed on 20 June.

23 Jönsson, *Soviet Bargaining Behavior*, chaps 10-13.
24 *Ibid*, 193.
25 Bloomfield et al, *Khrushchev and the Arms Race*, 236; Jönsson, *Soviet Bargaining Behavior*, 193.

Esoteric communications soon signalled changes of direction in Soviet policy across the board. On 11 April the annual May Day slogans were subject to an unprecedented correction which favoured reformist views. That same day a piece from the *Washington Post*, which lauded Kennedy's effort to reach agreement with the USSR, was reprinted in the Soviet press. The party's theoretical journal then brought to the surface a Lenin document on the utility of concessions to support realistic elements in the West, and the Lenin anniversary address of 22 April included direct references to Genoa and the need to differentiate between opposed tendencies in the capitalist countries. On 24 April, Khrushchev was openly critical of the Soviet defence industry. It was on this day that he received the Anglo-American proposal to send high-level representatives to see whether negotiations for a comprehensive test ban might be reopened.

An improved internal bargaining situation allowed Khrushchev greater leeway in pursuing a test ban as an instrument of Soviet-American accommodation and the varied advantages that would come from it. But was it to be a comprehensive or a limited ban? According to his own testimony, during his later years in office Khrushchev became increasingly interested in slowing the rate of military spending.[26] Indeed, he seems to have become wedded to the notion of demilitarizing and thereby accelerating the competition of opposed social systems. A comprehensive test ban, assuming one could be negotiated, offered a superior means of constraining the nuclear arms race and obliging rivals to rely more heavily on non-military forms of struggle. Correspondingly, its achievement required either a stronger internal bargaining position than a limited one did or offsetting concessions from the other parties. From April to the end of the prenegotiation in July 1963, Khrushchev's behaviour would seem on balance to have been influenced more by external than internal bargaining considerations.

In suggesting on 8 May a three-power negotiation in Mos-

26 N.S. Khrushchev, *Khrushchev Remembers* (Boston: Little Brown 1971), 534-5.

cow, and on 8 June the mid-July date for talks to begin, Khrushchev evidently moved towards a decision on the matter of underground nuclear testing. According to the Chinese, whose ideological dispute with the Communist Party of the Soviet Union (CPSU) had reached towering proportions by midsummer 1963, the Soviet Union told them on 9 June that a limited test ban was unacceptable. This point was not denied in the Soviet counterblast of 21 August.[27] Nevertheless, the United States Senate resolution of 27 May clearly indicated that Kennedy would encounter significant internal resistance in pursuing a comprehensive test ban. As to Khrushchev's reading of Kennedy's intentions, it may have improved following the Soviet leader's conversation with Norman Cousins on 12 April and almost certainly improved following the president's exceedingly conciliatory speech of 10 June at the American University.[28] As well, whereas a comprehensive ban was distinctly problematic in presenting the United States with perceived intelligence-gathering opportunities through on-site inspection, a limited ban was not wholly incompatible with the interest of the Soviet military establishment and its supporters in strategic nuclear force modernization.[29]

All things considered, by the second half of June at the latest, the Soviet leader could have anticipated that support in principle was to be had from his colleagues for a stabilization of East-West relations, and that things would go more smoothly all round if the agreement were for a limited ban as indicated in the East Berlin speech of 2 July. The stage was thus set at the Soviet end for a businesslike formal negotiation, and for

27 See 'A comment on the Soviet government's statement of August 3' and 'Soviet government statement of August 21, 1963,' in William E. Griffith, ed, *The Sino-Soviet Rift* (Cambridge MA: MIT Press 1964), 341 and 354-70. Nor was the matter taken up in the Soviet statement of 21 September (pp 426-61).

28 Seaborg, *Kennedy, Khrushchev, and the Test Ban*, 208, 212-15. On the American University speech, Khrushchev said later: 'I have been criticized for praising this speech of Kennedy's. But we must not take a primitive approach to events, we must not feel that we are clever and all our opponents are fools' (6 April 1964). Quoted in Bloomfield et al, *Khrushchev and the Arms Race*, 218.

29 Jönsson, *Soviet Bargaining Behavior*, 175; Bloomfield et al, *Khrushchev and the Arms Race*, 205-8.

escape by means of linkage to a non-aggression pact if the talks went wrong.

Throughout there were good reasons for Khrushchev to view negotiation and also prenegotiation for a nuclear test ban as a process centred on the technical characteristics of a possible agreement. It is clear however that alternative outcomes of the process were also evaluated in terms of their political effect on the wider context in which Soviet foreign and domestic objectives were pursued. We should as well consider whether the bargaining process as such was understood in terms that required a Soviet effort to shape the context in which formal negotiation took place. This brings us back to Genoa.

Beyond doubt the Genoa precedent was cited to counter criticism and to legitimize collaboration with the principal adversary in arms agreements. The Chinese were an obvious concern here, as were others in the international communist movement who might be swayed by Chinese sectarianism. By the same token, the conservatively minded, also referred to as sectarians and dogmatists, and those in the régime who might otherwise have followed their lead could equally well have been targets in the revelation of Lenin's decidedly reformist tactics of 1922. Internal and external bargaining may moreover have been interconnected in Sino-Soviet as well as United States-Soviet relations.

In launching a diatribe against Soviet conduct in domestic and foreign affairs, and against the Soviet propensity to collude with the United States in particular, the Chinese could have hoped to bolster Khrushchev's conservative opponents who themselves favoured 'leftist' slogans in contesting the priorities of the first secretary. Of special significance were the Chinese assertions that United States imperialism was wholly devoid of 'reason' and that to pin hope on negotiation with 'sensible' elements of the American leadership was entirely unjustified.[30] Whether or not Khrushchev and his advisers viewed Genoa as a guide to action, the Chinese acted as though this were the

30 Jönsson, *Soviet Bargaining Behavior*, 118-21.

case. In practice, however, the Chinese attempt to instruct the CPSU seems to have been viewed as an affront throughout the Soviet hierarchy. Accordingly, China's actions may actually have assisted Khrushchev in gaining legitimacy for his American policy by subverting the status of conservative thinking within the CPSU.[31] Not by chance were the two communist parties negotiating in Moscow when American and British representatives showed up to discuss a test ban treaty.

As to the operational significance of the Genoa precedent in Soviet prenegotiatory behaviour on a test ban, Khrushchev had visited the United States in 1959, presented himself as a man of peace, and put forward 'a very broad pacifist programme' with his proposal at the United Nations for general and complete disarmament. General disarmament occupied public attention and the time of negotiators until after the Soviet leader was removed from office in 1964. In underwriting liberal and 'pacifist' policy preferences, the Soviet campaign for general and complete disarmament could have been viewed in Moscow as creating a climate conducive to the negotiation of more modest measures.[32] Further, in commenting on the resolution of the Cuban crisis, Khrushchev noted that compromises and restraint had been required to improve the bargaining strength of more moderate American decision-makers.[33] There is little reason to doubt that an equivalent awareness persisted in the prenegotiation of the nuclear test ban, albeit within the confines

31 *Ibid*, 131-2.
32 The proposal for general and complete disarmament was accompanied by a statement of interest in partial measures. See Bernhard G. Bechhoefer, *Postwar Negotiations for Arms Control* (Washington: Brookings Institution 1961), 527. See also I. Kulkov and V. Trepelkov, 'Novye dokumenty o vneshnei politiki Sovetskogo gosudarstva,' *Mirovaya ekonomika i mezhdunarodnye otnosheniya*, no 4(1960), 146-9.
33 In a speech to the Supreme Soviet in December 1962, Khrushchev asked: 'Is it not clear that if we had adopted an uncompromising position it would only have helped the camp of the rabid ones to utilize the situation to inflict a blow against Cuba and to unleash a world war?' In the same address, he observed: 'The Soviet Government takes into account the complexity and many-sidedness of the problems facing various states, displays the necessary restraint, and adheres to constructive views.' Quoted in Bloomfield et al, *Khrushchev and the Arms Race*, 211-12.

of the Soviet leader's own internal bargaining space. Hence the Soviet readiness in 1963 to make reassuring moves that served to widen Kennedy's margin for manoeuvre: agreement on the hotline, Soviet entry into the United States grain market for the first time, suspension of jamming of Voice of America broadcasts, and so on. Hence also Khrushchev's willingness to opt for a limited test ban in deference to Kennedy's internal bargaining situation as well as his own. In addition, as the United States embarked upon an intensive series of underground nuclear tests after the Limited Nuclear Test Ban Treaty had been signed – this as part of the price Kennedy had to pay for a treaty – Moscow moved quickly to quell condemnation by Soviet-line peace movements.[34]

Above all, we have Khrushchev's claim, first made privately at the Vienna summit of 1961, that he had helped to elect Kennedy in 1960.[35] With this claim the Soviet leader acknowledged an interest in utilizing the American electoral process, and thus the relative autonomy of the American state, to alter the correlation of forces within the ruling class in a manner disadvantageous to the 'most bellicose circles of imperialism.' In my judgment, Khrushchev very probably believed that détente and arms control in 1963 would assist Kennedy and 'sensible' American opinion to prevail against a Republican challenger in the presidential election of the following year. And yet, all along Khrushchev remained fully committed to the eradication of capitalism.[36]

As in 1922, the Soviet leadership was obliged to reconcile revolutionary objectives with the need for collaboration with the principal adversary. Though Khrushchev did not enunciate the solution in so many words, it was evident in Soviet pronouncements on war and peace in the debate with the Chinese

34 *Ibid*, 197-8.
35 Khrushchev, *Khrushchev Remembers*, 491.
36 There was no reason to doubt Khrushchev when later he said: 'I sought to destroy capitalism and create a new social system based on the teachings of Marx, Engels, and Lenin.' *Ibid*, 514.

and in internal commentary on the foreign policy of the regime.[37] The thrust of the argument was that by influencing the politics of American foreign and military policies, Moscow could translate American-Soviet competition from the military to the economic and the ideological planes. Collaboration would gradually overwhelm conflict in a relationship that had priority over all others. American 'militaristic-aggressive' tendencies would progressively be constrained, as would the ability of the United States to rely upon military capabilities either in direct competition with the ussr or in intervening against national liberation movements in the developing countries. As had also been intended in 1922, the cumulative effects of co-operation and a diminished perception of a Soviet threat would serve at once to further Soviet state interests and to accelerate the world revolutionary process.

In Moscow, therefore, the external bargaining that led up to the final test ban talks was understood very largely in terms of extra-negotiatory interaction among opposed social systems. The essence of the process was reciprocal action and restraint that served to strengthen or weaken the internal bargaining positions of leaders interested in formal negotiation and agreement. Soviet policy-makers in 1922 had implicitly recognized that the parties to an arms negotiation were likely to be engaged in simultaneous internal and external bargaining. I say implicitly because Soviet decisions for Genoa were keyed to one-way influence on the internal bargaining of the principal adversary and did not acknowledge Soviet internal bargaining as being subject to external influence. Under Khrushchev, the sense of mutual dependence was substantially stronger.

Whereas conventional notions of negotiation tend to treat it as an exercise in formal external bargaining, the test ban

37 A selection of Soviet statements is available in Griffith, ed, *The Sino-Soviet Rift*. See also N.N. Inozemtsev, 'Rost mogushchestva mirovogo sotsializma i obshchestvennyi progress,' *Kommunist*, no 6(1963), 64-5; Yu. Arbatov, 'Borba za mir i perspektivy sotsialistichiskikh revolyutsii,' *Kommunist*, no 14(1963); esp. 61; and F.M. Burlatskii in *Pravda*, 25 July 1963.

prenegotiation highlighted the need for leaders to assist one another directly in the internal bargaining processes that very largely determined external bargaining behaviour. In 1962-3, Khrushchev needed measures that constrained conservatives simultaneously in the United States and the Soviet Union without compromising the core values of his own society. In this he had much in common with Kennedy.

SALT I

The negotiation that produced the Interim Agreement on Offensive Strategic Forces and the Anti-Ballistic Missile Treaty of May 1972 began in November 1969.[38] It was preceded by formal exchanges and tacit bargaining that reached back to Lyndon Johnson's first year in the White House.[39] By the end of 1968 the two sides had achieved certain understandings that were to persist. First, they alone would be parties to the negotiation. And, according to an American participant, it was agreed that the objective of the talks would be 'stable mutual strategic de-

38 Data and commentary relating to the SALT I preliminaries are to be found in the following: Lawrence T. Caldwell, *Soviet Attitudes to SALT*, Adelphi Papers 75 (London: International Institute for Strategic Studies 1971); Raymond L. Garthoff, *Detente and Confrontation: American-Soviet Relations from Nixon to Reagan* (Washington: Brookings Institution 1985); Henry Kissinger, *White House Years* (Boston: Little, Brown 1979); Glenn T. Seaborg, *Stemming the Tide: Arms Control in the Johnson Years* (Lexington MA: Lexington Books 1986); and Gerard Smith, *Doubletalk: The Story of the First Strategic Arms Limitation Talks* (New York: Doubleday 1980). Caldwell is especially useful.

39 As had been the case in the ultimate prenegotiation for the limited test ban, the United States cast itself in the role of *demandeur* throughout the SALT preliminaries to the end of 1968. In an announcement made jointly with Washington in July 1968, Moscow agreed to begin strategic arms talks in the near future, but then for some weeks declined to set a date. Only on 19 August was the Johnson administration informed of Soviet readiness to hold a summit and to commence negotiations in October. This arrangement was to be jointly announced on 21 August. But the Soviet Union invaded Czechoslovakia on 20 August, and the United States was obliged to cancel the summit and the arms talks. Continuing Soviet contacts with the Johnson administration on strategic arms control following the election of Richard Nixon in November were terminated the following month at the request of the incoming president. The story is laid out in Seaborg, *Stemming the Tide*.

terrence' based on a recognition of the 'integral interrelationship' between strategic offensive and defensive systems.[40] In significance and complexity, the Strategic Arms Limitation Talks (SALT) would differ from the test ban negotiations by orders of magnitude.

The ultimate prenegotiation that led to the commencement of SALT may be said to have begun with the first statement of official interest in 1969. It came at a Soviet Foreign Ministry press conference on 20 January, the day of Richard Nixon's inauguration, and was followed by a succession of Soviet statements of interest in formal negotiation without delay. Moscow's initiative left time, place, and details of agenda to be worked out. Certain basic conceptions were also undefined. If stable mutual deterrence was indeed the goal, what was meant by deterrence? If there were differences of opinion on this matter within as well as between the two sides, how were the ensuing force posture requirements to be reconciled in an agreement? Was there to be numerical equality, or were asymmetrical force structures to be allowed? What indeed was a strategic nuclear weapon?

Nixon had little interest in such matters and was in no mood to begin talks right away. Instead, he preferred to erect a larger bargaining structure that would see Washington deal with Moscow on an array of concurrent or linked issues of which such talks would be only one. Foremost among his priorities was an end to the war in Vietnam and the exploitation of the perceived Soviet interest in strategic arms control to secure Soviet pressure on the North Vietnamese. As well, he was determined to secure Senate approval of an improved ABM system before beginning arms talks with the Soviet Union.[41] Public pressure, bureaucratic leaks, and congressional demands for the commencement of

40 Raymond L. Garthoff, 'BMD and East-West relations,' in Ashton B. Carter and David N. Schwartz, eds, *Ballistic Missile Defence* (Washington: Brookings Institution 1984), 301.
41 Kissinger, *White House Years*, 148, 128-30 and 138, and 205 and 208-9.

talks proved irresistible, however.[42] On 11 June 1969 the Soviet Union was informed of American readiness to set a date for SALT.

Then the Soviet side delayed. Only on 20 October did Washington receive word of Moscow's willingness to agree on a date. A few days later the two sides jointly announced that talks would begin with a 'preliminary discussion' to be held in Helsinki.

The first round of SALT, which ran from 17 November to 22 December, may be regarded as an exercise in prenegotiation, since only then did the parties begin to hear one another out on goals, issues, concepts, and agenda. The behaviour of Soviet negotiators proved to be 'precise, nonpolemic, businesslike, and serious.'[43] There was, however, some evidence that Moscow was prepared to break off these 'preliminary' talks if the encounter seemed unpromising.[44] As well, there were esoteric signs of internal Soviet debate over the entire enterprise.

In the words of a Soviet historian, published soon after SALT had begun, 'when you familiarize yourself with the discussions in Soviet Russia concerning the preparations for Genoa, it seems that you are dealing with events of the present day.'[45] Translated to the context of 1969-70, this comment suggested three tendencies in the Soviet approach to SALT: to use formal negotiations as a platform for anti-imperialist propaganda; to engage in divisive conciliation aimed at creating the appearance of improved American-Soviet relations so as to assist in the cultivation of United States allies in Europe; and to attempt to come to terms with the principal adversary on matters of mutual interest. Further, if the parallel with 1922 held, by the end of 1969 the Soviet leadership had come down in favour of the third option, with the second as a possible but subsidiary preference.

To gain an understanding of what brought the Soviet Union to the table for SALT and how its decision-makers approached

42 *Ibid*, 130-8.
43 *Ibid*, 150.
44 Garthoff, *Detente and Confrontation*, 133.
45 Chubaryan, 'Lenin i Genuya,' 36.

the talks, we need to answer three questions. Why did they state an interest in formal negotiation on 20 January 1969? Why did they delay from 11 June to 20 October before finally committing themselves to a first round of bargaining? And if the first round was indeed an exploratory venture, why did they decide to continue?

Explanation

In the Soviet Union of today, the Brezhnev years are termed the era of stagnation. Leonid Brezhnev did not, however, gain visible status as first among equals until 1971. Until then, the collective Soviet leadership was represented jointly by Brezhnev and Aleksei Kosygin. The Brezhnev-Kosygin régime itself was significantly more conservative than its predecessor, so much so that unsuccessful bids could be made to rehabilitate Stalin in 1966 and again as SALT began late in 1969.[46] Nonetheless, the reformist impulses that reappeared under Khrushchev had persisted under the new management, albeit in unpromising circumstances. The result was significant ambiguity in the foreign and domestic conduct of the Brezhnev-Kosygin régime, an ambiguity that continued into the mid-1970s when conservative policy preferences more clearly prevailed and stagnation set in.

In relations with the United States, the Khrushchevian formula of minimum deterrence and attempted intervention into United States internal politics was soon repudiated.[47] In its place the new régime sought military strength and an improved world correlation of forces so as to deal with the principal adversary

46 Roy Medvedev, *Faut-il réhabiliter Staline?* (Paris: Editions du Seuil 1969), and Stephen F. Cohen, 'The Stalin question since Stalin,' in Cohen, ed, *An End to Silence* (New York: Norton 1982), 42-5.

47 See, for example, V.A. Golikov, 'Vazhnyi printsip leninskoi vneshnei politiki,' *Kommunist*, no 18(1965), 91-9. Golikov was a personal assistant to Brezhnev at the time. See also V.I. Popov, 'Vneshnyaya politika SSSR,' *Voprosy istorii*, no 10(1966), 157; and M. Gorokhov, 'Leninist diplomacy: principles and traditions,' *International Affairs*, no 4(1968), 43-4, where opposition is offered to the view that 'if the Soviet Union wants peaceful coexistence with the United States it should abstain from any action that could "hamper" the process of normalization of relations.'

essentially as it stood. American choices were to be shaped as it were 'from without,' and free of the political and ideological compromises entailed in the attempt to underwrite forces of moderation in United States policy-making 'from within' except on tactical matters.[48] Despite the Vietnam War, multilateral arms control agreements that included the United States – for example, the 1968 Non-Proliferation Treaty (NPT) – were by no means excluded. Nor, as Soviet dealings with the Johnson administration showed, was there a prohibition on bilateral negotiation for strategic nuclear arms control. But co-operation was to be had more by the imposition of external constraint on American choices than by Soviet 'good behaviour' and other stratagems designed to enhance the bargaining strength of American administrations. The United States was, on balance, to be compelled, not enabled, to co-operate. Objective forces, helped along by the Soviet Union, would do the compelling.

Though it would soon alter, the situation that prompted the Soviet statement of 20 January 1969 presented Soviet decision-makers with opportunities as well as constraints. The formidable build-up of Soviet strategic offensive forces was bringing the USSR to a position of quantitative parity with an opponent whose strategic launchers remained constant as Soviet numbers increased. Crises aside, for the first time since World War II Moscow would be able to negotiate with the United States on crucial security matters as an equal, and to threaten the attainment of superior power by continuing to build offensive weapons. Indeed, as the Soviet naval chief would before long observe, arms negotiations offered a 'diplomatic route' to superiority for a great power that sought to equal and then surpass the military might of a rival without war.[49] Whether parity or superiority

---

48 Franklyn Griffiths, 'The sources of American conduct: Soviet perspectives and their policy implications,' *International Security* 9(fall 1984), 9-10.

49 Admiral S.V. Gorshkov (August 1972), cited in Franklyn Griffiths, 'Tactical uses of naval arms control,' in Michael MccGwire et al, eds, *Soviet Naval Policy: Objectives and Constraints* (New York: Praeger 1975), 643.

was the Soviet strategic objective in January 1969 cannot be said. But either way, SALT made sense.

Political trends in the West may also have been promising, as viewed from the Soviet capital. Mired in Vietnam and faced with mounting internal disorder, the United States appeared to be a waning force in world affairs.[50] France had withdrawn from military participation in NATO. In the Federal Republic, Willy Brandt had made clear his intention to pursue a more vigorous Ostpolitik and to sign the NPT once, as seemed increasingly likely, he became chancellor. As well, Soviet decision-makers could not but note the potential of strategic nuclear parity to put stress on transatlantic ties by reinforcing doubt in Western Europe as to the credibility of United States security guarantees. The less viable the United States commitment to the defence of Europe, the more favourably its allies would view direct dealings with the USSR on the recognition of postwar European frontiers, on trade, and on transfers of technology. In these circumstances, the appearance first of a Soviet interest in strategic arms negotiations with the United States, and then of United States participation in SALT, stood to reduce the reluctance of European NATO countries, most notably the Federal Republic, to do business of their own with Moscow. By the same token, a Soviet policy of appearances on SALT could have been expected to ease the way for West European acceptance of the current proposal of the Warsaw Treaty Organization for a European security conference that was to be held without the participation of the United States or, for that matter, of Canada.

But Soviet interests in SALT were not confined to appearances. Partly because of the Johnson administration's insistence on the matter, the Soviet side had come to the conclusion that

---

50 See, for example, A.N. Yakovlev, *Ideologiya amerikanskoi 'imperii'* (Moscow: Mysl' 1967); E. Bugrov, 'Problemy "bolnogo" obshchestva,' *Mirovaya ekonomika i mezhdunarodnye otnosheniya*, no 1(1968), 81-90; V. Shamberg, 'Na poroge prezidentiskikh vyborov,' *ibid*, no 10(1968), 91-7; and A.N. Yakovlev, ed, *SShA: ot 'velikogo' k bolnomy* (Moscow: Politizdat 1969).

simultaneous competition in strategic offensive and defensive forces would be not only very expensive but also detrimental to deterrence and thus to Soviet security.[51] By early 1969, when work on their own ABM system had been curtailed,[52] the régime had evidently opted to rely upon offensive forces. Johnson had however committed the United States to a limited ABM capability whose quality and growth potential could not be ignored. In addition, a revision of Soviet military doctrine in the mid-1960s had accentuated both the opportunity and the need to avert the destruction of the homeland in a third world war. These objectives might be achieved by structuring Soviet forces so as to deter intercontinental nuclear exchanges and to permit victory through conventional and, if necessary, limited nuclear warfare in Europe, should war be forced upon the USSR.[53] Though the new doctrine was accompanied by bureaucratic dissonance and no little uncertainty, it made negotiated limitations on strategic intercontinental forces increasingly appropriate for the Soviet Union.

Accordingly, in fitting SALT into a political and military strategy towards the West, Soviet decision-makers would seem to have had two main options as of January 1969. They could have sought to bargain in earnest on ABM and offensive force limitations with a formidable but debilitated adversary. Or they could have gone through the motions of prenegotiation and negotiation in order to create a setting conducive to the achievement of strategic superiority and new security arrangements in Europe that served the long-term goal of decoupling the United States from its allies. Though evidence of internal Soviet bar-

---

51 Seaborg, *Stemming the Tide*, esp. 420-7; Garthoff, 'BMD and East-West relations,' 286-7, 294, and 301; Smith, *Doubletalk*, 32.

52 Garthoff, 'BMD and East-West relations,' 300.

53 Michael MccGwire, *Military Objectives in Soviet Foreign Policy* (Washington: Brookings Institution 1987), chaps 3 and 11. See also John G. Hines, Philip A. Petersen, and Notra Trulock III, 'Soviet military theory 1945-2000,' *Washington Quarterly* 9(fall 1986); Mary FitzGerald, 'Marshal Ogarkov on the modern theater operation,' *Naval War College Review* 39(autumn 1986), 6-25.

gaining is lacking, I suspect that in initially agreeing to SALT in July 1968, the Soviet leadership had come down in favour of the first option.

Treating arms control on its military-technical merits and without reformist political fanfare, Moscow had already gone so far as to collaborate with Washington in generating support for the NPT by extending joint guarantees to non-nuclear-weapons states, hostilities in Vietnam notwithstanding. And once the NPT was signed on 1 July, Soviet assent to begin SALT was quickly given. But then came the armed suppression of reformism in Czechoslovakia, American cancellation of a Johnson-Kosygin summit that was to launch the talks, and subsequently the election to the White House of a conservative Republican who had campaigned for American strategic superiority. These developments surely served to create new internal and external bargaining situations in Moscow as of January 1969.

Internally, Soviet advocates of negotiation in earnest were very likely confronted with heightened anti-reformist sentiment in Moscow and perceived intractability in Washington. Correspondingly, Soviet external bargaining preferences may have hardened to favour divisive détente in Europe and negotiation for appearances in SALT. But before Soviet policy could be recast, the measure of the new American administration had to be taken. The Soviet statement of 20 January in favour of SALT is therefore to be regarded as a tactical probe that initiated a prenegotiation whose preferred outcome had yet to be decided in Moscow.

First to be probed would be the new president's ability to carry forward the Johnson administration's controversial decision to field an ABM system. In urging an early start for SALT, Moscow could expect to reinforce anti-ABM opinion in the United States, principally in the Senate, and thus Soviet security to the extent that Nixon's capacity to deploy an ABM system was thereby impeded. This objective could be accomplished by substantiating the American view that real opportunities existed for strategic arms control which would be diminished by a decision to move ahead with the ABM programme.[54] Second, the commitment of the incoming administration to linkage made it in the Soviet interest to urge upon American public, congressional, and official opinion the view that the proposal for talks should not be delayed but dealt with promptly and on its own merits.[55] In pressing the case for SALT in January 1969 and in the months that followed, Moscow could therefore probe the intentions and determination of the new administration in a quiet test of wills. As it happened, the Soviet Union 'won' the test where linkage was concerned and came close on the ABM programme: American readiness to begin SALT was announced on 11 June 1969 without a quid pro quo from the USSR in Indochina or the Middle East; and the Senate was able to endorse Nixon's Safeguard ABM system on 6 August only when a tie vote was broken by the vice-president.

Having urged the commencement of talks until the United States agreed to set a date, why then did the Soviet Union delay until 20 October in stating its readiness to begin the negotiation? Tactical considerations surely entered the picture once again. If Moscow had agreed to start talks before the Senate vote on Safeguard, it would have undercut the ABM opponents' view that an agreement to deploy the system was a threat to negotiation. As well, in terms of Soviet arms bargaining objectives, it could have been thought necessary to all but eliminate the gap in strategic offensive launchers.[56] This had pretty well been accomplished by November 1969. But the real reason for Soviet delay seems to have lain elsewhere. Developments in the Soviet

54 Alexander O. Ghebhardt, 'Implications of Organizational and Bureaucratic Policy Models for Soviet ABM Decision-Making,' unpublished doctoral dissertation, Columbia University, 1975, 132-3.

55 In discussion with a KGB contact in New York on 18 December 1968, Kissinger had made a point of conveying to Moscow the elements of the linkage doctrine including the intention of the new administration not to be rushed into strategic arms talks: White House Years, 127.

56 Garthoff, 'BMD and East-West relations,' 297-9.

external and domestic situations after January 1969 prompted a review of its underlying political strategy towards the West. As in 1922 and 1963, the assimilation of new situational variables abroad and at home was mediated by conflict within the régime.

To begin with, there was an increase in the severity of external and domestic constraints on the ability of the Soviet Union to engage in global competition with the United States. In March and April 1969, armed clashes occurred along the border with China. Not only could China be seen to be moving towards a multipolar strategy including rapprochement with the United States – 'a complex political game,' as one observer put it[57] – but the threat to the physical security of the USSR in the east had clearly increased. These developments could not but affect the Soviet interest in employing SALT to stabilize political-military relations with the United States. Indeed, as in August 1963, the Soviet side was engaged in separate and unproductive negotiations with the Chinese as talks began with the United States in November 1969.

Preparations for the Twenty-Fourth Party Congress, scheduled for 1970 but delayed until the following year, would also seem to have uncovered the beginnings of the economic decline that Mikhail Gorbachev ultimately had to deal with. Defence expenditure was acknowledged to be a part of the problem in a reportedly forbidding economic report that was delivered by Brezhnev to the Central Committee in December 1969 but never published. Further, in March 1969, President Charles de Gaulle had been replaced by a French leader more inclined to accept British entry into the European Community, which now threatened to become increasingly inward-looking as a trading bloc and source of advanced technology for the USSR. Correspondingly, Soviet interest in the long-term development of economic

---

57 O. Nikanorov, 'Gruppa Mao i amerikanskii imperializm,' *Mirovaya ekonomika i mezhdunarodnye otnosheniya*, no 7(1979), 62.

relations with the United States may have appreciated. Potential adversity arising from the development of Anglo-French relations was offset, however, by the election of Brandt as chancellor of the Federal Republic on 28 September 1969. But could openings for economic renewal in relations with Western Europe be fully exploited if Moscow's underlying objective was to play upon West-West differences? Taken together, changing geopolitical and economic variables in 1969 served to throw doubt upon the advisability of subordinating SALT to the requirements of divisive détente.

Meanwhile the United States was sending signals that could not be ignored. Some came from the administration. Others from the Senate. Still others from the streets. Nixon and his national security adviser, Henry Kissinger, began to convey the message that the new administration was indeed committed to a negotiated end to the war in Vietnam. On strategic military matters, Nixon indicated in January 1969 that 'sufficiency' and not superiority was the American goal.[58] To the degree that the new administration was prepared to forgo United States requirements for strategic superiority in practice, it became possible for Moscow to contemplate strategic arms control arrangements that reduced the threat to the homeland, institutionalized parity, and rationalized Soviet weapons acquisition. The vote on Safeguard in the Senate suggested that the administration's ability to mount a strategic defence capability could be constrained through negotiation. Moreover, continuing domestic unrest served to underline American vulnerabilities. To the dispassionate Soviet observer, these and similar signals could only have meant that Moscow would be missing an opportunity to do vitally important business with the United States if policy on SALT were governed more by appearances than by substance. But passions seem to have been running high in the Soviet leadership by the autumn of 1969.

For reasons that remain obscure, policy preferences polar-

58 Smith, *Doubletalk*, 23-4.

ized within the régime.[59] Brezhnev, whose overall foreign affairs orientation had been more conservative than Kosygin's, had begun to make inroads into his colleague's power.[60] In the ensuing realignment, Brezhnev may have started to appropriate some of Kosygin's positions while others in the leadership took up vacant conservative ground. Russian nationalist sentiment with its anti-Western, chauvinist, and anti-semitic overtones had surfaced in the Soviet media with covert official sanction.[61] Stalinist opinion, no doubt bolstered by the decision against reformism in Czechoslovakia the preceding year, also experienced a resurgence. Though not coterminous, Stalinist and Russian nationalist preferences favoured a two-camp view of the world, strategic superiority, anti-American vigilance, and, if negotiation with the West were unavoidable, its use for accusatory propaganda. Amplified by institutional interests likely to lose from strategic arms control, conservative and indeed reactionary opinion within the régime stood behind a series of exceedingly pessimistic media evaluations of what could be accomplished in Soviet dealings with the United States and also with West Germany.

Possibly because centrists in the leadership and their sup-

---

59 Of interest here is the attack on party 'centrists' in V. Golikov et al, 'Za leninskuyu partiinost v osveshchenii istorii KPSS,' *Kommunist*, no 3(1969), 67-82.

60 George W. Breslauer, *Khrushchev and Brezhnev as Leaders: Building Authority in Soviet Politics* (London: Allen & Unwin 1982), esp. 179-83. It should also be noted that as of 1969, Brezhnev was citing the existence of 'a more moderate wing' in addition to the 'aggressive circles' in the United States and was stating that such tendencies were taken into account in the determination of Soviet foreign policy. L.I. Brezhnev, *Leninskim kursom* (Moscow: Politizdat 1970), II, 412-13. Subsequently, in the Lenin anniversary address of 22 April 1970, he asserted that Soviet foreign policy was based in part on the presence of 'realistically-minded circles in the bourgeois countries who in fact recognize the principle of peaceful coexistence' (which could of course been but a small group in Washington): *ibid*, 586. In Garthoff's view, Brezhnev had opted for détente with the United States as well as Western Europe in 1969, but had yet to carry the leadership on the matter: 'BMD and East-West relations,' 300-1. On Brezhnev's foreign economic preferences in 1969, see Bruce Parrott, *Politics and Technology in the Soviet Union* (Cambridge MA: MIT Press 1983), 239-41.

61 John B. Dunlop, *The Faces of Contemporary Russian Nationalism* (Princeton NJ: Princeton University Press 1983), 217-25 and chap 10.

porting coalitions faced a more active threat from the right, reformist opinion also strengthened in 1969. While conservative assessments insisted, for example, that the United States military-industrial complex 'inevitably' gained the upper hand, 'completely' directed American politics, formed the 'real' government, and by virtue of the ABM and other decisions had already committed the United States to a new round in the strategic arms race,[62] others argued that countervailing forces were capable of constraining the military-industrial complex in a country 'literally split into two camps' over the value of the ABM programme and the political utility of military power.[63] Even Genoa could now be cited in reformist criticism of 'pessimists, quite a few,' who saw little potential for success in negotiation.[64] Caught in the crossfire – and possibly inclined to increasingly reformist positions – were those who favoured a divisive détente that could hardly be obtained if Moscow's posture was one of shrill anti-imperialism.

Though little is known about the give-and-take of Soviet internal bargaining after 10 June 1969, a provisional resolution of conflict over the military, political, and economic uses of strategic arms control would seem to have been reached by 20 October. The thrust of the Soviet decision was clearly to reject extreme conservative views and possibly to reaffirm the order of preferences that had prevailed in July 1968. Businesslike Soviet behaviour and the maintenance of confidentiality during the Helsinki discussions offered indisputable evidence that the

---

62 Naysaying of this kind is evident in D. Druzhinin, Moscow Domestic Service in Russian, 11 November 1969; M. Sturua, *Izvestia*, 24 June 1969; Yu. Gudkov, Moscow Domestic Service, 22 June 1969; N. Karaev, *Dinstiya shtyka i dollara* (Moscow: Politizdat 1969); E. Cheporov, Moscow Domestic Service, 5 October 1969; A. Belyaev, *Sotsialisticheskii promyshlennost*, 30 October 1969; G. Vasiliev, *Pravda*, 22 November 1969; and E. Cheporov, Moscow Domestic Service, 10 December 1969. Items broadcast within the Soviet Union are to be found in Foreign Broadcast Information Service, *Daily Report: Soviet Union* (Washington: United States Department of Commerce).

63 V. Losev, Moscow Domestic Service, 26 November 1969; Col. Engineer M. Belousov, *Za rubezhom*, no 40(1969); V. Vladimirov, Moscow Domestic Service, 8 August 1969; D. Draminov, *Izvestia*, 28 August 1969; and S. Vishnevskii, *Pravda*, 5 October 1969.

64 N. Polyanov, Moscow Domestic Service, 2 September 1969.

preference for anti-imperialist propaganda had for the moment been repudiated.[65] Soviet conduct also suggested that substance was of greater importance than appearances to Moscow.

Soviet delay in setting a date for SALT may therefore be attributed largely to the need for time to resolve internal differences over external bargaining strategy. Soviet internal bargaining seems to have been directly influenced by American external bargaining behaviour and by perceived political developments within the United States. Electoral politics in the Federal Republic, external bargaining with China, and the growing salience of Soviet economic renewal also had a role in the shaping of Soviet choices. But communications originating from the principal adversary seem to have been central. Though the actions of the Nixon administration lent themselves to the view that SALT would be used merely to further the acquisition of new strategic military power in the form of bargaining chips, by October a dual message seems to have got through: Washington might indeed be prepared to negotiate for an agreement, and if Moscow failed to take up the opportunity, it could be faced with the many consequences of simultaneous competitions in defensive and offensive strategic systems. At the same time, while the Soviet leadership was divided over American intentions, Americans who opposed the ABM programme and questioned the political utility of military power almost certainly provided support for those in Moscow who sought to make the case for substantive negotiation. Arms policy debates unfolding in two solitudes were subtly linked as Moscow moved towards the table.

But Soviet internal bargaining was evidently incomplete as of 20 October. Based on comments by their Soviet counterparts, American SALT delegates believed that Moscow decided to con-

---

65 A preference for propaganda is evident in a September 1968 article by the notorious Col. Rybkin, in which he asserted that 'it is impossible to agree that disarmament can be realized by *quiet* discussion of this acute and complex problem by representatives of opposing social systems' (emphasis added). Hope of success in such talks was an illusion in the view of Rybkin, who also inveighed against a 'utopian tranquillization' of the arms race and international political conflict. Quoted in Garthoff, 'BMD and East-West relations,' 299-300.

tinue the negotiation only in the course of the Helsinki round. As the chief American negotiator reported: 'Several Soviets had emphasized the importance of their decision to continue the talks. After the final plenary, one of their advisers said that, while "old hands" knew that discussions were possible between the United States and the u.s.s.r., a very great result of the session was that others now had this impression.'[66] In the final analysis, American external bargaining behaviour at Helsinki seems to have brought the internal Soviet bargaining process to its conclusion. There is a curious irony here. A régime that limited itself to tactical interventions in the American policy process ultimately left it to the United States to determine Soviet strategy on arms control.

The Soviet negotiating strategy was to emphasize substance over appearances and to eschew two-camp confrontation. Diminished interest in divisive détente was promptly signalled when very early in December 1969 Moscow modified its proposal for a European security conference to allow for American participation.[67] Concrete evidence, literally, of a preference for a stabilizing arms agreement with the principal adversary was to be had in April 1970, when the ussr unilaterally ceased construction of an estimated 78 launch sites so as to hold its land-based missile force to numerical parity with that of the Americans.[68] But strategic force modernization continued unabated. While prepared to reduce the risks and costs of military competition through negotiation, the Soviet leadership was determined to avoid constraints on its ability to compete, especially constraints that Nixon might gain through linkage. Moscow accordingly exercised its subsidiary option to exploit West-West differences by moving rapidly to a series of accommodations with the Federal Republic and, primarily through Bonn, to

66 Smith, *Doubletalk,* 106.
67 'Press conference at the Soviet Foreign Ministry,' *New Times,* no 4(1970), 17. The new position was communicated by the Soviet ambassador in Washington 'early in December' and before the nato Council meeting which began in Brussels on 4 December 1969.
68 See MccGwire, *Military Objectives,* 239, and his 'Gorbachev's arms policy rooted in past,' *Bulletin of the Atomic Scientists* 44(March 1988), 44.

détente in Europe. As well, the flow of arms to North Vietnam continued and the Soviet military presence in Egypt was substantially enlarged in 1969-70.

The United States administration was thus left to maintain its own internal bargaining strength as the Soviet Union endeavoured to constrain American choices by improving its own position through self-help and negotiation. For a time this procedure worked as Brezhnev joined Nixon in surprising adaptations of traditional national security policy. But eventually the predisposition of the Brezhnev régime to slight the need of American administrations to maintain domestic support for cooperation with the Soviet Union figured heavily in the undoing of superpower détente and strategic arms control.

NUCLEAR AND SPACE TALKS

The treaty of December 1987 that eliminated intermediate-range nuclear forces (INF) and shorter-range missiles had its origins in the exclusion of forward-based systems from the SALT I agreement. Seemingly permitted and clearly determined to modernize their strategic forces targeted against NATO Europe, the Soviet leadership began in 1977 to deploy the ss-20 missile in European areas of the USSR and then in the Far East.[69] The NATO decision of December 1979 to field offsetting American weapons in Europe led to American-Soviet negotiations on INF, which commenced in November 1981. Months later, parallel talks on the reduction of strategic intercontinental arms (the Strategic Arms Reduction Talks – START) were also begun. Then, in March 1983, Ronald Reagan proceeded to challenge the basic assumptions of nuclear deterrence and arms control with his announcement of the Strategic Defense Initiative (SDI). This programme aimed to create a space-based ballistic missile

---

69 Garthoff, *Detente and Confrontation*, 872-6. Discussions of the INF issue to early 1984 are also to be found in MccGwire, *Military Objectives*, and, above all, in Strobe Talbott, *Deadly Gambits: The Reagan Administration and the Stalemate in Nuclear Arms Control* (New York: Knopf 1984). Talbott's *The Master of the Game: Paul Nitze and the Nuclear Peace* (New York: Knopf 1988) provides a brief account of arms politics within the Reagan administration during the preliminaries of the nuclear and space talks.

defence which Moscow and many in the West seized upon as an egregious threat to peace. As the NATO deployment of Pershing II and ground-launched cruise missiles began in November 1983, the Soviet Union quit the INF talks and refused to resume START. Between November 1983 and March 1985, the Soviet Union found its way back to the table, and to the formal negotiation that produced the INF treaty some 30 months and several summits later.

The table to which the Soviets came in March 1985 was not the one they had left. Known as the Nuclear and Space Talks (NST), the new negotiation was to deal with a 'complex of questions concerning space and nuclear arms, both strategic and medium-range, with all these questions considered and resolved in their interrelationship.' The objective in discussing such matters was 'to work out effective agreements aimed at preventing an arms race in space and terminating it on earth, at limiting and reducing nuclear arms, and at strengthening strategic stability.' These goals were to be pursued by means of three concurrent negotiations, on INF, on strategic nuclear arms, and on space weapons. The Soviet Union and the United States further agreed that 'ultimately the following negotiations, just as efforts in general to limit and reduce arms, should lead to the complete elimination of nuclear weapons everywhere.'[70] The INF talks had thus been folded into an omnibus negotiation that envisaged complete nuclear disarmament and some form of accommodation on the military uses of space. Just as the SALT I agreements had represented a formidable increase in the scope of nuclear arms control when compared with negotiations for a test ban, NST signalled a further extension of the arms bargaining agenda. Though the INF treaty was to be the first fruit of these revived talks, considerably more than intermediate-range missiles was at stake as American and Soviet decision-makers reverted to wrangling and then explicit prenegotiation after November 1983.

70 The joint statement is available in *Pravda*, 9 January 1985.

Process as well as substance proved to be complex in the NST preliminaries. Broadly, the thrust of United States actions was to bring the Soviet Union back to the table for talks on the reduction of offensive forces even as deployments of American INF continued and work began on SDI. For its part, the Soviet Union sought to raise public opposition to INF in the NATO countries and, as of 28 June 1984, to commit the United States to negotiations (beginning in Vienna in September) that would prohibit the militarization of outer space.[71] Washington promptly accepted talks on space weapons in principle, but called as well for the resumption of those on INF and strategic nuclear arms. This the Soviet Union resisted until 16 November 1984. On that date Moscow conceded to the American bargaining position in privately proposing a ministerial meeting to work out details for the resumption of arms talks without precondition.[72] Several days later the two sides jointly announced that Andrei Gromyko and George Shultz would meet in Geneva to discuss the agenda for a negotiation on 'the entire range of questions relating to the nuclear and space arms.'[73] The ministers met as appointed, negotiated for two days, and on 8 January 1985 produced the joint statement on the 'subject and objectives' of the new talks. Soon thereafter date and place for the beginning of NST were announced: 12 March 1985 in Geneva.

From start to finish, Soviet participation in the prenegotiation for NST, and for the INF treaty, was presided over by a succession of three leaders – Yuri Andropov, Konstantin Chernenko, and Mikhail Gorbachev. The Nuclear and Space Talks began the day after Gorbachev assumed the general secretaryship and was in the following months affected by increasingly

71 *Pravda*, 29 June 1984. The Soviet proposal also called for a ban on the testing of anti-satellite (ASAT) systems, this at a time when there was opposition in the United States Congress to the testing of the F-15 in an ASAT mode.

72 Bernard Gwertzman, 'Moscow reported to suggest Shultz and Gromyko talk,' *New York Times*, 21 November 1984. The Soviet proposal was received in Washington on 17 November 1984.

73 Clyde Farnsworth, 'U.S. and Russians agree to resume armaments talks,' *New York Times*, 23 November 1984.

radical departures in Soviet domestic and foreign policy which in the ensemble marked a repudiation of the practices of the Brezhnev era. But for most of the prenegotiation phase, Gorbachev's status was that of heir presumptive to the ailing Chernenko and a prime mover in a régime that continued to revere the foreign policy accomplishments of Brezhnev. As of 12 March 1985, Gorbachev was himself unlikely to have fully thought through the new directions in internal and external affairs that eventually helped bring the USSR to the asymmetrical missile reductions (roughly 1700/800) and the intrusive verification arrangements of the INF treaty. He and his advisers had nevertheless reflected upon a new international security policy. In speaking to the British parliament on 18 December 1984, he referred to the need for 'new political thinking' and the dissolution of 'outdated stereotypes' — hallmarks of the security policy to come — and linked these notions to the Soviet proposal to start 'completely new talks' on nuclear and space arms.[74] In short, Soviet arms bargaining behaviour between 23 November 1984 and 12 March 1985 was not merely complex in substance and process, but transitional.

To simplify an otherwise unmanageable task, we need to understand only one Soviet move in the prenegotiation for NST: Moscow's proposal of 16 November 1984. This proposal came as a striking concession to the United States bargaining position and to the continued deployment of American INF in Europe. In return, the Soviet Union gained only a minor increment in the readiness of the Reagan administration to negotiate over SDI and the abolition of nuclear weapons. According to the conventional wisdom in the West, the USSR returned to the table for NST because the military strength and political cohesion of the Atlantic alliance left it no choice. This judgment makes sense when Soviet actions leading to the proposal of 16 November 1984 are viewed through the lens of 'old' thinking about international security. But when the precepts of a nascent

74 *Pravda*, 19 December 1984.

'new political thinking' are brought to the fore, the Soviet move to the table acquires a different meaning.

Explanation
Throughout 1984 and for months thereafter, many in the West believed that the Reagan administration had no serious interest in strategic arms control. Despite the president's acquiescence in extraordinary cleavages within his administration over the utility of arms control, it appeared that Washington was still wedded to the use of non-negotiable proposals to shift blame for the corrosion of East-West relations onto the Soviet Union as the United States military build-up continued. This also seemed to be the governing perception in Moscow until September 1984, when the Soviet assessment began to change.[75] To the extent that the United States was seen in Moscow to be an obdurate and deceitful bargaining partner, Soviet behaviour in turn had to be confined to non-negotiable proposals designed for public consumption. And yet Moscow had compelling interests in a resumption of arms talks.

Soviet military strategy, oriented to a homeland-sparing doctrine in the event of a world war, continued to favour a reduction of intercontinental nuclear forces.[76] But START had been suspended by Soviet decision. Meanwhile, American intermediate-range missiles, particularly the Pershing II with its short time to target, offered a new threat to the homeland. The same applied to SDI, which if pursued with vigour could face the USSR with a triple setback: a simultaneous build-up of offensive and defensive forces, an enhanced risk of nuclear attack in the event the United States achieved an effective anti-missile defence, and a transfer of the arms competition into the realm of exceedingly expensive high technology in which the Soviet Union suffered a competitive disadvantage. As it was, the

75 For the hard line, see, for example, Gromyko, *Pravda*, 3 July 1984; editorial, *ibid*, 6 August 1984; Yuri Zhukov, *ibid*, 6 September 1984.
76 MccGwire, *Military Objectives*, chap 13, and 'New directions in Soviet arms control policy,' *Washington Quarterly* 11(summer 1988), 188, 196.

revolution in military technology was presenting Moscow with radically new and highly demanding conventional force requirements.[77] Meanwhile, the Soviet economy continued to operate at a deficit, possibly a 'critically large' shortfall at about this time.[78] To cap it all, as of midsummer 1984 Soviet fulminations against INF deployment and SDI were producing no favourable results either in American policy or in public opinion within the European NATO countries.

But after all that had occurred since the NATO decision to deploy American INF in Europe, was Moscow finally to humble itself by returning to the INF talks and START as the United States demanded? And was Moscow to make this kind of concession to an American government deemed unwilling to negotiate in good faith? These questions received a twofold answer in the Soviet proposal of 28 June 1984 for negotiations to prevent the militarization of outer space. By seeking to change the subject of arms bargaining from INF and strategic nuclear arms to SDI, Soviet decision-makers moved towards a new basis for negotiation. At the same time, by proposing to prohibit space weapons and by underlining the extraordinary deterioration of American-Soviet relations, Moscow evidently hoped to strengthen the appeal of the Democratic nominee in the 1984 presidential election[79] and to amplify public opposition to NATO nuclear strategy in Western Europe.

The deft American response, in calling for the resumption of INF talks and START while allowing for some discussion of space weapons, served to deny the Soviet Union any substantial gains in turning American and European opinion. Despite con-

---

77 M.A. Gareyev, *M.V. Frunze – voennyi teoretik* (Moscow: Voenizdat 1985), 239-40. This volume was sent to press on 17 November 1984.

78 Finance Minister Boris Gostev, as quoted in Jeff Sallot, 'Soviets hope lack of price rises will fend off economic anarchy,' Toronto *Globe and Mail*, 2 November 1988, B17.

79 Gromyko, for example, denounced the administration's negotiating position and went on to say: 'We do not think that ... many in the United States will be taken in by a deception that is obviously calculated to gain votes.' *Pravda*, 3 July 1984.

tinuing conflict within the administration, by early September Washington seemed increasingly prepared to add space weapons to the agenda of any would-be negotiation. Indeed, as the presidential election gained momentum, Reagan became more insistent that nuclear arms control would rank high in his priorities during a second term. Given his continued vehemence in stating that SDI was not negotiable, the evident aim of the United States was to resume the INF talks and START, and to get the USSR to go along with SDI. Nevertheless, even as Chernenko asserted on 2 September 1984 that the American position was 'directly opposite' to the Soviet one,[80] the bargaining agenda had already begun to alter.

At some point in September, Soviet expectations started to change. Not only was American and European opinion holding firm, but the prospect of a Republican victory on 6 November may have begun to dawn on Moscow. Almost certainly Soviet decision-makers saw new evidence of serious American interest in negotiation when Reagan proposed that 'umbrella talks' be considered. Presented on 24 September at the United Nations, Reagan's vague thought was 'to extend the arms control process to build a bigger umbrella under which we can operate – a road map if you will, showing where, during the next twenty years or so, these individual efforts can lead.'[81] More immediately significant was Moscow's agreement to an American proposal that Gromyko meet for the first time with Reagan in Washington following the foreign minister's address to the United Nations on 27 September. At this meeting Gromyko began to explore the 'umbrella' concept. According to the United States national security adviser, Robert McFarlane, the meeting also resulted in 'acceptance on both sides that we have no hostile intents.'[82] Soviet assent to such an encounter, and inevitably to

---

80 Chernenko in *Pravda*, 2 September 1984.

81 Bernard Gwertzman, 'Soviet has queries on arms proposal,' *New York Times*, 10 November 1984, 3.

82 *Ibid*; Farnsworth, 'U.S. and Russians agree.' McFarlane dated the beginnings of the breakthrough from the time of Gromyko's meeting with Reagan in Washington.

a session between Gromyko and Walter Mondale (the Democratic candidate for president), indicated a correction of course in Moscow. The Soviet leadership now seemed slightly less interested in creating public pressure on the United States by 'exposing' the administration to American and European publics and more prepared to consider what the American administration itself had to offer. The new inclination in Soviet policy was made official on 18 October when, in answers to questions posed by the *Washington Post*, Chernenko or those preparing replies for him acknowledged in passing that 'a change for the better' was possible in American-Soviet relations.[83]

Between mid-October and 16 November, Soviet behaviour towards the United States became increasingly differentiated. Publicly, the Soviet line remained accusatory (and broadly would continue so until 1987). But now Moscow also began to explore the potential of the 'umbrella talks' idea in private exchanges.[84] By the time of Reagan's re-election, the two sides were discussing a ministerial meeting in January to settle the framework and procedures for a resumed negotiation.[85] Trade-offs in defining the 'subject' and 'objectives' of the talks had no doubt become a key Soviet concern by this time.

If Moscow was to concede on the matter of subject by returning to talks that dealt with INF as American deployments continued, it no doubt sought a measure of compensation in the definition of objectives. In particular, if the United States could be brought to accept not only a linkage between offensive and defensive weapons but the need to abolish nuclear weapons, a variety of long-term Soviet goals could be advanced. Not the least of these would be the exploitation of differences between the Americans and their allies. Be that as it may, on 16 Novem-

---

83 *Pravda*, 18 October 1984 (issued by Tass the day before).
84 Exchanges occurred 26 October in Washington, 31 October in Moscow, and early in November in Moscow. Gwertzman, 'Soviet has queries,' and 'U.S. says it has begun to "flesh out" the idea of umbrella talks,' *New York Times*, 16 November 1984, 12.
85 Gwertzman, 'Soviet has queries.'

ber, soon before a series of conciliatory remarks on the restoration of détente in American-Soviet relations was issued by Chernenko, the Soviet leadership took it upon itself to propose privately to Washington that talks be held between their foreign ministers, Gromyko and Shultz, to establish a 'new' negotiation on space and nuclear arms.[86]

Widely regarded in the West as an abrupt cave-in to Western strength and American insistence, the Soviet concession of 16 November turns out to have been the culmination of a series of moves that began with the proposal of 28 June and that included American actions which helped Moscow return to the table. Having failed to force the United States into altering the substance of its arms and arms control policies as of early September, Moscow was nevertheless presented with a changing American attitude towards negotiation as such. Indeed, given the administration's desire to prevent arms control from becoming a negative electoral issue, the Soviet bargaining stance after 28 June may have prompted the Americans to be more forthcoming on the negotiability of SDI in particular. By the same token, Soviet public diplomacy could have contributed to the efforts of those within the administration who sought to create a framework for the resumption of negotiations.

Whether or not Soviet actions indeed played into the United States internal bargaining process, Soviet monitoring of the presidential election and of internal American bargaining over arms control appears to have modified prevailing expectations and preferences in Moscow by September. Presidential statements, including the 'umbrella talks' proposal and the face-to-face encounter with Gromyko, could well have been critical in reinforcing the thought among Soviet decision-makers that the interplay of contending forces in Washington might after all produce an American willingness to negotiate in something like

---

86 The Soviet proposal was received in Washington on 17 November: Gwertzman, 'Moscow reported to suggest.' Chernenko commented in response to questions from Marvin Kalb of NBC: *Pravda*, 18 November 1984.

good faith. Those in Moscow who preferred a posture of continuing confrontation towards the United States may thus have been placed at a disadvantage relative to those who favoured negotiation in earnest or negotiation for appearances in Western Europe.

For the Soviet Union, however, the basic problem was not so much the productivity of prospective talks or their offensive uses, but the necessity to concede to the Americans. Where face was concerned, American handling of SDI and the 'umbrella' concept presumably played into the Soviet decision process in ways that made it easier for the leadership to claim it was entering 'completely new talks.' But the real difficulty in conceding to the United States was the all-but-explicit admission that Soviet security policies of recent years had been fatally flawed. At stake were basic questions of domestic as well as foreign affairs – questions of principle – that could hardly be resolved on the basis of arms bargaining considerations alone.

Gorbachev tells us that well before he assumed office he and others were committed to a fundamental reformation of Soviet ways, foreign policy included.[87] Domestic reform was of course the prime concern, but it could not be separated from the economic and political consequences of foreign policy keyed to the goal of Soviet domination in global conflict between opposed social systems. In citing the need for new political thinking in his speech to the British parliament in December, Gorbachev was very likely drawing upon an incipient foreign policy belief system that would have the USSR renounce predominance and domination in favour of new international relationships based upon progressive Western concepts of mutual security and the realities of interdependence.

As well and if only as an avid student of Lenin's practice, Gorbachev could hardly have been unaware of the political use of appeals to liberal and 'pacifist' sentiment in combating con-

---

87 Gorbachev emphasizes that a reappraisal of Soviet policies across the board had begun well before the April 1985 Central Committee plenum: *Perestroika: New Thinking for Our Country and the World* (New York: Harper & Row 1987), esp. 24-7.

servative policy predispositions abroad. Moreover, there was an unusual twist to the situation in 1984: a conservative American president was personally committed to the goal of making nuclear weapons impotent and obsolete. Though space-based ballistic missile defences were unacceptable as the means to this end, Reagan's interest in nuclear abolition raised the possibility of constraining conservative policy arguments in the West by committing the American state to a contemporary equivalent of the 'very broad pacifist programme' favoured by Lenin in 1922. In fact, when it came, the joint American-Soviet statement of 8 January 1985 on the subject and objectives of NST represented initial progress in solidifying the American commitment to nuclear abolition. But before the joint statement was reached and began to make things harder for the 'war party' in the West, a setback had to be administered to the 'war party' in a Soviet régime still headed by Chernenko.

Though Soviet succession politics in the late summer and autumn of 1984 remain obscure, several things are more or less certain. Chernenko, whose tenure was marked by 'relative political inactivity within the era of aspiration for reform initiated by Andropov,' was surrendering to emphysema and related disorders.[88] In his absence, Gorbachev, possibly by arrangement at the time of Andropov's death, chaired sessions of the Politburo and Central Committee Secretariat, as second in command.[89] But while Gorbachev was well placed to accede to the general secretaryship and had acquired broad responsibility in external as well as domestic affairs, Gromyko had seniority in matters of foreign policy and Gorbachev's claim to office had yet to be ratified. When that ratification came, on 11 March 1985, it was Gromyko who, with great personal conviction, gave the nominating speech.[90] As a principal architect of the foreign policy that had brought the USSR to a dead end in strategic

88 The quotation is from Baruch A. Hazan, *From Brezhnev to Gorbachev: Infighting in the Kremlin* (Boulder CO: Westview 1987), 140.
89 Archie Brown, 'Gorbachëv: new man in the Kremlin,' *Problems of Communism* 24(May-June 1985), 8, 14.
90 The speech is reproduced in Hazan, *From Brezhnev to Gorbachev*, 144-5.

arms control and so much else, Gromyko was likely to have
favoured a course correction as distinct from a transformation
of Soviet foreign conduct. Others, however, and Grigoryi Romanov would seem to have been their leading spokesman, evidently favoured continuity and strength as opposed to concessions. In these circumstances, Gorbachev could only have
kept his reformist proclivities in check, which is what he did in
his pronouncements to Soviet audiences through February 1985.

When we consider the pattern of Chernenko's public appearances to 16 November 1984, we note that the general secretary was up and about and presumably 'leading' at key moments
in the process that finally brought Moscow to the table for NST.[91]
Also apparent is the fact that Gromyko's stature rose in October
and November, as did Romanov's, whereas Gorbachev seems
to have fallen under a cloud.[92] Indeed, there is good evidence
that Gorbachev was not present at the Politburo session of 15
November which seems to have authorized the negotiating
concession of the following day and Chernenko's conciliatory
interview with NBC soon thereafter. To obscure the picture still
further, Chernenko's published interviews of 18 October and
18 November struck an increasingly moderate tone on relations
with the United States, whereas the October anniversary address as read by Gromyko on 6 November was hostile. Only
late in November did Gorbachev's standing improve visibly and
then surge upwards as the Soviet media covered his visit to
Britain in December.[93]

91 Having been in Moscow at the time the Soviet negotiating proposal of 28 June
was made, Chernenko left for vacation on 15 July and was not seen in public
until 5 September. On that date he, with difficulty, awarded medals to a group
of Soviet cosmonauts. Gorbachev, not Chernenko, had opened the Friendship
Games in Moscow not long before. Chernenko was in evidence prior to and
during Gromyko's visit to the United States at the end of September. On 17
October, a television clip showed him giving the *Washington Post* interview of
that day. As well, he appears to have been at the Politburo meeting of 15
November. Hazan, *From Brezhnev to Gorbachev*, 122-30.

92 *Ibid*, 127-31. Gorbachev's visit to Britain had, however, been announced by Mrs
Thatcher on 7 November.

93 *Ibid*, 130-2.

We therefore have reason to believe that it was not Gorbachev but Gromyko and Chernenko who were principally responsible for the Soviet negotiating concession of 16 November. Given the personal quality of the nominating speech for Gorbachev a few months later, Gromyko may have been fronting for Gorbachev at a difficult moment in the latter's rise to primacy. The clear losers in the Politburo decision of 15 November were Romanov and other irreconcilables who favoured a continuation of Brezhnev-style international security and domestic policies. Though Gorbachev's ensuing rise to pre-eminence is not to be attributed to a single foreign policy decision, Politburo proceedings on strategic nuclear arms control must have had an effect on his leadership prospects and hence on overall Soviet strategy.

The key Soviet prenegotiatory concession of 16 November may therefore be seen as the outcome of intersecting internal and external bargaining processes. The effect of the American posture of strength and constrained flexibility in negotiation, coupled with Reagan's resounding election victory over Mondale, left the Soviet leadership with little real alternative but to concede that past policy had indeed been misguided. In particular, SDI and the potential it offered to those in Washington who sought offensive missile reductions[94] presented counterparts in Moscow with good reason to moderate political-military conflict with the United States, and with opportunities to exploit public opposition in the West to military modernization and indeed to the very existence of nuclear weapons.

In making the concession of 16 November 1984, Moscow

---

94 Though we have no way of knowing how conflict within the Reagan administration over strategic arms was assessed in Moscow, we may assume that they had much current information and, once Strobe Talbott's *Deadly Gambits* appeared early in November 1984, more than they needed on the background. In particular, Gromyko's personal evaluation of Reagan and the president's commitment to arms control must have made a difference. Some detail on the goings on in Washington during this period is provided in Talbott's *Master of the Game* (pp 200-16), which depicts McFarlane and Paul Nitze as prepared to negotiate constraints on SDI.

began to extricate itself from the hole into which it had fallen with the deployment of the ss-20 and the related misadventures of the Brezhnev years. In assisting this turn in Soviet policy, the United States assisted in the rise of a man whose endeavour to make a wasting asset of military strength would pose a radical challenge to American security policy. American 'strength' certainly helped bring the Soviet Union to the negotiating table for NST. But it also opened the way for Soviet threat-reducing activity that would subvert the military power of the United States and its allies.

CONCLUSIONS

Why then has the Soviet Union come to the table to negotiate in earnest with the United States on matters of nuclear arms control? Are there patterns to be observed in Soviet prenegotiatory behaviour? And what might Soviet conduct suggest for an understanding of negotiation as well as prenegotiation? In answering these questions, we should be clear about what we mean by the term 'Soviet Union.'

As referred to here, 'Soviet Union' signifies an authoritarian and highly centralized political system, the heart of which is a single-party régime. The foreign behaviour of the system is expressed in an array of established predispositions or tendencies whose relative influence alters under the impact of domestic and international situational variables. Situational variables have status but no force unless they are perceived and acted upon in the light of the régime's goals. Political co-operation and conflict within the régime is all-important in determining the system's responses, including those on arms bargaining, to situational change. Significant foreign policy responses to change typically take the form of adjustments in the relative strength or correlation of the system's tendencies.

Four basic tendencies are to be observed in the cases considered here.[95] Indeed, they are to be seen in Soviet conduct towards the West on most issues. Stated very briefly, these tend-

95 For detail, see Griffiths, 'Sources of American conduct.'

encies are *coercive isolationism* (confrontational and ultimately self-isolating use of proposals and negotiations to 'expose' the innate aggressiveness of imperialism); *expansionist internationalism* (use of proposals and negotiations to mask the acquisition of military strength and to assist in the conciliation of the principal adversary's allies and the uncommitted); *reformative internationalism* (use of negotiations with the principal adversary to achieve substantive agreements that stabilize and ultimately demilitarize the struggle of opposed social systems while easing the way for increasingly rapid social change at home and abroad); and *democratic isolationism* (use of negotiations and agreements to achieve a fundamental settlement of differences with capitalist states and thereby to create conditions conducive to radical reform of the Soviet economy and democratization of the political system). Only under Gorbachev, it should be noted, has democratic isolationism been converted from a current of opinion to the status of a tendency of the system. The origins of the other three tendencies can be traced back to Genoa, to the debate of 1918 over Brest-Litovsk, and to diverging orientations among Russian socialists prior to 1917.

Each of these tendencies has of course evolved and has also made for a different approach to arms prenegotiation, negotiation, and agreements. Only very rarely has unanimity within the régime been such that one tendency prevails to the exclusion of all others in the repertoire of Soviet arms bargaining practice. Which is to say that Soviet behaviour is usually ambiguous. What is not ambiguous is the highly instrumental Soviet approach to negotiation as a tool of political as well as military strategy.

Though all four tendencies incline the Soviet Union to engage in arms bargaining of one kind or another, only reformative internationalism and democratic isolationism represent a predisposition to negotiate *in earnest* with the principal adversary. So, the question is not so much what brings the Soviet Union to the table for nuclear arms talks with the United States. The question is what serves to strengthen reformist responses in the overall correlation of Soviet tendencies.

The four cases considered here suggest that economic stress

has been a perennial and in recent decades an increasingly potent factor in the moderation of Soviet arms bargaining behaviour. The persistent failure of social and political development within advanced capitalist societies to conform to Soviet expectations has also been a force in the appreciation of reformative and democratic isolationist tendencies. Fear of war, above all nuclear war, and the growing recognition since the mid-1960s that nuclear arms control could meet the military-strategic interests of the country have further moderated the arms bargaining predispositions of the régime. Finally, the emergence of political and economic, if not military-strategic, multipolarity since the late 1950s has prompted Soviet decision-makers to better their relations with the United States through strategic arms control.

But if there is a single precondition for the growing readiness of the Soviet Union to negotiate in earnest with the principal adversary, it is the stubborn and unrealistic optimism of Soviet leaders in estimating their capacity to transform the external environment. When this optimism is punctured, and when the public or the government of the opposing society or both show signs of interest in negotiation, the Soviet Union moves to the bargaining table with substance and not merely appearances in mind.

The conjuncture of policy failure and opportunity for accommodation is to be seen in each of our cases. Under Lenin, the unexpected deferral of socialist revolution in Europe, for which October was to have been the spark, was accompanied by perceived opportunities to employ arms proposals to moderate the behaviour of the leading adversary. In 1963, the failure of Khrushchev's excessively ambitious foreign policy strategy was driven home at a time when the Kennedy administration seemed capable of entering into potentially reformative agreements. In 1969, America's troubles served to heighten the sense of opportunity. In bargaining from what appeared to be greater strength, the Brezhnev-Kosygin régime seemed nevertheless to respond to the shadow of crisis in Soviet economic performance.

The unrealistic expectation of the Brezhnev leadership that the global correlation of forces could be altered to favour the Soviet Union while co-operation continued with the United States was in turn a contributing factor to the next conjuncture of failure and opportunity. Under Gorbachev, an impending economic crisis and an untenable international strategy of domination joined with perceived opportunities to transform Western opinion of the Soviet Union to bring the USSR back to the table for the Nuclear and Space Talks in 1985. *If* history is any guide, Gorbachev's far-reaching expectations of international change will sooner or later be proven unrealistic, and the Soviet Union will settle for less as the illusion is revealed.

Failure and opportunity have thus combined to create situations that evoke reformist tendencies in Soviet conduct and move the régime into progressively deeper collaboration with the principal adversary on arms control and disarmament. Reformism in Soviet arms bargaining behaviour has of course been reversible. Lenin's decisions were undone by Stalin, Khrushchev's by Brezhnev and Kosygin, and Brezhnev's by Brezhnev. Nevertheless, the capacity to collaborate has grown markedly since 1917. Moreover, if coming to terms with the principal adversary on means to reduce the risks and opportunity costs of an adversarial relationship adds up to learning, our cases suggest that it is in prenegotiatory interaction that much Soviet learning occurs.

Though the significance of formal negotiation and agreements should not be slighted, the record demonstrates that Moscow decides on the basic issues in the process of getting to the table. Soviet decision-makers enter formal bargaining encounters knowing what they want and prepared to stay the course. They do not go in expecting to improvise. Typically, what they want is not so much a specific agreement as a modification of the overall relationship with the adversary. This was the case with Lenin's decision in principle on a reformative approach to arms bargaining in 1922. It was the case in 1963, when only a few days of formal negotiation were required to bring to fruition the reformative preferences that had taken shape under Khrushchev's guidance. Similarly, by the end of the first round of SALT in December 1969, Moscow seemed to have decided to mute the expansionist predisposition to negotiate for appearances and to undertake instead to bargain in earnest. And as of March 1985, Gorbachev and some of his colleagues had probably resolved not only to get American INF out of Europe but to pursue a reformation of East-West relations according to the principle that the real enemy is the image of the enemy.

Our cases also suggest that learning occurs through internal bargaining processes that serve to moderate the tendencies of the Soviet system. Each tendency may be said to represent a distinct variant of the régime's goals, situational assessments, and action preferences in dealing with the West. Though what happened in practice has been far less tidy than this, incremental learning has occurred as the correlation of Soviet tendencies was repeatedly altered to accentuate reformative and more recently democratic isolationist goals, perceptual biases, and policy preferences. Again, it is in the preliminaries to formal negotiation, and not in formal bargaining as such, that most Soviet learning may well be found.

This much allowed, we are well on the way to identifying patterns in Soviet behaviour prior to the negotiation of substantive arms agreements with the United States. The underlying pattern is one of tendency shifts in processes of internal bargaining whose outcomes favour reformist approaches to formal negotiation. External bargaining, both tacit and face to face, has by no means been insignificant in the determination of Soviet predispositions before talks begin. Indeed, Soviet decision-makers have typically found themselves engaged in simultaneous internal and external bargaining as they contemplate moving to the table. But the essence of Soviet prenegotiatory behaviour is internal bargaining which serves to convert situational variables into political action by the régime.

As our cases make clear, Soviet leaders have been in no

position to issue orders on major matters of disarmament and arms control. Lenin had to reconcile conflicting predispositions within the régime to obtain a course correction of some 90 degrees in the Soviet approach to arms talks. Khrushchev's internal bargaining position would seem to have been improved by the chance occurrence of another's heart attack, but he was left with a situation in which a limited nuclear test ban was the most that could be sustained. The prenegotiation of 1969 was accompanied by coalition politics in which Brezhnev's personal position may have been improved by decisions that gave greater weight to reformative tactics in promoting favourable change in the global correlation of forces. An equally murky bargaining process, now beginning to take the shape of a contest between 'new' and 'old' in Soviet domestic as well as foreign policy, seems to have produced the return to the table and an enhancement of democratic isolationist preferences in March 1985.

If Soviet prenegotiatory behaviour has been shaped primarily by the happenstance of internal bargaining within a secretive régime, what might the role of external bargaining have been? As I see it, two-way communications have been at work. On the one hand, both intended and involuntary signals from the United States have played into the Soviet internal bargaining process to affect goal determination, situational assessments, action preferences, and thus the correlation of tendencies. On the other hand, Soviet actions have fed into the American policy process to produce effects or lack of them, which have also been monitored in Moscow and fed back into Soviet decision-making. Either way, relevant information appears to have been highly contextual and concerned far more than the nuts and bolts of prospective arms talks.

Our data indicate that communications originating in the West, above all from the United States, have reverberated within the Soviet system to affect internal bargaining there. These communications, in the phrase of Lenin, have been both 'nasty and nice.' To cite 'nice' influences, if there had been little or no pacifist reaction to the World War I, there would have been no real way for Lenin to have taken the steps he did in committing the Soviet state to a conciliatory but anti-imperialist arms bargaining posture in 1922. Had the Kennedy administration and the American people showed less interest in an improved relationship with the USSR and in a test ban treaty, Khrushchev's effort to obtain even a limited test ban might well have been denied on grounds of appeasement. More particularly, the Anglo-American letter of 24 April 1963 proposing a resumption of talks reached Moscow at exactly the right moment and permitted Khrushchev to present himself to colleagues as responding to foreign applicants. Similar considerations, notably the Nixon administration's stated interest in negotiation, its behaviour in the first round of SALT, and evident public opposition not only to the ABM programme but to reliance on armed force, would seem together to have influenced the outcome of internal Soviet bargaining over relations with the United States in 1969. The same applies to the repeated American injunctions after 1966 that no advantage was to be had from simultaneous competitions in strategic defensive and offensive systems. Equivalent Soviet assessments of American and European opinion on nuclear war and the nuclear arms race undoubtedly figured in the formation of 'new' thinking and Gorbachev's evident determination as of early 1985 to secure an INF agreement. Indeed, European as well as American reformist views, as contained for example in the report of the Palme Commission, were not only observed but absorbed wholesale into the new thinking and increasingly into Soviet practice after 1985.

But 'nice' alone from the West was not enough in the decades between 1917 and 1987. Whether or not 'nasty' is the right word, communications from the West that also threatened or delivered deprivations were equally important in bringing the Soviet Union around. Denials abound in our cases: of world socialist revolution after 1917, of the Khrushchev and Brezhnev foreign policy offensives, of authentic military parity (one might say parody), of military stability (the American ABM potential in 1969 and SDI in 1984). Notwithstanding the primacy of internal bargaining, the unilateral signalling of inducements and threats coupled with the bilateral exchanges that together constitute external bargaining helped Moscow not only to come to the table but to come prepared to deal. As well, Soviet decisions have been affected by attempts to 'help' the adversary to co-operate.

Though the Brezhnev-Kosygin régime seems to have confined itself to tactical interventions in American foreign and defence policy making, the effect of Moscow's actions in 1969 was to improve the long-range Soviet bargaining outlook by helping to contain the Safeguard system and the administration's ability to use its ABM programme as a bargaining chip. The Soviet posture in the first half of the year was consistent with expansionist international preferences to secure unilateral advantage through atmospheric effects. But when Moscow opted for negotiations in earnest, it could well have been judged that Soviet actions had served to bolster an arms control coalition in the United States which would continue to benefit the cause of co-operation.

Similar efforts to help the adversary to co-operate are to be observed in the remaining three cases. Lenin authorized the practice of attuning Soviet diplomacy to the task of strengthening the advocacy of co-operation with Moscow. Under Khrushchev, a series of Soviet moves after 1958 served to improve the outlook for negotiation of a test ban treaty and conceivably, as of midsummer 1963, for improved American-Soviet relations through to the end of a second Kennedy administration in 1968. And in 1984-5, Gorbachev hinted at a similar inclination to create an international setting that helped to build support in the West for progressively more ambitious arms agreements with the USSR. All of which brings us to a final pattern that emerges from the Soviet experience of prenegotiation for arms control and disarmament.

In greater or lesser measure, the Soviet exponent of collaboration with the principal adversary has found himself engaged in an informal alliance with counterparts on the other side.

This happens quite simply because he is engaged in simultaneous internal and external bargaining. His need, and the need of his analogue, have ultimately been the same: to help and gain help from the other side in reducing the strength of conservative policy preferences in both polities simultaneously. Conversely, the opponents of collaboration work together informally by doing what comes naturally to resist it.

This was the pattern in 1922, when Lenin dealt simultaneously with Soviet sectarians and the Winston Churchills of Great Britain in seeking to further both his own preferences for accommodation and those of British liberals and pacifists. The situation was broadly the same for Khrushchev and Kennedy in 1963: they had more in common on the main arms bargaining issue of the day than they did with the Kozlovs and Barry Goldwaters who pursued parallel unilateral courses to the same end of 'no deal.' The picture was somewhat but not wholly different in 1969 and 1984-5. In the former case Brezhnev, who seems at the time to have been appropriating some of Kosygin's policy agenda, occupied more common ground with Nixon on the matter of strategic arms control than either leader shared with the Henry Jacksons and Soviet diehards. In the 1984-5 prenegotiation, Gorbachev and the emerging exponents of the 'new' apparently believed that there were sufficient commonalities between their arms policy preferences and those of the American public and key United States officials to permit joint action that would impose increasingly effective constraints upon American and Soviet reactionaries.

Accordingly, the model of arms bargaining that emerges from the Soviet prenegotiatory experience is not one that pits the Soviet Union against the United States. Instead we find highly informal transnational coalitions of Americans and Russians who are pursuing parallel goals in separate internal bargaining exercises which are loosely linked by external bargaining.[96]

96 Franklyn Griffiths, 'Transnational politics and arms control,' *International Journal* 25(autumn 1971), 640-74.

Though we have been concerned here with the preliminaries to formal bargaining, there is little reason to doubt that similar transnational interactions figure in formal negotiation as well.

What then do these observations about Soviet prenegotiatory behaviour suggest for our understanding of prenegotiation and negotiation as such? To return to my opening remarks, it seems to me that we in the West have paid excessive attention to the give-and-take of formal bargaining. Our interest has been captured by the figure of formal negotiation as a thing in itself. Processes that very largely determine negotiating outcomes have been relegated to background or extra-negotiatory status. To understand more clearly what is going on, we need to reverse the relationship in our mind's eye and pay greater attention to the ground on which the superpower arms bargaining table rests.

The ground is to be found not so much in Geneva or another European capital, but in concurrent bargaining processes centred in Moscow and Washington. It is these processes that give the negotiators their mandates. They are shaped by an array of variables that would seem to have little or nothing to do with arms control and disarmament as conventionally understood, but that have in some measure been understood by the Soviet Union. Discussions of strategic arms bargaining that centre on the number and quality of weapons, the implications of proposals and agreements for crisis and arms race stability, and so on are to a degree inevitable. But they tell us nothing about where the political will to collaborate might come from.

The Soviet experience directs us to the question of political will. It tells us that something is to be gained by doing away with a truncated conception of superpower external bargaining that stresses what happens or might happen at the table. It urges us to pay more attention to ways in which American and Soviet actions on a wide range of issues – everything from consular arrangements to involvement in distant wars – play into one another's internal bargaining and influence the interplay of tendencies in the conduct of each towards the other.

As well, the objectives of strategic arms control ought not to be defined primarily in military-technical terms. There is no need to rehearse the variety of objectives that have been pursued by Soviet leaders in arms bargaining over the years. Suffice it to say that they have been highly political and have included the provision of help to counterparts as well as the pursuit of unilateral gain, military-technical advantage included. To the degree that the inner workings of the Soviet political system become more transparent in the years ahead, it will be increasingly possible for Westerners to take a leaf from the Soviet book and begin to pursue extra-negotiatory objectives in arms bargaining with the USSR. To begin with, American and Soviet advocates of co-operation in nuclear and conventional arms arrangements could well embark upon a systematic discussion of what it takes to reinforce one another's positions and to avoid doing unintended damage to the arguments of one's counterpart.

In sum, the extra-negotiatory environment is the prime source and should also be regarded as the prime concern of prenegotiation and negotiation for superpower collaboration in major matters of arms control and disarmament. Until the United States and the Soviet Union begin to regulate the way they intervene in one another's policy processes and together insulate their bilateral interaction against ups and downs produced by local conflicts, East-West arms bargaining will remain hostage to events, and today's 'up' will sooner or later be followed by a 'down.' American-Soviet entente, not détente, is required for truly substantial progress in disarmament and arms control.

5. Headed for the Table: United States Approaches to Arms Control Prenegotiation

FEN OSLER HAMPSON

Arms control got a new lease on life at the end of Ronald Reagan's presidency. Six months after signing an agreement with the Soviet Union to ban intermediate-range nuclear forces (INF), the United States president went to Moscow for his fourth summit where he expressed strong hopes for the speedy conclusion of an agreement in the Strategic Arms Reduction Talks (START) which would halve the intercontinental arsenals of the two superpowers.[1] All this from a president who had won the White House eight years before on a platform that rejected arms control and who had promoted the biggest military build-up in United States history. What brought the United States back to the negotiating table? Why have arms control negotiations come to be viewed by successive administrations as an important element of relations with the Soviet Union? What factors influence any administration, no matter how pro-military and hawkish, to participate in formal arms control negotiations?

The pursuit of arms control has been surprisingly uneven. Until the early 1960s, there was no serious progress, and it was not until the end of the decade that the two superpowers ac-

Associate Professor of International Affairs, The Norman Paterson School of International Affairs, Carleton University, and research associate at the Canadian Institute for International Peace and Security, Ottawa, Ontario.

I would like to thank Steven Miller, Sean Lynn-Jones, Steven Lee, and the members of the Project on Prenegotiation for their extremely helpful comments on earlier drafts of this paper.

1 Because of the counting rules in START, the agreement would effectively only reduce the number of strategic nuclear charges by one-third.

tually sat down at the negotiating table to commence serious discussions about limiting strategic forces. The Strategic Arms Limitation Talks (SALT) continued throughout the 1970s, but there was another hiatus after the Reagan administration, less committed to arms control, took over the White House. As one recent study notes, progress in managing and limiting strategic competition and in seeking ways to avoid accidental war has been of 'a limited, fragile character,' and once developments in the 1970s and 1980s challenged the 'belief that the United States has a long-range interest in maintaining the strategic arms regime ... the issue became a highly divisive one within the influential elite in the United States.'[2]

This article addresses three questions. First of all, why do states choose to become involved in arms control negotiation? Or, phrased somewhat differently, when do they believe it to be in their interest to pursue negotiation? Second, why did the four cases examined here get to the table? Third, what factors shaped the United States government's substantive position prior to the negotiations themselves? That is to say, what determined the boundaries and agenda for the negotiations that followed? Did the agenda for formal negotiation expand or narrow during the prenegotiation process? This is not the same as asking why a government changes its position in a negotiation, what factors determine the pace of a negotiation, or what factors determine the likelihood of reaching agreement in a negotiation. And it is worth noting that involvement in a negotiation is not, in and of itself, an indication of a desire to reach agreement. Instead, we are concerned with asking why negotiation is considered in the first place and why states choose negotiation as a policy option.

A number of different domestic political, military policy, and foreign policy motivations can be identified to explain why states will choose to engage in arms control negotiation. One

2 Alexander L. George, Philip J. Farley, and Alexander Dallin, eds, *U.S.-Soviet Security Cooperation: Achievements, Failures, Lessons* (New York: Oxford University Press 1988), 715.

set of reasons emerges from military and geostrategic considerations. A recent study of United States-Soviet arms control notes that 'arms control agreements have been concluded only when neither side had an appreciable advantage – that is, only when there already existed rough parity in the relevant forces of the two sides.'[3] Moreover, the study concludes that meaningful constraints on any particular category of weapons cannot be achieved 'if either side strongly prefers unfettered freedom of action with regard to the weapons in question ... If either party has tested the weapon or invested heavily in it, the difficulties confronting arms control are compounded.'[4] While these conditions define the possibility of success in reaching arms control agreements, they do not explain why the parties went to the negotiating table in the first place. The decision to enter into negotiation may well be influenced by a broader range of factors than those just mentioned, including a perceived change in the military balance of forces, the emergence of new technologies that threaten current military capabilities, and a sense of impending (or actual) crisis that threatens the current political, military, or geostrategic status quo. For example, some believed that the purpose behind the SALT II negotiation was to solve the problem of the vulnerability of United States intercontinental ballistic missiles (ICBMs) and to slow the Soviet military build-up. Negotiation may also create a safer and more predictable military environment by managing the arms competition. One of the objectives behind the negotiation leading to the Anti-Ballistic Missile (ABM) Treaty in SALT I was to avert a potentially destabilizing and costly race to deploy ballistic missile defences.

It is important to note that a negotiation may also be important in the context of alliance relations and military politics. It may be necessary to get allies off one's back, especially if these allies are pushing vigorously for arms control. Concession to

3 Albert Carnesale and Richard N. Haas, eds, *Superpower Arms Control: Setting the Record Straight* (Cambridge MA: Ballinger 1987), 330.
4 *Ibid*, 33.

To identify the potential domestic political, military policy, and foreign policy motivations for engaging in arms control negotiation, this paper examines four cases of arms control prenegotiation. For the United States arms control began well before the nuclear age, and our story therefore begins with the Washington Naval Treaties of 1922. The other cases considered are the Limited Nuclear Test Ban Treaty of 1963, the beginnings of the SALT process in the 1960s and early 1970s, and the prenegotiation phase of START in President Reagan's first term (1981-4). These cases were chosen with the aim of assessing the cumulative but also relative explanatory power of the factors influencing United States policies and whether they are similar or have changed over time (and if so why).[9] Cases of prenegotiation that led to successful negotiation of arms control agreements are considered in addition to a case in which prenegotiation did not or has yet to result in a formal agreement.

THE INTERWAR PERIOD AND THE WASHINGTON CONFERENCE 1921-2

The United States approach to the Washington Naval Treaties reveals many ingredients common to much of the subsequent

---

9 The obvious difficulty is deciding which combination and sequence of variables are most important in any given case(s) of prenegotiation, particularly in the absence of direct or first-hand evidence about the thoughts and motivations of the key policy-makers. Moreover, anecdotal information, personal recollections, memoirs, and such may contain incomplete or inaccurate information about the motivations of the players and actual course of events. The historical case-study method has obvious drawbacks which derive from the inherent limitations of circumstantial inference: see Donald J. Moon, 'The logic of political inquiry: a synthesis of opposed perspectives,' in Fred I. Greenstein and Nelson W. Polsby, eds, *Micropolitical Theory: Handbook of Political Science* (Reading MA: Addison-Wesley 1975), I, 145-51. Where possible, I have tried to use first-hand accounts and recollections of the prenegotiation period. In the absence of such information, I have relied on secondary sources and I have tried to reconstruct the choices and consequences of political action in an attempt to judge the motives of the political élites, given the context and forces pressing on them. This method explores both ends of a causal chain – context → motive → choice – to determine the characteristic of the intermediate link, motive. Accordingly, it inclines us to think in terms of men constrained by outer circumstances rather than men acting under internal compulsions. Historical events, rather than instincts, appear as the starting point of behaviour, and actions are often interpreted as reactions.

American experience with arms control. It is a story of a new administration (in this case a Republican one) intent on increasing defence spending in the face of mounting domestic and international pressure for arms control and disarmament. It is the story of a president eventually forced to strike a compromise with Congress in order to secure approval of his new defence programme. It is a story of changing public attitudes and values towards the arms race because of growing fears about the destabilizing consequences of new weapons and military technology. It is a story where key allies helped bring the United States to the negotiating table.

Origins

Before World War I, Germany and Great Britain had been involved in a major arms race to build heavy battleships. The race began with Germany's ambitious programme to rearm its navy with a new fleet of battleships at the turn of the century. Matched by Britain's deployment of a new class of heavily armed battleships, the Dreadnought, Germany responded with its own programme. Britain nevertheless managed to maintain numerical superiority over the German fleet. Efforts to stop this naval arms race at the Hague Conferences of 1899 and 1907 failed. In 1908, the British suggested voluntary restraints on construction of new ships, but these were rejected by Germany, and subsequent efforts to bring a halt to naval construction programmes were a dismal failure. Many believed that the naval arms race had raised international tensions and contributed to the outbreak of World War I.

The Washington agreements

After the Great War people the world over did not want such a war to happen again. 'The Covenant of the new League of Nations expressed the founders' vague hope that the organization would reduce armaments and eliminate the pressures of arms producers on governments.'[10] The major postwar effort

---

10 Coit D. Blacker and Gloria Duffy, eds, *International Arms Control: Issues and Agreements* (2nd ed; Stanford CA: Stanford University Press 1984), 87.

to control naval arms was the Washington Naval Conference of 1921-2 which placed limitations on naval shipbuilding by the great powers. Under the Five-Power Treaty for the Limitation of Armaments, the signatories agreed to stop construction of capital ships for ten years and to limit total tonnage: for the United States 525,000 tons, for the British empire 525,000, for France 175,000 tons, for Italy 175,000 tons, for Japan 315,000 tons.[11] The agreement did not apply to cruisers and submarines, which would play a decisive role in World War II, but it established naval parity between Britain and the United States, neither of which wanted to get into an arms race. For Japan the agreement replaced the Anglo-Japanese alliance of 1902 and established it as the predominant power in the northwest Pacific.

Prenegotiation

In 1914, the United States stood third among the naval powers. By the end of the war, it was second only to Britain. The Department of the Navy had ambitious plans for expansion after the war, but it encountered stiff domestic opposition after the armistice. The former president, Theodore Roosevelt, argued that the United States should 'not ... try to build a navy in rivalry to [Britain],' but should be satisfied to 'have the second navy in the world.'[12] The *New York Times* was opposed to any build-up that might threaten ties with Great Britain. Efforts by the administration in 1919 to secure congressional approval for an ambitious naval building programme encountered stubborn resistance. Representative E.W. Saunders captured the mood of the house: why 'at this time when our enemies are prostrate,' should we 'increase the burdens in the name of the national defense? What are the dangers that render necessary these prodigious preparations? ... England has deferred her naval program. Neither in France, Italy, or Spain do we find lurking dangers, or any quickening activities ... Germany is in sackcloth

11 Harold Sprout and Margaret Sprout, *Toward a New Order of Sea Power: American Naval Policy and the World Scene, 1918-1922* (Princeton NJ: Princeton University Press 1946), 174.
12 Quoted in *ibid*, 106.

and ashes. Look to Japan, China, South America, take in the whole circle of the world, and tell me where you find evidence of any present, or prospective preparation so extensive, and so alarming, as to make it necessary for this Congress to proceed with feverish haste to establish new armaments in the name of proper and adequate defense.'[13] In the end, the government was forced to scale down its programme.

The reaction against navalism continued into the early 1920s, but began to take on a new form: 'It now evolved rapidly into a positive, well directed popular movement for international action to check the competitive struggle for naval primacy which, according to a widespread and growing fear, was driving the great naval Powers towards bankruptcy or war, or both together.'[14] In December 1920, the Department of the Navy proposed a major programme to build 88 new vessels within three years, including 4 capital ships and 30 light cruisers. Britain, in turn, announced in March 1921 a building programme to keep pace with United States expansion. Many predicted the outbreak of war unless this race was brought to a halt.

The navy's plan clashed with public demands to limit government spending as the United States fell into recession. 'Peace groups, churches of all denominations, the recently founded National League of Women Voters, the American Federation of Labor, a large and influential group of daily newspapers, and eventually also the conservative editorial spokesmen of American industry and finance' entered the debate to limit defence spending. In December 1920 Senator William E. Borah introduced a joint resolution in the debate over the naval appropriations bill calling upon the president to begin negotiations with Great Britain and Japan on 'the question of disarmament, with a view of quickly coming to an understanding by which the building naval programs of each ... shall be reduced annually during the next five years by 50 percent of the present

13 Quoted in *ibid*, 109-10.
14 *Ibid*, 114.

estimates or figures.'[15] As Roger Dingman explains, Senator Borah's resolution was controversial even though it enjoyed widespread public support: 'First the *Philadelphia Public Ledger*, then the *New York World* conducted polls which showed strong international interest and overwhelming congressional support for disarmament ... But old enemies like Josephus Daniels rejected Borah's proposal. The Navy Secretary turned the senator's isolationist arguments against him when he insisted that a naval limitation agreement outside the League would amount to an entangling alliance.'[16]

The Borah resolution tied the hands of the president-elect, Warren G. Harding. During the presidential campaign, Harding, who had been a 'big navy' supporter in the Senate, had expressed some desire for 'partial, but not permanent' disarmament. In his inaugural address on 4 March 1921, Harding ruled out the possibility of entangling alliances or membership in the League of Nations. But his support for isolationism was a qualified one. The president indicated that the United States would continue to associate with other nations 'for conference, for counsel ... to recommend a way to approximate disarmament and relieve the crushing burdens of military and naval establishments.'[17] Nevertheless, Harding opposed Borah's amendment as an invasion of presidential prerogative. Harding's spokesmen in Congress argued that international developments had taken a turn for the worse and they successfully defeated efforts to slash funding for work on ships authorized earlier. Harding continued to lobby to have the Borah amendment defeated. But on 17 May 1921, he decided to drop his opposition and promised negotiations 'at the earliest possible date.'[18]

---

15 Quoted in *ibid*, 117.
16 Roger Dingman, *Power in the Pacific: The Origins of Naval Arms Limitation, 1914-1922* (Chicago IL: University of Chicago Press 1976), 144.
17 Thomas H. Buckley, *The United States and the Washington Conference, 1921-1922* (Knoxville: University of Tennessee Press 1970), 11, 14.
18 Dingman, *Power in the Pacific*, 150.

Harding had realized that if the naval appropriations bill was to secure congressional approval some sort of compromise was necessary. The Borah resolution passed both houses along with congressional approval of the naval appropriations bill, thus allowing work to continue on the navy's ambitious shipbuilding programme. On 11 July, the day after the house passed the bill, Harding announced that he would summon a conference in Washington as soon as possible. As Christopher Hall explains, there were good reasons for this:

The first was that it seized the initiative in domestic politics for the president, whose prestige in the control of foreign policy and in the leadership of the Republican Party had been shaken by the Borah resolutions. The second was that it seized the initiative in international diplomacy for the United States which would derive a number of advantages, psychological, and organizational, from having the conference held in Washington; it might also partly restore American prestige after the unhappy battle over the League. The third was that it enabled the United States to control the Conference's agenda ... [The secretary of state, Charles Evans Hughes] was determined that Far Eastern affairs should take a place on the agenda at the forthcoming conference.'[19]

The president would thus also take political credit for the conference away from Borah who opposed including east Asian affairs in discussions about naval matters. Hughes was also keen to replace the Anglo-Japanese alliance with a broader agreement on Pacific security. Although London and Tokyo were supportive of this idea, the British had encountered strong opposition from the prime ministers of the British dominions at the 1921 Imperial Conference.

External pressures also played an important role in the president's decision to call the conference. Great Britain viewed

19 Christopher Hall, *Britain, America and Arms Control 1921-37* (New York: St Martin's Press 1987), 25-6.

the United States naval build-up with consternation and worried about the impact of a loss of British naval supremacy on the empire. Great Britain's weakened economic position after the war also meant it would have difficulty increasing the size of its navy. The prime minister, David Lloyd George, was keen to find a solution to the 'alternatives of new naval building and financial entrenchment ... a conference might get both the Treasury and the Admiralty off his back.'[20] In early June 1921, Lloyd George had therefore begun to explore with Washington and Tokyo the possibility of holding an international conference to nip the budding arms race.

But it was the United States which took the initiative to issue invitations to Britain, Japan, France, and Italy – the world's major maritime powers – for such a conference. Invitations were also sent to China, the Netherlands, Portugal, and Belgium. Within a month all had accepted. The Washington Naval Conference began on 12 November 1921.

Explaining outcomes
The threat of a new naval arms race among the great powers was a prime moving force in the process of prenegotiation of the Washington Naval Conference. Some of the great powers saw the need to avert the impending crisis of unrestrained military competition. Behind strong, though by no means unanimous, public support for the Borah resolution was a genuine belief that arms races had been an important factor in the outbreak of World War I. This belief had a powerful grip on the popular imagination, as did concerns about increased military spending in a war-weakened economy. Pressure from allies to halt naval construction also played an important, if indirect, role in prenegotiation politics. Ultimately, however, it was Congress and not the allies which tipped the scales in the United States debate about the desirability of an international naval

20 Quoted in *ibid*, 26.

conference. The only way Harding could secure congressional approval of his naval bill was to support the idea of a conference. He was willing to entertain a compromise to ease passage of the naval appropriations bill. By seizing the initiative from Borah, Harding also saw important gains to be reaped for his presidency and for the United States that went well beyond immediate political considerations. Thus domestic politics was an important 'intervening' or 'mediating' variable in the United States decision to enter negotiations.

This pattern would repeat itself later – a pattern characterized by the threat or crisis of an impending arms race, a desire to manage the risks of arms competition and reduce uncertainty in the military-strategic environment, and strong domestic political pressure in support of arms control which forced a sometimes all-too-reluctant administration to the negotiating table.

THE LIMITED NUCLEAR TEST BAN TREATY 1963

The Limited Nuclear Test Ban Treaty was the first major arms control agreement to be concluded between the superpowers after World War II. The treaty was signed less than a year after the Cuban missiles crisis, which had marked the height of the Cold War; there is little doubt that that crisis played a central role in changing American attitudes and perceptions about the need to place the United States-Soviet relationship on a more co-operative footing. However, it was not the only factor. From the early 1950s scientific and public fears about the biological dangers of atmospheric testing had grown in light of dramatic new evidence about the harmful effects of radioactive fallout. These concerns, along with growing fears about the risks of nuclear proliferation, were important to the prenegotiation debate about a test ban. But scientific, public, and congressional opinion were far from unanimous. President John Kennedy failed to secure a comprehensive, as opposed to a limited, test ban treaty. That failure was linked not only to Soviet intransigence on the issue of on-site verification but also to congressional and bureaucratic opposition to a comprehensive ban.

These constraints shaped the prenegotiation agenda and ultimately the negotiation leading to the final agreement itself.

Treaty

The Limited Nuclear Test Ban Treaty was signed on 5 August 1963 in Moscow by the foreign ministers of the United States, the Soviet Union, and Great Britain after a mere twelve days of negotiation. The treaty, ratified by the United States Senate on 7 October 1963, banned nuclear testing in the atmosphere, in outer space, and under water.

Origins

The detonation of the first fission-fusion-fission bomb at Bikini atoll in the Pacific in 1954 dramatized the dangers of radioactive fallout from atmospheric testing. The unfortunate crew of the Japanese fishing boat, *Lucky Dragon*, which was downwind from the test, sailed into the 'ashen rain.' India's prime minister, Jawaharlal Nehru, and members of the British Labour party used the incident to call for a moratorium on nuclear testing. In the years that followed, a spate of scientific studies uncovered the dangers of strontium 90, carbon 14, cesium 137, and other radioactive materials produced from nuclear explosions. Scientific arguments were soon reinforced by political arguments that the only way to achieve co-operation with the Soviet Union was through partial rather than comprehensive schemes for disarmament. A test ban would be a good first step.[21]

Prenegotiation in this case is a troublesome concept particularly because negotiations for a ban on nuclear testing began in 1955 when the Sub-Committee of Five (the United States, the Soviet Union, the United Kingdom, France, and Canada) of the United Nations Disarmament Commission took up the issue. However, these 'negotiations' were erratic and protracted,

---

21 Harold Karan Jacobson and Eric Stein, *Diplomats, Scientists, and Politicians: The United States and the Nuclear Test Ban Negotiations* (Ann Arbor: University of Michigan Press 1966), 88-9; and Arthur M. Schlesinger, *A Thousand Days: John F. Kennedy in the White House* (Cambridge MA: Houghton Mifflin 1965), 450-1.

and it is more appropriate to consider them part of the prenegotiation phase. These early discussions covered two functional aspects of prenegotiation: an attempt to define the problem
and an attempt by the parties to develop a commitment to
further negotiation in order to make the problem susceptible
to mutually satisfactory management. They helped pave the
way for separate negotiations among the United States, the
Soviet Union, and the United Kingdom, which began in October 1958 following the convening of an international conference of experts to study ways of monitoring and verifying a
nuclear test ban. The three nuclear powers also agreed to an
informal moratorium on nuclear testing. The discussions became deadlocked over verification, however, with the West
pressing for some form of on-site inspection which the Soviet
Union opposed. On 30 August 1961, the Soviet Union announced it would resume atmospheric testing. Barely a week
later, it broke the moratorium with the first of an extensive
series of atmospheric tests.

The Soviet action dismayed United States officials. As Soviet
nuclear testing continued unabated into 1962, opposition in the
United States to arms control negotiations grew. In November
1961, the Presidential Committee on Atmospheric Testing recommended that a vigorous nuclear testing programme was
needed in order to develop anti-ballistic missile defences, to
ensure the reliability of United States missiles against a Soviet
attack, and to acquire further knowledge about the effects of
nuclear explosions. In view of this recommendation and the
lack of Soviet compliance with the moratorium, President Kennedy decided that the United States would resume atmospheric
testing, which it did on 25 April 1962.[22]

Crisis and response
On 15 October 1962 the Cuban missiles crisis began when United
States intelligence discovered that the Soviet Union was con-

22 Ivo H. Daalder, 'The limited test ban,' in Carnesale and Haas, eds, *Superpower
Arms Control*, 10-12, and Schlesinger, *A Thousand Days*, 454-61.

structing sites for medium-range missiles in western Cuba. The crisis, which brought the world closer than it had ever been to nuclear war, dramatized the dangers of brinksmanship while illustrating the need for better communications and crisis control. It is also played a major role in resumption of negotiations for a limited test ban treaty. As the crisis wound down, Nikita Khrushchev wrote to President Kennedy: 'We would like to continue the exchange of views on the prohibition of atomic and thermonuclear weapons, on general disarmament and other problems relating to the relaxation of international tension.' In his reply Kennedy agreed that 'perhaps now, as we step back from danger, we can make some real progress in this vital field. I think we should give priority to questions relating to the proliferation of nuclear weapons ... and to the great effort for a nuclear test ban.'[23] Theodore Sorensen explains: 'In response to Khrushchev's talk of new accords after the Cuban crisis, Kennedy put the test-ban treaty first. Indeed, since the day of his inauguration, a test ban had been his principal hope for a first step towards disarmament and other pacts. He had termed the collapse of the Geneva talks in 1961 "the most disappointing event" of his first year. He had hopes that a new treaty would be the most rewarding event of his third. The time was right.'[24]

These communications engendered optimism that a test ban agreement could be reached. The United Nations General Assembly lent additional support with the passage of two resolutions on 6 November 1962. The first, introduced by thirty-seven non-nuclear states including all eight neutrals on the Disarmament Committee, called for a cessation of atmospheric nuclear tests by 1 January 1963 and a comprehensive or limited treaty accompanied by an interim suspension of underground testing. The second, introduced by the United States and the United Kingdom, called for a comprehensive treaty with international verification or a limited treaty covering the atmosphere, the oceans, and space. These proposals formed the basis

23 Quoted in Glenn T. Seaborg, *Kennedy, Khrushchev, and the Test Ban* (Berkeley: University of California Press 1981), 176.
24 Theodore C. Sorensen, *Kennedy* (New York: Harper & Row 1965), 727-8.

of the test ban treaty negotiated in 1963. The third session of the Eighteen-Nation Disarmament Committee (ENDC), which ran from 26 November to 20 December 1962, was stimulated by the United Nations resolution calling for a complete halt to all testing by 1 January 1963. However, the conference stalled on the question of on-site inspection and the difficulty of monitoring underground explosions.

On 19 December 1962, Khrushchev sent Kennedy a letter on the test ban. On the crucial issue of on-site inspection, he indicated that the Soviet Union was 'prepared to agree to two to three inspections a year being carried out in the territory of each of the nuclear powers.' Khrushchev stated 'that the time has come to put an end once and for all to nuclear tests, to draw a line through such tests.' However, Kennedy was concerned that Congress, and Senator Henry Jackson in particular, would not agree to this lower figure and wrote back to Khrushchev saying that two or three inspections were insufficient. But he added: 'notwithstanding these problems, I am encouraged by your letter.'[25]

Informal talks began between the United States and Soviet representatives in Washington on 14 January 1963.[26] They were later moved to New York and British representatives were included. These discussions proved unproductive and stalled over the number of on-site inspections and the location of unmanned

25 Quoted in Seaborg, *Kennedy, Khrushchev, and the Test Ban*, 179, 181.
26 Kennedy was also anxious that a test ban be negotiated soon in order to bring about a halt to the Chinese nuclear programme. At a White House meeting on 22 January 1963, Glenn Seaborg (chairman of the United States Atomic Energy Commission) recalls (*ibid*, 182): 'The president then went on to talk about his recent correspondence with Khrushchev and the importance of a test ban in the world situation. An important consideration was the power that the Chinese would have with nuclear weapons and how they would use that power. If a test ban treaty could lessen this prospect, the U.S. should take much forethought before turning it down. He suspected that the Soviets were thinking much the same way about it. He said that a test ban that affected only the Russians and the United States would have only limited value but, if there was a chance it could affect the Chinese, it could be worth very much indeed. In this sense it was more important to the world situation than it had been a year or two ago. He said that the C[entral] I[ntelligence] A[gency] agreed with this assessment.' The treaty that was eventually negotiated did not include the People's Republic of China and it failed to bring a halt to the Chinese programme.

seismic stations to monitor underground testing. The United States wanted more inspections than the Soviet Union was prepared to accept and once more negotiations were broken off. The Soviet Union moved these discussions to the ENDC which had resumed its work on 12 February. It hoped to use world opinion to force the United States to accept a lower number of inspections.

Congressional opinion on a test ban was divided. The Joint Committee on Atomic Energy attacked its verification aspects while expressing support for a vigorous programme of nuclear testing. Senators Jackson, Richard Russell, Bourke Hickenlooper, and Thomas Dodd led the opposition in the Senate. In February, the United States resumed underground testing. In the ENDC, the United States and the Soviet Union lobbied neutral members to support their respective positions regarding on-site inspection. However the talks made no progress, and the United States planned a new round of atmospheric tests.

On 8 February President Kennedy stated at a press conference that the main reason to pursue a test ban was to arrest the spread of nuclear weapons: 'I think people who attack the effort should bear in mind that the alternative is the spread of these weapons to a government which may be irresponsible, or which by accident may initiate a general nuclear war.'[27] At a subsequent press conference on 21 March, he declared that 'the reason why we keep moving and working on this question [of a test ban], taking up a good deal of energy and effort, is because personally I am haunted by the feeling that by 1970, unless we are successful, there may be 10 nuclear powers instead of 4, and by 1975, 15 or 20.'[28] Kennedy's view was supported by the Arms Control and Disarmament Agency (ACDA), although the chairman of the Joint Committee on Atomic Energy was more sceptical. With the deadlock in Geneva and the impending threat of Chinese nuclear tests, hope for a test ban began to fade.

On 8 May 1963 Khrushchev sent a letter to the British and

27 Quoted in *ibid*, 193.
28 Harold W. Chase and Allen H. Lerman, eds, *Kennedy and the Press: The News Conferences* (New York: Thomas Y. Crowell 1965), 410.

Americans indicating that he would be prepared to receive emissaries to discuss a test ban. In a subsequent letter of 8 June he agreed to set a formal date for the negotiation in Moscow and suggested 15 July. The Soviet final push obviously proved critical to the prenegotiation phase of the test ban.

In the meantime, congressional attitudes towards a test ban began to shift. Senator Dodd had had an extensive exchange with Adrian Fisher of ACDA. As Arthur Schlesinger Jr explains: 'The correspondence brought new points to Dodd's attention, and the Connecticut Senator had the grace to change his mind. On May 27 he joined with Hubert Humphrey and thirty-two other Senators in introducing a resolution declaring it "the sense of the Senate" that the United States should again offer the Soviet Union a limited test ban; if the Russians rejected the plan, the United States should nevertheless "pursue it with vigor, seeking the widest possible international support." '[29]

Public interest in the test ban also intensified. In May 1963 the Women's Strike for Peace and the Women's International League for Peace and Freedom lobbied members of Congress on behalf of the test ban. Numerous peace groups made serious efforts to alert the public to the dangers of future testing, fallout, and the arms race. The Senate was showered with letters, phone calls, and petitions.[30] Public opinion had supported the moratorium on nuclear testing during the second Eisenhower administration. In a poll taken in November 1959, four out of five people supported an extension of the moratorium for another year. But the U-2 crisis, the Cuban revolution, and the cancellation of a United States-Soviet summit in Paris had helped bring about a change in public attitudes. By December 1960, 50 per cent of the American public believed it was impossible to reach a peaceful settlement with the Soviet Union. In June 1961, only 27 per cent of the American public believed that the United States should not resume its nuclear testing programme.

29 Schlesinger, *A Thousand Days*, 899.
30 Ronald J. Terchek, *The Making of the Test Ban Treaty* (The Hague: Martinus Nijhoff 1970), 82-3.

In a March 1962 poll, 67 per cent of Americans approved of atmospheric testing and only 21 per cent expressed concern about radioactive fallout in the atmosphere. But by July 1963, in the aftermath of the Cuban missiles crisis, 52 per cent of the public was expressing its unqualified support for a test ban; after the treaty was negotiated and signed, 81 per cent would take this position.[31]

On 10 June President Kennedy gave the commencement address at the American University in Washington. He reaffirmed his desire for a test ban and announced that high-level discussions on a comprehensive test ban treaty would begin soon with the Soviet Union and the United Kingdom. The under secretary of state, Averell Harriman, who had been the ambassador to Moscow in 1943-6, was chosen to head the United States negotiating team.

In the preparatory meetings for these negotiations it became clear that bureaucratic and congressional support for a comprehensive test ban was lacking. The Joint Chiefs of Staff opposed a comprehensive ban because they thought the Soviet Union might cheat and could make important gains through clandestine testing. The air force was concerned about treaty restrictions which might prevent study of missile site vulnerability and the development of very high yield nuclear weapons. The navy did not want to compromise its ability to test nuclear devices under water. The army worried about the prohibitions on the use of tactical nuclear weapons in training and the development of an anti-missile missile system which was under army jurisdiction. The Atomic Energy Commission feared that a test ban would increase technical uncertainty, weaken the United States nuclear stockpile, and reduce the efficiency of its laboratories. In the Senate, it was clear there was not enough support for a comprehensive treaty although support for a ban on testing in the oceans and atmosphere was widespread.[32]

31 *Ibid*, 115-16, 119.
32 *Ibid*, 42-3, 37-8.

The Soviet Union backed down from its proposals for limited on-site inspection. In a speech given in East Berlin on 2 July, Khrushchev proposed the idea of a partial test ban limited to the oceans and atmosphere. At a White House meeting on 9 July, just before Harriman was to leave for the Soviet Union, the joint chiefs expressed doubts about their ability to support even a limited test ban. Nevertheless, Kennedy instructed Harriman to try to achieve a comprehensive treaty but, failing that, to seek a limited treaty banning nuclear testing in the oceans, air, and space.[33] On 15 July the formal negotiation for a limited test ban began. It was concluded a mere twelve days later.

Explaining outcomes

The prenegotiation phase of the Limited Nuclear Test Ban Treaty was triggered by the Cuban missiles crisis. The ostensible purpose of the treaty was to improve United States-Soviet relations in the aftermath of a crisis that had brought the two superpowers to the brink of nuclear disaster. However, other developments helped break the logjam in discussions that had taken place prior to the formal negotiation itself. The apparent lack of any sort of scientific or military breakthrough in the testing programmes of the two superpowers and the United Kingdom removed a potential obstacle to the ban. An accumulation of scientific evidence pointed to the growing dangers of nuclear testing in the atmosphere. Kennedy was increasingly concerned about nuclear proliferation and China's nuclear programme. The major obstacle was the Soviet objection to on-site verification. Discussions in the Eighteen-Nation Disarmament Committee had stalled on this issue. The Cuban missiles crisis, however, created a new sense of urgency and dramatized the need for Soviet-American co-operation to reduce the risks of nuclear war. Kennedy and Khrushchev seized on the test ban as an important symbol of de-escalation and a tangible way to improve United States-Soviet relations. Although the treaty it-

33 Seaborg, *Kennedy, Khrushchev, and the Test Ban*, 227-9.

self did little to stop the arms race and halt the nuclear weapons programmes of the superpowers, it was an important confidence-building measure intended to help place the superpower relationship on a more stable and predictable footing while paving the way for future arms control agreements.

DÉTENTE AND THE ORIGINS OF SALT I

Administration fears about the Soviet strategic build-up and the emergence of military parity between the superpowers played an important role in the prenegotiation phase of SALT I. However, arms control negotiations were also viewed by Washington as a way to place the strategic-military relationship with the Soviet Union on firmer ground and to halt a potentially destabilizing race to develop ABM defences. SALT I was also a response to political pressures for arms control from Congress and the general public. The timing of the negotiation was affected significantly by these pressures and also by mounting pressure from a coalition of forces within the bureaucracy for the new administration to begin talks.

SALT I agreements

The election of Richard Nixon to the presidency in 1968 marked the revival of the SALT process which had begun under Lyndon Johnson. Talks began in November 1969. These discussions were directed at limiting the major build-up in strategic offensive systems and the emerging competition in ballistic missile defensive systems. On 26 May 1972, the United States and the Soviet Union signed a five-year interim agreement that took the first step towards limiting strategic offensive arms by placing ceilings on both land-based and submarine-based offensive nuclear forces.[34] The United States and the Soviet Union also

---

34 The United States was allowed 1054 ICBMs operational or under construction and the Soviet Union 1618. Both parties were prohibited from converting light ICBM launchers deployed before 1964 to heavy launchers. The United States was limited to 710 launchers for submarine-launched ballistic missiles (SLBMs) and 44 ballistic-missile-carrying submarines and the Soviet Union to 950 launch-

signed the ABM Treaty, an agreement of unlimited duration severely restricting deployment of anti-missile systems.[35]

Origins

SALT I had its beginnings in the Johnson administration. The official announcement of strategic arms limitation talks between the United States and the Soviet Union came with the signing of the Non-Proliferation Treaty on 1 July 1968. This agreement secured a commitment from the superpowers to reduce the 'vertical proliferation' of their nuclear arsenals. However, the seeds of SALT I had been sown with the United States build-up of ICBMs and submarine-launched ballistic missiles (SLBMs) in the early 1960s, which may have led, directly or indirectly, to a similar build-up on the Soviet side starting in 1964 after the Soviet attempt to place medium-range missiles in Cuba was foiled. The growing arms race in the mid-1960s was a source of concern to senior defence and arms control officials in the United States as was the Soviet construction of a crude defence system around Leningrad in 1962. Although this construction stopped two years later, it was shortly followed by the construction of a similar system around Moscow. The United States feared that the Soviet Union might be constructing a nation-wide ABM system, and this helped to accelerate the Pentagon's development of the multiple independently targetable re-entry vehicle (MIRV) and eventual work on an ABM system for the

---

ers and 62 submarines. Within these limitations, modernization and replacement missiles were permitted. Among the systems and characteristics not limited by the agreement were strategic bombers, forward-based systems, mobile ICBMs, multiple independently targetable re-entry vehicles (MIRVs), and missile accuracy.

35 The two countries agreed not to deploy ABM systems for national or regional defence. Each side would be allowed two ABM deployment areas, subsequently reduced to one. The treaty specifically prohibited the development, testing, or deployment of sea-, air-, space-, or mobile land-based ABM systems and their components. It also imposed restraints on radars and interceptor missiles. The SALT agreement contained extensive provisions to facilitate verification by national technical means including satellites. It also provided for a United States-Soviet Standing Consultative Commission to deal with compliance questions and to ensure implementation.

United States. These developments also precipitated a spate of studies within the Joint Chiefs of Staff and the Arms Control and Disarmament Agency about the desirability of controlling nuclear weapons through arms control.[36]

In December 1966 President Johnson instructed the United States ambassador to the Soviet Union, Llewellyn Thompson, to sound out the Soviet Union about bilateral talks on strategic arms limitation. Johnson had been persuaded by the secretary of defense, Robert McNamara, that there was growing danger of an ABM race between the United States and the Soviet Union which had considerable potential to lead to a new offensive arms race as well. McNamara also feared that ABM defences would be strategically destabilizing if they impaired the assured destruction capabilities of the United States and its ability to retaliate in the event of a Soviet first strike. He urged Johnson to begin serious negotiation with the Soviet Union to limit or ban ABM systems on both sides. Whether Johnson agreed because of the strategic merits of these arguments or for domestic political reasons (or both) is unclear. However, he did face growing pressure on Capitol Hill and in the Pentagon to move forward with ABM deployments.[37] With an election coming up in 1968, the president may have felt that talks with the Soviet Union would be a campaign asset in view of his mounting political difficulties over the war in Vietnam.

In January 1967 the Soviet Union agreed in principle to offensive and defensive arms limitation talks, but the date for their initiation was left open. McNamara pressed the Soviet prime minister, Aleksei Kosygin, for a date at the Glassboro summit meeting but without success. Talks were delayed for almost a year and a half while the Kremlin wrestled with the problem of deciding whether such talks were indeed desirable

36 Fen Osler Hampson, 'SALT I: Interim Agreement and the ABM treaty,' in Carnesale and Haas, eds, *Superpower Arms Control*, 65-7; and Thomas W. Wolfe, *The SALT Experience* (Cambridge MA: Ballinger 1979), 23-4.

37 Jerome Kahan, *Security in the Nuclear Age* (Washington: Brookings Institution 1975), 123.

and awaited the outcome of the United States presidential election.

The domestic debate in the United States during this period was marked by growing differences of opinion about the desirability of strategic defences. Some feared that ballistic missile defences would threaten strategic stability. Others – notably civilian analysts in the Department of Defense – were keen on developing such defences. The administration also found itself under growing congressional pressure to provide defences to counter Soviet ABM deployments. In September 1967 McNamara announced that the administration had decided to deploy a 'thin' ABM system to protect the United States from a missile attack by China or some other third party or from an accidental missile launch.[38] It was quite apparent that the administration rejected the notion that an ABM system could limit damage from a Soviet missile attack. This viewpoint prevailed until the end of the Johnson administration. The idea of using ABM systems as 'a bargaining chip' for arms control also gained credence in the 1968 congressional debate on the Sentinel system, even though the term had not yet entered political discourse. It was reinforced as the Soviet position on defences began to shift in June 1968, when the Soviet foreign minister, Andrei Gromyko, announced that his country was ready for 'an exchange of opinion' on limiting strategic arms, including ABMs. But progress came to an abrupt halt in August 1968 when the Soviet Union moved into Czechoslovakia.

Prenegotiation

Both President Nixon and his national security adviser, Henry Kissinger, came to office firmly convinced that arms control would help exert a positive restraining influence on Soviet behaviour in other areas of the globe. Their approach to SALT was intimately tied to a broader strategy of 'linkage.' However, both were reluctant to jump into talks with the Soviet Union

38 *Ibid*, 123-4.

until they had conducted a formal review of United States strategic requirements. If the Soviet Union was anxious for talks, all the more reason to wait, and in the view of Nixon and Kissinger, any progress on SALT would depend on acceptable Soviet behaviour in the Middle East, Vietnam, and other areas.

Nixon also had strong political reasons for not rushing into negotiation with the Soviet Union. Kissinger recalls his meetings with the president-elect during the transition period:

Nixon had come to the problem by a more political route than I. Having made his reputation through tough, occasionally strident anti-Communism, he was committed to maintaining his traditional conservative constituency ... But he understood that as President he would need to stretch his political base towards the political center; indeed, he shrewdly saw in East-West relations a long-term opportunity to build his new majority ... He had been afraid that the Glassboro summit might restore Johnson's fortunes – hence he considered that the Soviets had colluded with the Democrats to thwart him. But he had also seen how the inconclusive outcome caused Johnson's popularity to dissipate as rapidly as it had spurted – hence his determination not to have a summit unless success could be guaranteed.

Kissinger's own reasons were more geopolitical:

Our past policy had often been one of 'confidence building' for its own sake, in the belief that as confidence grew tensions would lessen. But if one took the view that tensions arose as a result of differences over concrete issues, then the way to approach the problem was to begin working on those differences. A lasting peace depended on the settlement of the political issues that were dividing the two nuclear superpowers.[39]

There were other reasons for the new administration's reluctance to plunge immediately into strategic talks with the Soviet Union. The United States was no longer as deeply worried about a nation-wide deployment of ABM systems by the Soviet

39 Henry Kissinger, *White House Years* (Boston: Little, Brown 1979), 126-7.

such pressures may also be desirable to secure continued public support for alliance policies and to maintain alliance cohesion.

A second set of reasons for engaging in arms control negotiation has to do with domestic politics. As some scholars note, the willingness to negotiate (or not to negotiate) international agreements may be affected in the first instance by domestic political pressures.[5] These can take several forms: catering to public opinion; appeasing or deflating domestic opponents; dealing with bureaucratic warfare; or positioning for electoral campaigns. Negotiation, for example, may help secure passage of the defence budget in Congress or save some valued programme (like the MX missile). An agreement might help ease economic and budgetary pressures. One might also want to improve relations with an opponent in order to achieve a major foreign policy 'success' that would have important pay-offs domestically.

The fragmentation and decentralization of power in the American political system creates its own special pressures and constraints. Congress enjoys 'a broad set of legitimate means to block, divert, or alter foreign policy initiatives.'[6] Power over appropriations, general legislation, ratification of treaties, and confirmation of appointments enables Congress to exercise significant control over the agenda in any arms control prenegotiation as well as over other foreign policy and defence matters.[7] Policy outcomes thus reflect the interaction between Congress and the executive as well as what goes on within each branch of the government – what Robert Pastor calls 'interbranch politics.'[8] Executive-legislative politics and bargaining processes may therefore influence not only the choice of arms control negotiation as a policy option but also the subsequent agenda for and boundaries to the negotiation itself.

5 See Lloyd Etheridge, *Can Governments Learn?* (New York: Pergamon 1986).

6 Joseph S. Nye Jr, 'Can America manage its Soviet policy?' in Nye, ed, *The Making of America's Soviet Policy* (New Haven CT: Yale University Press 1984), 334.

7 I.M. Destler, 'Congress,' in Nye, ed, *The Making of America's Soviet Policy*, 400.

8 Robert A. Pastor, *Congress and the Politics of U.S. Foreign Economic Policy, 1929-1976* (Berkeley: University of California Press 1980), 61.

Union because construction of new sites had halted. The Soviet Union, which hitherto was not especially worried about ABM systems, was now deeply concerned and anxious to see some sort of limitation established. Soviet views had undergone an important change: 'It was now accepted that [ABMS] could play an offensive as well as defensive role, and that an effective (or comparatively more effective) American ABM system would disrupt the nuclear balance by enabling the United States to lessen the effectiveness of a Soviet nuclear strike.'⁴⁰

But while Nixon and Kissinger chose to move slowly, countervailing domestic political pressures to begin arms control talks grew quickly. Public and congressional attitudes towards the deployment of new strategic systems had changed. Congress was no longer forcing the ABM programme on a reluctant administration. Opposition to ABMS had grown considerably in Congress and also within the academic and scientific communities. In part, this scepticism was based on a growing appreciation of the costs and technical limitations of the system, but it also reflected political worries in Congress about the location of future ABM sites. Members of the scientific community appearing before Congress argued that an ABM system was not technically reliable and could be defeated by Soviet countermeasures. The deployment of defences might also spark a new arms race and weaken the deterrent effect of strategic weapons. The underlying assumption in these arguments was that unilateral restraint by the United States would induce reciprocal restraint by the Soviet Union and increase the likelihood of achieving bilateral arms control.

Moreover, Safeguard (a ballistic missile defence system that was the follow-on to Sentinel) was not popular with some sectors of the public. People living near designated ABM sites believed that they would be more not less vulnerable to Soviet attack. But it is also true that most people did not have especially strong

---

40 David Holloway, *The Soviet Union and the Arms Race* (2nd ed; New Haven CT: Yale University Press 1984), 45.

opinions about the issue one way or the other. In a 1969 Gallup poll – in response to the question 'Have you heard or read about discussions on the ABM program – that is, the antiballistic missile program?' – 69 per cent answered yes, and 31 per cent said no. Those who had heard about the programme were asked: 'Do you happen to have an opinion about the ABM program as submitted to Congress by President Nixon?' Forty per cent said yes, 60 per cent no. Of those who had an opinion and were asked 'Do you favour or oppose the ABM program as submitted by President Nixon?' 25 per cent were in favour and 15 per cent opposed, but the majority, 60 per cent, were undecided.[41]

The MIRV did not arouse the same intense passions as the debate over the ABM, but it was, nevertheless, the focus of some concern in Congress. The genie was already out of the bottle, insofar as Congress had appropriated funds for MIRV testing in 1968, but the final round of tests, due to begin in May 1969, sparked debate. There were amendments to the MX appropriations bill calling for an end to MIRV testing and calls for a moratorium. On 12 June the *New York Times* argued that unilateral suspension of MIRV testing would invite reciprocal restraint by the Soviet Union. Just over a week later the *Times* gravely predicted: 'No decision Richard Nixon will face as President is likely to be more momentous than the decision he faces within the next few days on the proposals to suspend the flight testing of MIRV ... Continued testing for even a few more weeks threatens to take the world past a point of no return into an expensive and dangerous new round in the missile race.'[42]

Increasing pressure from the public and Congress for arms control was coupled with the growing belief that emerging parity in strategic forces had created a new opportunity to freeze the arms race; and there was some feeling that the administra-

41 George D. Gallup, *The Gallup Poll: Public Opinion 1935-1971* (New York: Random House 1979), 2190, 2207.
42 *New York Times*, 12 June and 20 June 1969, as quoted in Kissinger, *White House Years*, 211.

tion should not use arms control as a lever to resolve other disputes with the Soviet Union. Senator Albert Gore declared: 'It may be that we have an unparalleled opportunity to arrest a developing escalation of another nuclear armaments race.' The former secretary of defense, Clark Clifford, who himself had approved funding for the ABM and MIRV programmes, called for a freeze: 'The hard fact is that we may never again expect to be in as favorable a position as we enjoy for entry into talks about a freeze in strategic nuclear armaments. Technological developments may well make any arms limitation agreement more difficult to develop and enforce a year from now, or 6 months from now, than it is today.'[43]

Nixon's critics saw his mandate as a chance to put United States-Soviet relations on a new footing. Some urged a 'get acquainted summit' to initiate strategic arms limitation talks while others urged the removal of barriers to East-West trade. A Council on Foreign Relations study group, chaired by Carl Kaysen (the deputy national security adviser during the Kennedy administration), argued that 'a rare opportunity might slip away, and called for a unilateral moratorium on American deployment of antiballistic missiles (ABMs) and multiple independently targetable reentry vehicles (MIRVs) in order to make a strategic arms limitation agreement possible.' A United Nations panel chaired by Arthur Goldberg also urged 'necessary and urgent initiation of bilateral strategic missile negotiations with the Soviet Union.'[44]

From a strategic standpoint it was evident that the Soviet Union was entering a major build-up of its ICBM and SLBM forces and that these programmes were gaining momentum. This was reflected in the changes in the strategic balance. By the late 1960s the United States had tested the MIRV and was beginning to develop plans to outfit its ICBM forces with new MIRVed warhead packages. In January 1967 the United States

43 Cited in Kissinger, *White House Years*, 134.
44 Cited in *ibid*, 131.

had 1630 operational ICBMS and SLBMS versus 600 for the Soviet Union. By September 1968, the date SALT had originally been scheduled to begin, the ratio of operational ICBMS and SLBMS was reduced to 1710 to 1500 in the United States' favour. The balance was beginning to shift towards the Soviet Union. By November 1969 when the talks began, the Soviet Union had 1900 missiles operational and under construction. (When the talks concluded in May 1972, the figure stood at 2348, while the United States count remained unchanged at 1710).[45]

The Nixon administration also found itself under strong pressure from the State Department to begin negotiations. On 19 March 1969, Gerard Smith, the head of ACDA, told his Soviet counterpart, Aleksei Roshchin, in Geneva that the start of SALT 'need not be tied, in some sort of package formula, to the settlement of specific international problems.' On 27 March the secretary of state, William Rogers, told the Senate Foreign Relations Committee that 'we hope such talks can begin within the next few months ... We have already agreed with the Soviet Union that we will have these talks fairly soon.'[46] The State Department draft for a presidential address to the North Atlantic Council in April had the president announcing that talks would begin in Geneva immediately. The administration quickly found that its policy of deferring negotiation was being undermined by the bureaucracy. As Kissinger writes:

Day after day that spring the bureaucracy chipped away at the President's declared policy, feeding expectations of arms talks. In the *New York Times* of April 18, 'officials' were contending that arms agreements with the Soviet Union 'are an overriding goal of the Nixon foreign policy.' On April 22 the *Times* cited 'American diplomats' speculating about SALT talks in June. On May 4, Llewellyn Thompson told Dobrynin that Rogers hoped to discuss a date and place with Dobrynin before Rogers left May 12 on his trip to Asia ... On May 14, UPI reported from Geneva that the United States was ready to

45 Raymond Garthoff, 'SALT I: an evaluation,' *World Politics* 31(October 1978), 8.
46 Quoted in Kissinger, *White House Years*, 137.

start SALT in early July. On May 14, the British government approached the State Department for guidance on how to comment publicly on SALT ... Other NATO allies, under the same impression, followed suit. ...

These preemptive statements and cumulative pressures were not the result of an articulated conceptual difference between the Secretary of State and the President. They were a series of tactical day-to-day deviations from White House policy. They were intended to crystallize a decision. ...

The cumulative impact of all the bureaucratic indiscipline, with media and Congressional pressures added, was that we had to abandon our attempt to use the opening of SALT talks as a lever for other negotiations. On June 11 we authorized Rogers to inform the Soviets that we were ready to start SALT.[47]

The first round of discussion in SALT began at Helsinki in November 1969. Although the prenegotiation phase in this study is defined to include informal bilateral (or multilateral) discussions *prior to* the tabling of formal proposals and the designation of official negotiators, it would be a mistake to cast this distinction too narrowly. This first set of talks was much more of an exploratory discussion than a negotiation. As the chief American negotiator in SALT I, Gerard Smith, observed, his delegation faced a monumental task: 'We knew from earlier exchanges that the Soviets were interested in limitations on offensive as well as defensive systems (ABMs). Beyond that we were in the dark. I learned indirectly that the White House had advised Soviet Ambassador Dobrynin not to expect any specific proposals at the opening round.'[48] And it was not until after this lengthy first round of exploratory discussions lasting two months that an agenda – and a very rough one at that – emerged. As Smith noted in a personal report to the president:

My hunch at this very early stage of the talks is that Soviet purposes

47 *Ibid*, 137-8.
48 Gerard Smith, *Doubletalk: The Story of SALT* (Lanham MD: University Press of America 1985), 79-80.

are a mix of at least three possible main ingredients: a) To see if an arrangement can be negotiated that would improve their prospects, or stabilize the strategic balance at lower cost; b) To 'cover' their ICBM/SLBM build-up and hopefully to defer, if not defeat, a U.S. reaction; c) To advance their general arms control image as well as their specific non-proliferation interests by appearing to meet the obligations of Article VI (NPT).

According to Smith, it also became apparent to the United States delegation 'that the Soviet commitment to proceed with the negotiations had been made only after the Helsinki talks were well under way ... After the final plenary, one of their advisers said that, while "old hands" knew that discussions were possible between the United States and the U.S.S.R., a very important result of the sessions was that others now had this impression.'[49]

Explaining outcomes

The most important precondition for SALT I was the changing strategic balance between the United States and the Soviet Union. As the Soviet Union approached strategic parity with the United States, some saw a new opportunity to halt the arms race. President Johnson began preliminary discussions with the Soviet Union on arms limitation but the Soviet invasion of Czechoslovakia put these talks on the back burner. The new Republican administration of President Nixon entered office worried that the Soviet Union would soon overtake the United States in military power and strategic arms because the American public, wearied by the Vietnam War, would not support increases in defence spending. Nixon and Kissinger saw an impending crisis in the Soviet arms build-up. Although the two men saw an important opportunity in arms control to halt that build-up, they were both reluctant to jump into talks with the Soviet Union, if perhaps for different reasons. Nixon was fearful of the domestic political consequences of negotiations that bore

49 *Ibid*, 106.

no fruit. Kissinger was more concerned about laying the groundwork for arms control and incorporating it into a broader strategy of 'linkage' before entering negotiations.

In the wider arms control community and in Congress worries about the strategic balance were reinforced by growing awareness and concern about the destabilizing consequences of new technology, in particular the ABM and the MIRV.[50] The United States had gone from hot to cold on ABM deployments and, coupled with the apparent lack of Soviet interest in further ABM deployments, this increased the possibilities for an arms control agreement on defences. As pressures in Congress grew, and a manipulative bureaucracy helped accelerate the timetable for talks, the administration found itself headed to the negotiating table earlier than it expected. It was also unclear when the talks first began just what the Soviet Union itself hoped to get out of the negotiation. The first round of SALT I was thus crucial to defining the agenda and ensuring a commitment by both sides to the negotiation that followed.

NUCLEAR AND SPACE TALKS 1982-

The final case in this study concerns the origins of the nuclear and space talks, also known as START, which began in 1982 and resumed after a brief hiatus in 1985. Although the two sides have yet to reach an agreement, progress of sorts on strategic arms reduction was made at the Reykjavik summit in October 1986 and in subsequent talks in Washington and Geneva. The agreement on intermediate-range force reductions, signed at the Washington summit in December 1987, gave added momentum to the possibilities of an agreement on strategic weapons. It is indeed ironic that Reagan, who had rejected the possibilities of arms control as a presidential candidate in 1980,

50 In spite of concerns expressed by the arms control community, the momentum behind the MIRV programme by the time the talks got started made it impossible to negotiate meaningful and verifiable constraints, and it is noteworthy that the issue was never put on the table for discussion in SALT.

had become one of its seeming champions by the end of the decade.[51] Why did the Reagan administration reject and then initiate arms control talks with the Soviet Union? Why did the administration begin START in 1982? Was it in response to domestic political pressures and the 'nuclear freeze' movement? Was it because the administration believed it could only negotiate with the Soviet Union from a position of military strength? What effect, if any, did a desire to place the strategic relationship with the Soviet Union on a more stable footing play in the prenegotiation process? What impact did pressures from the allies play in bringing the United States to the table?

Origins of START

By the end of the 1970s, arms control had become the favourite whipping boy of critics from the right. They complained that the SALT agreements did not have adequate verification provisions and that the intelligence community had seriously underestimated the size and capability of Soviet missile forces. The loss of Iranian intelligence-gathering posts in 1979 had further compromised the ability of United States intelligence to provide timely assessments. Critics argued that the SALT II treaty did not limit Soviet missile production and that the size of the Soviet stockpile of missiles was therefore unknown. Limits on ICBM silos and SLBM launchers did not address the real threat. They charged that subceilings on MIRVed missile launchers and constraints on modernization regarding throw-weight or launch-weight could not be adequately verified, nor could SALT II restrictions on new missile development. Amid growing charges of violations, the record of Soviet compliance became a key issue in the Senate ratification hearings on SALT II.[52]

---

51 Not all would agree with this assessment. Many would argue that Reagan's policies on arms control, including the Strategic Defense Initiative, verification, and the repudiation of SALT, were basically damaging to arms control and that Reagan was on the road to a bad agreement in START.

52 National Academy of Sciences, *Nuclear Arms Control: Background and Issues* (Washington: National Academy Press 1985), 49-52.

In the 1980 presidential campaign, Ronald Reagan said that he would withdraw the 'fatally flawed' SALT II treaty from the Senate ratification process. He criticized the treaty for its failure to limit Soviet throw-weight and to close the 'window of vulnerability' which threatened United States ICBMs. The new administration offered no new ideas for arms control. Instead, its priority was to redress the strategic 'balance' with a military build-up of unprecedented proportions. President Reagan announced a 10-per-cent annual increase in the military budget for the next five years.

However, the administration soon found itself under strong domestic and allied pressure to pursue arms control. The most pressing issue on the agenda was how to deal with the 'two-track' decision of December 1979.[53] That decision had committed the North Atlantic Treaty Organization (NATO) to proceed with the deployment of new intermediate-range nuclear forces while pursuing reductions in Soviet missiles. On 26 February 1981, the British prime minister, Margaret Thatcher, in Washington for talks with Reagan, secured the new president's commitment to the two-track policy.[54]

Although the State Department was keen to get arms control talks under way, it faced heavy opposition from the anti-arms control lobby in the Pentagon, led by the assistant secretary, Richard Perle, and the under secretary of defense for policy, Fred Iklé. They did not want to commit the administration to negotiation. Pressures from the allies continued to grow. The governments of both the Federal Republic of Germany and

---

53 For a further discussion of NATO, arms control, and the 'two-track' decision, see Raymond Garthoff, 'Brezhnev's opening: the TNF tangle,' *Foreign Policy*, no 41(winter 1980-1), 82-94; William G. Hyland, 'U.S.-Soviet relations: the long road back' and Flora Lewis, 'Alarm bells in the West,' *Foreign Affairs* (winter 1982), 525-50 and 551-72; and Gregory F. Treverton, *Making the Alliance Work: The United States and Western Europe* (Ithaca NY: Cornell University Press 1985), 25-58.

54 Strobe Talbott, *Deadly Gambits: The Reagan Administration and the Stalemate in Nuclear Arms Control* (New York: Vintage Books 1985), 45.

Italy let it be known that they would not deploy new intermediate-range missiles until Washington set a date for talks. At a National Security Council meeting on 30 April, the president authorized the secretary of state, Alexander Haig, to commit the United States publicly to negotiations on INF by the end of the year.[55] The talks began in November 1981. Like Harding some sixty years earlier, Reagan had made a reluctant concession to pressing political realities.

In November 1981 Reagan also announced that the United States might enter into negotiation with the Soviet Union on strategic arms reduction the following year. However, the Polish crisis would defer negotiations for another eight months. Pressure from the nuclear freeze movement, which had begun the year before the president was sworn into office, also forced the administration to set a date for strategic arms control negotiations. Initially a grass-roots campaign, the movement gathered momentum and by 1982 had acquired substantial political support in Congress.[56] The principal architect of the freeze was Randall Forsberg, head of the Institute for Defense and Disarmament Studies in Massachusetts. In 1980 she published a paper, 'Call to halt the nuclear arms race,' which urged a comprehensive freeze on the testing, production, and deployment of nuclear weapons and their delivery systems.

Initially there was little public interest in the idea of a freeze. During 1980-1, public support for increases in defence spending was strong as a consequence of disillusionment with détente after Soviet aggression in Afghanistan and Soviet actions in the Horn of Africa. Two-thirds of the American public (67 per cent), in a poll conducted by the Public Agenda Foundation, endorsed the view that the 'Soviet Union used detente as an opportunity to build up their armed forces while lulling [the United States] ... into a sense of false security.' 'The public mood

---

55 *Ibid*, 45-51.
56 See Adam M. Garfinkle, *The Politics of the Nuclear Freeze* (Philadelphia: Foreign Policy Research Institute 1984).

was characterized by injured national pride, unqualified support for increasing the defense budget, and a general desire to see American power become more assertive.'[57]

However, that mood quickly shifted with Reagan's defence build-up. In early 1981, state senatorial districts in western Massachusetts passed freeze resolutions. In March 1981, the national conference of peace groups, meeting in Washington, decided to promote the freeze. In early 1982, freeze resolutions found their way onto ballots in town meetings in Vermont and California. By the end of the year there were freeze movements in every state and two-thirds of the congressional districts nation-wide. An AP/ABC poll of 6 April 1982 reported that 74 per cent of those polled supported a bilateral verifiable freeze, 18 per cent were opposed, and 8 per cent were not sure.[58]

On 10 March 1982, nuclear freeze resolutions had been introduced in the Senate by Edward Kennedy and Mark Hatfield and in the House of Representatives by Edward Markey and Silvio Conte.[59] Although the resolutions were eventually passed by both houses, they were heavily amended.[60] The administration expressed its own opposition to a freeze on the grounds that it would lock the United States into a position of strategic inferiority vis-à-vis the Soviet Union. But it was clearly on the defensive. On 31 March 1982, in a televised news conference, the president invited the Soviet Union to join in negotiations to bring about substantial reductions in nuclear arsenals. He also endorsed a resolution introduced by Senators Henry Jackson and John Warner which called for the reduction of United States and Soviet strategic arms to equal levels prior to a freeze.[61]

57 Daniel Yankelovitch and John Doble, 'The public mood: nuclear weapons and the u.s.s.r.,' *Foreign Affairs* 63(fall 1984), 82-3.
58 *Nuclear Arms Control*, 84.
59 See Edward Kennedy and Mark O. Hatfield, *Freeze! How You Can Help Prevent Nuclear War* (Toronto: Bantam Books 1982).
60 *Nuclear Arms Control*, 82-3.
61 *Ibid*, 58-9.

In the absence of visible progress on arms control, pressure in Congress to veto increases in defence spending and put key programmes on hold was growing. As Blacker and Duffy note: 'Specifically, the fate of the MX, to which the administration attached so much importance, seemed to hinge both on the development of a "survivable" basing mode and on the maintenance of significant constraints on Soviet ICBMs.'[62] Again, the situation was similar to that in the 1920s when an administration had seized on arms control to protect a military build-up from domestic opponents.

On 9 May 1982, President Reagan outlined his START proposal at an address at his alma mater, Eureka College. The first phase would see reductions of nuclear warheads and land-based missiles from 8000 to 5000 with no more than 2500 warheads on land-based missiles. The first phase would also include a limit of 850 on 'deployed ballistic missiles.' The second phase would see equal ceilings on the throw-weight of all nuclear missiles. Reductions on strategic bombers and cruise missiles would be left to later phases.[63] The president stated that his goal was to enhance deterrence and achieve stability through substantial reductions in 'the most destabilizing nuclear systems – ballistic missiles, and especially intercontinental ballistic missiles – while maintaining a nuclear capability sufficient to deter conflict, underwrite our national security and meet our commitment to our allies and friends.'[64] The emphasis on reductions was central to the administration's entire thinking about arms control. As Strobe Talbott explains: 'From the beginning of the Reagan administration, there had been two cardinal rules governing strategic arms control policy. First, START must be – and must be seen to be – very different from SALT. Second, the R in START, which distinguished the new initials from the old, stood for reduction as opposed to mere limitation. Whatever

62 Blacker and Duffy, eds, *International Arms Control*, 273.
63 *Ibid*; *Nuclear Arms Control*, 59-60.
64 *Nuclear Arms Control*, 60.

else START achieved, it must achieve reductions, the deeper and more drastic the better.'[65]

The two-step decision was a bureaucratic compromise engineered by Richard Burt, director of the Bureau of Politico-Military Affairs in the Department of State. Whereas Perle believed that what mattered most in the strategic balance was Soviet missile throw-weight, Burt was worried that a proposal limited to throw-weight reductions would be viewed by the Soviet Union as asymmetrical and kill any chances for agreement. Burt favoured limits on launchers combined with limits on the numbers of warheads each side could deploy. The compromise proposal limited reductions in the first phase to launchers and warheads while working towards throw-weight reductions in the second.[66]

The Soviet Union did not like the idea. On 18 May President Leonid Brezhnev declared that the proposed United States approach would require a unilateral reduction in the Soviet arsenal. Instead, he proposed a ban on the development of any new strategic weapons and a nuclear freeze as soon as talks began. As a sign of good will, President Reagan pledged not to take any actions that would undercut the agreement arising from SALT II so long as the Soviet Union showed similar restraint. The secretary of defense, Caspar Weinberger, warned that the Soviet Union would take advantage of a freeze and blackmail the United States. Nevertheless, on 31 May 1982, President Reagan announced that START would begin in June.

On 29 June 1982 the negotiations officially began in Geneva. In response to United States proposals, the Soviet Union proposed an interim freeze on strategic arms and limits based on the SALT II framework, that is, 20-per-cent reductions from SALT II ceilings on central strategic systems and unspecified subceiling reductions.

On 4 October 1983 Reagan unveiled a new 'build-down'

65 Talbott, *Deadly Gambits*, 234.
66 *Ibid*, 253-64 and 233-40.

proposal as the United States negotiating position. The United States proposed a reduction to 5000 missile warheads. New warheads could only be introduced if 'old' ones were withdrawn to guarantee annual reductions of 5 per cent in the total number of missile warheads. Build-down provisions specifically called for the removal of two warheads for each new MIRVed land-based missile, three old warheads for every two new SLBM warheads, and one old warhead for each new single-warhead land-based missile.[67] The president's build-down proposal received strong congressional support. But critics pointed out that build-down would still permit deployment of destabilizing first-strike systems and that the build-down ratios discriminated against the Soviet Union whose land-based missile force accounted for 70 per cent of its total force. The Soviet Union reacted to the new initiative unfavourably.

In December 1983 START stalled after the Soviet Union walked out of the INF talks. Talks did not resume until March 1985 when the Soviet Union decided to come back to the negotiating table after it was clear that its 'temper tantrum' had backfired badly with public opinion in both the United States and Western Europe.[68] These matters are explored more fully in Franklyn Griffiths's paper in this volume.

Explaining outcomes
Reagan's early allergy to arms control was based on the view that the SALT process had been profoundly inimical to United States interests. It was a view shared by many members of his administration. The president's priority was to restore American military superiority before entering into any kind of negotiation with the Soviet Union. It was a strategy of bargaining from strength rather than weakness. But it was a strategy that was not shared either by Congress or, increasingly, by broad sectors of the American public. Nor was it a strategy supported

67 *Nuclear Arms Control*, 64.
68 Arnold Horelick, 'U.S.-Soviet relations: the return of arms control,' *Foreign Affairs* 63(winter 1984/5), 511-37.

by the NATO allies which had decided that arms control and military improvements had to proceed in tandem. This was the logic of the December 1979 two-track decision. It was also the logic behind the decision of Congress to link support for Reagan's military build-up to progress in arms control.

The context of prenegotiation bore a striking resemblance to that prior to the Washington Naval Conference some sixty years earlier: a growing public belief that the world was on the edge of crisis and the threshold of a major new arms race, an administration intent on increasing United States defence spending, and a Congress reluctant to sanction increases without, at the same time, securing a formal commitment from the administration to pursue arms control.

Faced with the growing momentum of the nuclear freeze movement and congressional pressure, the Reagan administration was more or less forced into arms control negotiations. But it explicitly distanced itself from the past, emphasizing 'reductions' in both START and the INF talks as opposed to the 'limitations' and 'ceilings' characteristic of the SALT process. Reagan's own view of SALT played a key role in the definition of START, although many disagreed with the 'lessons' he drew from the historical record.[69]

Thus, domestic politics as much as international power politics were critical in the prenegotiation phase of START. In the absence of the freeze movement, it is quite likely that the 'start' of START would have been delayed. In the case of the INF talks, the views of the allies were obviously the key factor behind the administration's decision to enter negotiations.

CONCLUSIONS

The four cases of arms control prenegotiation examined here exhibit some common modalities or recurrent patterns of behaviour. The trigger for negotiations in each case was a 'crisis'

---

69 See Philip J. Farley, 'Strategic arms control, 1967-87,' in George, Farley, and Dallin, eds, *U.S.-Soviet Security Cooperation*, 215-53.

– either a crisis that had just passed or a sense of impending crisis based on the belief that the military-strategic balance was about to shift swiftly and dramatically against the United States.

The Washington Naval Treaties were prenegotiated against the background of a growing challenge to British naval supremacy by the United States. Fears that a naval arms race would precipitate the outbreak of another war spurred public and congressional activism in the prenegotiation phase of the Washington Naval Conference. The subsequent agreement established parity between British and United States naval forces and froze French, Italian, and Japanese forces at lower levels. Similarly, the Limited Nuclear Test Ban Treaty was negotiated in the aftermath of the Cuban missiles crisis which had brought the superpowers to the brink of nuclear disaster. The SALT I agreements were prenegotiated in the context of mounting concerns, especially of Nixon and Kissinger, that the Soviet Union was about to deploy a major anti-ballistic missile defence system and was on the threshold of achieving strategic superiority over the United States. United States aims in SALT I were intimately connected with the desire to establish strategic 'parity' and to foster a combination of greater 'strategic' and 'crisis' stability in the force postures of the two sides.[70] Similar objectives informed United States policies in SALT II and START.[71] In the case of START, the Reagan administration perceived that the Soviet Union had exploited loopholes in the SALT agreements and was acquiring a force posture that increasingly threatened the land-based leg of the United States strategic triad. The objective of the process of prenegotiation in START was to achieve asymmetrical reductions that would limit Soviet throw-weight and close the 'window of vulnerability.'

In these four cases, the prenegotiation game has been played on two levels in the United States: the international and the domestic. Although changing military power balances have de-

70 Smith, *Doubletalk*, 85-6.
71 See, for example, Stephen J. Flanagan, 'SALT II,' in Carnesale and Haas, eds, *Superpower Arms Control*, 105-38.

fined prenegotiation possibilities and opportunities in arms control, domestic influences, including bureaucratic politics, public opinion, and executive-congressional conflicts, have figured prominently in the timing of United States decisions to enter formal negotiation. Arms control prenegotiation has thus had a specifically domestic political orientation and the United States willingness to begin negotiations has been affected by the emergence of strong public and congressional pressures in support of arms control.

In all four cases, domestic pressures played a decisive 'intervening' role in the prenegotiation. Without the domestic political context it is difficult – in fact impossible – to explain why Washington initiated formal negotiations. From the Washington Naval Conference on, Congress has been instrumental in setting the date and agenda for subsequent arms control negotiations. Bureaucratic interests have likewise played a key role in building pressure for negotiation. Scientific evidence that atmospheric testing was harmful to health and the environment was instrumental in growing public pressure to conclude a treaty that would ban atmospheric testing. Fears among scientists, defence intellectuals, and Congress about the destabilizing consequences of ABM technologies were also important in the United States domestic debate prior to SALT I and led to a political climate generally supportive of arms control. A coalition of bureaucratic interests which favoured early negotiations with the Soviet Union brought the Nixon administration to the table in SALT I before it wanted to be there. In a story that is strikingly similar to that of the Washington Naval Treaties some sixty years earlier, congressional action on the defence budget along with mounting public pressure brought the Reagan administration to the negotiating table in 1982. The linkage established by Congress between increases in defence spending and arms control has figured prominently in the prenegotiation phase. Although American public opinion has shown considerable dissatisfaction with the results of specific agreements (like SALT I and SALT II), presidents from Warren Harding on have learned

that during times of peace Americans will not sanction unbri-
dled increases in defence spending without a concomitant commitment to arms control.

Pressure from allies was also important in the prenegotiation
phase of each negotiation. America's allies strongly supported
naval arms limitation prior to the Washington Conference. Similarly, there was growing international pressure to ban atmospheric testing, once the health risks became known. Although
less evident in the case of SALT I, there is little doubt that
pressure from the allies was important in the origins of START
and the INF talks. Thus the allies have played and will undoubtedly continue to play an important role in determining
the timing of new arms control negotiations.

The pattern to emerge from these four cases is characterized
by the following interaction of structural and independent (or
intervening) influences on prenegotiation: perception of crisis
(impending or actual) resulting from politico-military confrontation or change (or threat of change) to the military-strategic
balance → growing domestic public and congressional (and
sometimes bureaucratic) pressures for arms control → pressure
from allies for arms control → a decision to begin or initiate
formal arms control negotiations. This characterization, though
admittedly artificial, suggests a sequence of events and interactions characteristic of all four cases. It should be noted that
domestic coalition politics and the bargains struck between different competing institutional interests (in particular, between
those of Congress and those of the executive) are also important
in explaining outcomes.

The boundary- and agenda-setting functions of the prenegotiation process are worth noting as well. Discussions in the
United Nations Disarmament Commission and the Eighteen-
Nation Disarmament Committee were instrumental in laying
much of the groundwork for the Limited Nuclear Test Ban
Treaty by helping to define certain options while eliminating
others. Congressional and bureaucratic objections to a comprehensive as opposed to a limited test ban also helped define

the parameters of the negotiating agenda and the final agreement which resulted in a limited as opposed to a comprehensive test ban. By contrast, the prenegotiation phase of SALT I was characterized by little apparent consensus at the outset about what kind of negotiating proposals or arms agreements were desirable or feasible. There was also little information about the kinds of concessions or proposals the Soviet Union would be willing to consider when the formal negotiation began. Thus the first round of SALT I was crucial not only to delimiting the agenda for the subsequent rounds of talks but also in confirming the Soviet commitment to the negotiation itself. The prenegotiation phase in SALT I left the agenda for the formal negotiation wide open.

The same cannot be said about the situation when the two sides came to the table in START. In his 1980 election campaign, Ronald Reagan had made clear his profound dissatisfaction with the negotiating record of SALT I and SALT II. The initial prenegotiation objective of his administration was not to consider negotiation with the Soviet Union at all.[72] But when it became apparent that Congress and the American public would not sanction increases in defence spending without progress in arms control, the administration's fall-back position was to agree to negotiation but to seek asymmetrical cuts in Soviet forces in order to close the much-touted 'window of vulnerability' in United States strategic forces. These concerns, which were reflected in much of the political rhetoric of the 1980 presidential race, were instrumental in shaping the prenegotiating agenda of the Reagan administration in arms control.

All four cases also suggest that learning was an important characteristic of the prenegotiation phase and instrumental in defining the kinds of issues that eventually came to the table. Fears that a naval arms race would precipitate the outbreak of

72 Some of the reasons underlying the Reagan administration's scepticism towards arms control are explained by Kenneth L. Adelman, former director of the Arms Control and Disarmament Agency, in 'Arms control: with and without agreements,' *Foreign Affairs* 63(winter 1984/5), 240-63.

another war, as it was perceived to have done in World War I, spurred public and congressional activism in the prenegotiation phase of the Washington Naval Conference. Accumulating scientific evidence that atmospheric testing was harmful to health and the environment was instrumental in growing pressure to conclude an atmospheric test ban treaty. Arms controllers and some scientists worried openly about the implications of new technologies for ballistic missile defence and raised this issue prior to SALT I. But there were significant limits to learning as well. Although the destabilizing consequences of MIRV technologies for the arms race were well understood before SALT, limitations on MIRVs did not make it onto the negotiating agenda. And many would argue that concerns in the late 1970s and early 1980s about the 'window of vulnerability' in the United States ICBM force were exaggerated or misplaced.[73]

These preliminary findings suggest that changes in the military power balance are a necessary but not sufficient condition to explain why the United States has entered into arms control negotiations when it has. In superpower arms control, the United States decision to negotiate has been affected by a number of intervening factors, including Congress, public opinion, and pressure from allies. In addition, executive-congressional bargaining and bureaucratic pressures have been important in delimiting the negotiating agenda at the start (or resumption) of formal negotiation, and significant 'learning' has occurred prior to the onset of formal negotiation. It is therefore important to include the prenegotiation phase in any consideration of the processes and requirements for superpower arms control and the development of a more general theory of negotiating behaviour.

73 See, for example, Albert Carnesale and Charles Glaser, 'ICBM vulnerability: the cures are worse than the disease,' *International Security* 7(summer 1982), 70-85.

6. *Prenegotiation in the Arab-Israeli Conflict: the Paradoxes of Success and Failure*

JANICE GROSS STEIN

Prenegotiation has been extraordinarily important in the Arab-Israeli conflict. Throughout much of its history, direct contact was impossible and formal negotiation very difficult, even when it was done through intermediaries. Consequently, the testing of the intentions of one party by another, the examination of negotiation as an option, and the tentative assessment of the likelihood of agreement have all occurred frequently between Israel and Arab states. Indeed, prenegotiation has preceded all attempts at negotiation that have occurred throughout the forty years of the conflict. It is difficult to exaggerate the importance of prenegotiation in establishing channels of indirect communication, in setting the boundaries for the negotiations that did occur, in delimiting agendas, in determining the eligibility of participants, in clarifying core trade-offs, and in structuring bargaining strategies. Both when it succeeded and when it failed, prenegotiation had significant and unanticipated short-term and long-term consequences.

THE IDENTIFICATION AND CLASSIFICATION OF CASES
This study looks at two cases of prenegotiation which were briefly interrupted by a period of negotiation. The first began among the United States, Israel, Egypt, Jordan, Saudi Arabia, Syria, the Palestine Liberation Organization (PLO), and the

Professor Political Science, University of Toronto, Toronto, Ontario, and co-author (with Robert Jervis and Richard Ned Lebow) of *Psychology and Deterrence* (Baltimore MD: Johns Hopkins University Press 1985).

Soviet Union in January 1977 and ended in November 1977 in failure. Only two of the parties who had participated in the larger multilateral process of prenegotiation, Egypt and Israel, went on to negotiate, with the United States largely as observer rather than participant, but this negotiation failed as well. The second attempt at prenegotiation began three months later, in January 1978, among the United States, Egypt, Israel, Jordan, and Saudi Arabia and terminated in August 1978 when the first three agreed to a very different kind of negotiation at Camp David.

The identification of these two cases of prenegotiation and the classification of their outcomes are not obvious. The first process, initiated by the United States early in the term of President Jimmy Carter, was explicitly considered by American participants as prenegotiation designed to explore the positions of the parties, their willingness to negotiate, and the appropriate forum of negotiation.[1] They also acknowledged its termination after President Sadat of Egypt went to Jerusalem to break the impasse and move the parties to a very different kind of negotiation.[2] The second case of prenegotiation, which began after three months of negotiation between Egypt and Israel had ended in failure, is more difficult to classify. Leaders were now considering a very different kind of negotiation and some participants had been eliminated from the process. At the same time, the parties were becoming much more specific in their proposals and, indeed, were preparing draft documents for consideration by others. As they began to commit their ideas to paper, the process of prenegotiation shaded into negotiation. The evidence suggests, however, that these documents were

---

1 William Quandt, the member of the National Security Council staff charged with responsibility for the Arab-Israeli conflict, uses the term 'prenegotiation' to describe the process initiated by the Carter administration. William B. Quandt, *Camp David: Peacemaking and Politics* (Washington: Brookings Institution 1986), 74.

2 Cyrus Vance, *Hard Choices* (New York: Simon & Shuster 1983), 195.

not treated as serious negotiating positions, but were prenegotiation manoeuvres designed to influence the boundaries, form, format, and agenda of the anticipated negotiation.[3] For this reason, we treat this second case as a process of prenegotiation rather than as negotiation itself.

The classification of the outcomes of these two cases of prenegotiation is even more problematic. The first is technically a failure, because the process of negotiation that was under consideration was aborted by President Anwar el-Sadat's visit to Jerusalem. Yet, it was Sadat's low estimate of the prospects of success if prenegotiation continued that led him to initiate a process of negotiation with Israel. Moreover, significant learning did take place during this first prenegotiation which prepared some of the parties both for the negotiation that followed and for the process of prenegotiation that would begin in January 1978. The second prenegotiation did lead to formal negotiation, but only when the process threatened to collapse. Moreover, one of the principal participants in that process of prenegotiation, Jordan, did not participate in the negotiation that followed. Ultimately, the outcomes of these two processes are better judged in the first instance as part of an alternating sequence of prenegotiation and negotiation and, in the longer term, by the learning that occurred.

WHY DID PRENEGOTIATION BEGIN?

The first process of prenegotiation began not in the aftermath of a crisis, as some analysts suggest, but as a deliberate strategy of crisis avoidance.[4] It was initiated in early 1977 by the newly elected American president because of Carter's memory of the

---

3 In describing Sadat's draft proposals, Quandt observed: 'He lets his officials turn out worthless legalistic documents in the guise of serious negotiating proposals' (*Camp David*, 191). Only after the meeting at Leeds Castle in July 1978 did the United States recognize the need to develop far more concrete proposals (Harold Saunders, personal communication).

4 Daniel Druckman, 'Stages, turning points, and crises: negotiating military base rights, Spain and the United States,' *Journal of Conflict Resolution* 30(June 1986), 327-60.

adverse consequences of the war between Egypt, Syria, and Israel in 1973, the priority he attached to the development of a comprehensive domestic energy policy, and his fear of the consequences of renewed war.[5] His judgment was widely shared by members of both the old and new administrations. The transition papers prepared by State Department and National Security Council specialists warned that the status quo in the Middle East was inherently unstable; only progress in negotiation would avoid a slide towards confrontation.[6] Zbigniew Brzezinski, the new national security adviser, argued that the Arab-Israeli conflict required 'urgent' attention. In short, even before his term in office began, the attention of President-elect Carter was captured and sustained by a rare degree of consensus among his principal advisers that immediate action was required if adverse domestic and international consequences were to be avoided.

Arab leaders, especially Sadat, also expected that the new administration would seriously attempt to begin a process of negotiation. Indeed, Sadat told Carter during their first meeting that an agreement must be reached in 1977 and implemented before the second disengagement agreement then in place between Egypt and Israel came to an end in September 1978.[7] Although that agreement technically did not expire because it could be superseded only by another, the October deadline nevertheless served as a 'forcing mechanism' for a process of prenegotiation. The urgency of negotiation was heightened

5 In his speech to the United Nations General Assembly in October 1977, Carter made these concerns explicit: 'Of all the regional conflicts in the world, none holds more menace than the Middle East. War there has already carried the world to the edge of nuclear confrontation. It has already disrupted the world economy and imposed severe hardships on the people in the developed and developing nations alike.' 'United Nations: Address before the General Assembly, October 4, 1977,' *Public Papers of the Presidents of the United States: Carter, 1977*, II, 1720. See also his 'Speech to Town Meeting, Clinton, Massachusetts,' *Public Papers: Carter 1977*, I, 387, and Quandt, *Camp David*, 32.

6 Three relevant documents are 'Arab peace offensive,' 4 January 1977, a paper on the Arab-Israel dispute dated 14 January 1977, and an undated paper, 'Inter-Arab politics and a peace settlement.' See Quandt, *Camp David*, 36, note 8.

7 Quandt, *Camp David*, 51.

by an escalating domestic crisis in Egypt. Food riots, student strikes, and growing political opposition to the régime intensified the need for crisis avoidance.[8] An option of negotiation was especially attractive because the obvious alternative, renewal of military action, was unappealing in the light of the mixed military outcome of the 1973 war. Moreover, lower military expenditures would allow Sadat to channel additional resources to the urban poor. The president could thus balance the needs of an army tied in large part to the rural middle class with the conflicting needs of the urban poor.[9]

Israel's leaders also faced an increasing economic crisis. The balance-of-payments deficit had soared and inflationary pressures had created a particularly acute burden for the urban poor who were supporters of the principal opposition party.[10] The government of Yitzhak Rabin was weak and its three principal ministers were bitterly divided. Thus, in Jerusalem and in Cairo as well as in Washington, domestic and strategic factors interacted to promote movement towards prenegotiation. Estimates of the adverse consequences of inaction were widely shared.

8 Throughout 1976 Egypt suffered sustained shortages in its foreign currency reserves and imbalances in foreign trade. In response to demands by the International Monetary Fund, Dr Abd al-Moneim al Qaissuni, newly designated minister of finance and economy and former chairman of the Arab National Bank, announced on 18 January 1977 that the government would end or substantially reduce subsidies on sugar, flour, rice, oil, bottled gas, cigarettes, and beer. Riots erupted in major Egyptian cities the next day and order was restored only after a curfew was imposed. John Waterbury, *Egypt: Burdens of the Past, Options for the Future* (Bloomington: University of Indiana Press 1978), 315-16. President Sadat attacked the left for inspiring the riots and, in April 1977, dismissed Mohamed Heikal, the most articulate spokesman of the left, from the editorship of *Al-Ahram*, Egypt's official newspaper. Simultaneously, he encouraged the growth of Islamic forces in Egypt in an effort to build support for his régime. See Munir K. Nasser, *Press, Politics, and Power: Egypt's Heikal and Al-Ahram* (Ames: Iowa State University Press 1979), 100-2.

9 Melvin A. Friedlander, *Sadat and Begin: The Domestic Politics of Peacemaking* (Boulder CO: Westview 1983).

10 The massive increase in defence spending following the October 1973 War exacerbated Israel's economic difficulties and its balance-of-payments deficit soared to almost US$4 billion in 1976. Ann Crittenden, 'Israel's economic plight,' *Foreign Affairs* 57(summer 1979), 1005.

In the second case of prenegotiation which began in January 1978, the same kinds of incentives operated with even greater intensity. As well, there were additional factors in play. First, the secret meeting the previous September in Morocco between Israel's new foreign minister, Moshe Dayan, and Egypt's deputy prime minister, Hassan Tuhamy, had increased the confidence of both sides that negotiation was a credible option. Although the meeting produced no agreement on the principles or procedures of negotiation or on the terms of an agreement, both sides were persuaded that success was possible.[11] The subsequent failure of three months of negotiation between Egypt and Israel, with the United States largely as observer rather than as participant, convinced Sadat and, in particular, Dayan that any further process of negotiation must involve the United States as a principal participant, if it was to succeed.[12]

By January 1978 domestic political incentives were even greater in Cairo than they had been a year earlier. President Sadat had incurred heavy costs, at home and abroad, from his trip to Jerusalem.[13] The Muslim Brotherhood had been implicated in plots to overthrow the régime and had won an overwhelming victory in student elections at Egyptian universities in December 1977. To counter these pressures, Sadat encouraged the resurgence of the Wafd, a nationalist party that sup-

11 Moshe Dayan, *Breakthrough: A Personal Account of the Egypt-Israel Peace Negotiations* (New York: Knopf 1981); Anwar el-Sadat, *In Search of Identity: An Autobiography* (New York: Harper & Row 1977); Ismail Fahmy, *Negotiating for Peace in the Middle East* (Baltimore MD: Johns Hopkins University Press 1983); and Muhammad Ibrahim Kamil, *The Lost Peace in the Camp David Accords* (Jiddah: Saudi Research and Marketing Co 1984; in Arabic).

12 Quandt, *Camp David*, 166-7.

13 The civilian technocracy and the military were the principal centres of power in Egypt after the presidency. The vice-president, Hosni Mubarak, championed the junior officers who worried about the country's future military-industrial complex and supply of arms. He opposed a negotiated agreement that would align Egypt closely with the United States. Abd el-Ghani Gamasy, the deputy prime minister and minister of war, actively sought closer relations with the United States to secure access to American weapons. The rivalry between the two men gave President Sadat some room for manoeuvre, because neither could unify the armed forces. Ehud Ya'ari, 'Sadat's pyramid of power,' *Jerusalem Quarterly* 11(winter 1980), 113-14.

ported the return of the Sinai.[14] A negotiated agreement had become even more important by January 1978 than it had been a year earlier.

Carter was receptive to another attempt. The president had little to show for his heavy involvement in prenegotiation in 1977; the pressure to achieve a significant foreign policy 'success' was growing. As William Quandt observes: 'So unwilling was the American team to see the past year's investment produce nothing at all, that it spared no effort.'[15] Sunk political costs increased the attractiveness of a second process of prenegotiation in January 1978.

Finally, the prospects for successful prenegotiation had improved somewhat since the previous attempt. Sadat's visit to Jerusalem had fractured the Arab coalition and, in so doing, given him greater flexibility. Indeed, one of the principal purposes of his trip had been to eliminate the possibility of a multilateral conference that had been the focus of the first process of prenegotiation and thereby remove the possibility of a veto by those members of the coalition least willing to make concessions. Sadat also anticipated two other consequences from his trip to Jerusalem which would improve the prospects of negotiation. First, he hoped to speak over the heads of Israel's leaders to its people and create a constituency for negotiation. Second, he hoped to influence American public opinion and help counteract Carter's obvious political weakness at home.[16] The Egyptian president succeeded in both aims. In attempting to break through the obstacles imposed by the domestic and

14 Army officers feared that religious leaders might gain unwelcome influence among enlisted men and in the state bureaucracy. See Israel Atman, 'Islamic movements in Egypt,' *Jerusalem Quarterly* 10(winter 1979), 99, and P.J. Vatikiotis, *The History of Egypt* (2nd ed; Baltimore MD: Johns Hopkins University Press 1980), 414.

15 Quandt, *Camp David*, 170.

16 President Carter, at a meeting at Camp David with President Sadat, quoted the Egyptian president as saying that he had taken his initiative in part to overcome the influence of powerful lobby groups in the United States and to convince Americans that the Arabs were ready for peace with Israel. Sadat added that he had felt the weight of the Zionist lobby in the United States and had wanted to ease that burden on Carter by some bold action. *Ibid*, 173.

regional constraints to negotiation, he created the conditions for success.[17]

The principal participants in these two prenegotiations responded to the likely strategic and domestic consequences of inaction. Almost all feared a renewal of war, yet judged such a war likely in the absence of diplomatic progress. Moreover, they identified not only the adverse strategic consequences of war but also the negative political consequences of inaction. In this context, prenegotiation seemed a reasonable risk. Action was facilitated, moreover, by the approaching expiration of the disengagement agreement between Israel and Egypt in the autumn of 1978, which focussed the attention of all the parties on an obvious deadline.

THE FUNCTIONS OF PRENEGOTIATION
Prenegotiation as risk management:
the definition of boundaries, participants, and agendas

In both cases, the process of prenegotiation was critical in reducing the risks of negotiation for the parties that came to the table. It did so by defining the boundaries, selecting the participants, and setting the agenda for the negotiation that followed. Indeed, it is impossible to understand the boundaries of the negotiations that followed, what was put on the agendas and, more significantly, what was kept off, without considering the impact of the prior processes of prenegotiation.

The first process of prenegotiation was dominated by the search for principles to guide the negotiation of a comprehensive settlement of the Arab-Israeli conflict. The United States undertook to explore the attitudes of all the participants on two central questions. Were the parties to the conflict disposed to negotiate with one another, directly or indirectly? Was there

17 For a more detailed analysis of why Sadat's strategy succeeded, see Janice Gross Stein, 'Deterrence and reassurance,' in Paul Stern, Jo. L. Husbands, Robert Jervis, Philip Tetlock, and Charles Tilly, eds, *Behavior, Society, and Nuclear War* (New York: Oxford University Press 1989, forthcoming), and Zeev Maoz and Dan Felsenthal, 'Self-binding commitments, the inducement of trust, social choice, and the theory of international cooperation,' *International Studies Quarterly* 31(June 1987), 177-200.

common ground in the form of certain key principles that could guide the talks?[18]

At the outset, the strong preference of President Carter and his advisers was for a multilateral conference at Geneva at which all the outstanding issues would be negotiated. As the secretary of state, Cyrus Vance, subsequently acknowledged, the consensus on the appropriateness of a multilateral conference as the basic bargaining structure concealed a series of complex issues, some procedural and some substantive.[19] The president defined the key substantive agenda items as peace, borders, and the Palestinians.[20]

The parties would also have to agree on the eligibility of participants before a conference could be convened. The number of eligible parties was relatively large. The two superpowers, Egypt, Israel, Syria, Jordan, Saudi Arabia, and the PLO were all involved directly or indirectly in the process of prenegotiation. The large number of parties permitted a broad focus on the appropriate forum for negotiation and the modalities of representation of the interested parties. In the first six months, first Vance and then Carter met personally with most of the major participants: Prime Minister Rabin of Israel, President Sadat of Egypt, Syria's foreign minister, Abd al-Halim Khaddam, King Hussein of Jordan, President Hafiz al-Asad of Syria, Crown Prince Fahd of Saudi Arabia, and (after the Israeli election in May 1977) Prime Minister Begin.

Agreement on the organizing principles for a multilateral conference was impossible to achieve and attention shifted to procedures and participants. Here too disagreement was sharp. Surprisingly, from the United States administration's perspective, positions within the Arab coalition did not coincide but cut across the division between the Arab participants and Israel. As the secretary of state noted, Egypt, with Arab 'great power' status and experienced in negotiating with Israel, preferred to

18 Quandt, *Camp David*, 40.
19 Vance, *Hard Choices*, 163.
20 'Speech to Town Meeting, Clinton,' 386-7.

send a national Egyptian delegation to deal bilaterally with Israel as soon as the conference formalities were over. Precisely to prevent the creation of bilateral bargaining units, Syria insisted on a single pan-Arab delegation to pre-empt any further agreement between Egypt and Israel before the outstanding issues with the rest of the Arab world were resolved. On the closely related matter of the agenda, Syria and Jordan demanded a functional delimitation of the issues while Egypt strongly preferred a geographical delimitation, which would be far more suitable to bilateral bargaining.[21] After a week-long exploratory trip to the Middle East in February of 1977, Vance described the curious configuration of agreement and disagreement already apparent in the process of prenegotiation: 'On the procedural problem of how to organize a Geneva conference to negotiate specific issues, Sadat and Rabin stood firm on their demand for a bilateral approach to the negotiating arrangements. Asad and Hussein were just as unyielding in insisting that the Arabs should attend as a single body, and negotiate "functional" rather than geographical issues together, as Egypt and Israel wanted ... Egypt and Israel were not very far apart on procedural matters.'[22]

Closely linked to the issue of procedures was the far more difficult question of the eligibility of participants. It was far more difficult because it touched one of the core issues of the conflict, the status and future of the Palestinians. Israel adamantly refused to negotiate with the PLO, which had been declared the sole legitimate representative of the Palestinian people by the Arab summit meeting at Rabat in 1974. Arabs and Israelis were deadlocked on the appropriate representation of the Palestinians.

Early in the Carter presidency, senior officials in the administration decided to initiate exploratory talks with the PLO to see whether a commitment to United Nations Security Council

21 Vance, *Hard Choices*, 169.
22 *Ibid*, 171.

resolutions 242 and 338, passed after the wars in 1967 and 1973 respectively, might be forthcoming.[23] Using the good offices of Saudi Arabia, on 19 April the United States attempted to entice the PLO into the negotiating process by offering to begin discussions with the PLO immediately if its leadership was prepared to make the requisite public statement. Indeed, the administration hinted that it might be flexible on the language and terms of that commitment. Such an effort was wholly consistent with the effort to convene a multilateral conference with broadranging participation which would seek to achieve a comprehensive settlement. The secretary of state admitted disappointment when Saudi leaders were unable to persuade the PLO to join the negotiating process.

Carter subsequently decided to contact the PLO directly in an effort to persuade its leaders to participate in a multilateral conference. On 6 September, the president's personal representative, Landrum Bolling, met with Brzezinski and was given a message for Yasir Arafat. At the same time Carter sent a letter to President Asad of Syria, asking for his help in persuading the PLO to accept resolution 242, the precondition for an American dialogue with the PLO. Bolling met twice with Arafat who, while complaining of conflicting messages from Egypt, Syria, and Saudi Arabia, finally replied that the PLO could not accept resolution 242, even with reservations, unless the United States could guarantee that the negotiations would lead to a Palestinian state under PLO leadership.[24] On receipt of this message, the United States abruptly ended its dialogue with the PLO. By the end of September, the Carter administration had eliminated the PLO as a possible participant in any negotiation and shifted

---

23 Zbigniew Brzezinski, *Power and Principle* (New York: Farrar, Strauss, Giroux 1983), 94. Israel had extracted a commitment from the United States to refrain from negotiating with the PLO until it recognized the existence of Israel and accepted resolutions 242 and 338. The commitment had been made by Kissinger in September 1975 as diplomatic payment to Israel in exchange for Israel's withdrawal from the passes and oil fields in the Sinai.

24 Quandt, *Camp David*, 101-2.

its attention to the question of Palestinian representation within a broader Arab delegation.

By the time this preliminary round of consultations had concluded, the president was openly committed to an active American role in promoting a process of negotiation. The Policy Review Committee of the Department of State had met on 10 June and had recommended that the United States should emphasize the importance of a multilateral conference in Geneva and that the secretary of state should visit the Middle East in August and then arrange for further informal meetings with foreign ministers in September before the conference was convened.

During the autumn, the focus of American attention shifted to reaching agreement among Arab leaders and Israel on appropriate Palestinian representation. Progress was torturous. As Brzezinski observed: 'Geneva was beginning to look more as an end in itself rather than as a device to pressure or induce the parties to move on substantive issues. In effect, substance was giving way to procedure.'[25] As planned, the secretary of state met with Arab foreign ministers at the United Nations in New York and with Israel's foreign minister in Washington. The outline of a procedural agreement seemed in sight: the Arab participants would attend the opening session as a single delegation which would include Palestinian Arabs and the conference would then break into teams to negotiate bilateral peace treaties. The future of the West Bank and Gaza would be discussed in a separate working group consisting of Israel, Jordan, the Palestinian Arabs, and Egypt.[26]

At about the same time, however, two secret meetings took place. The first, between Dayan of Israel and King Hussein of Jordan, generated little new information, but the second, between Dayan and Hassan Tuhamy of Egypt, was far more im-

25 Brzezinski, *Power and Principle*, 102.
26 Vance, *Hard Choices*, 192-4.

portant in the exploration of the negotiating positions of Egypt and Israel. President Sadat wanted to explore Israel's willingness to make serious concessions.[27] Tuhamy told Dayan that Sadat was ready to meet with Begin, provided Israel gave a prior commitment to full withdrawal from all Arab territory. Moreover, the Egyptian president was ready to negotiate secretly, not in a multilateral forum at Geneva. Although Sadat's terms were unacceptable, Israel's foreign minister learned a great deal from the meeting. First, a bilateral agreement with Egypt would require, at a minimum, Israel's complete withdrawal from the Sinai; what additional concessions might be necessary remained unclear. Second, Dayan discovered that a multilateral conference was a matter of secondary concern to Egypt's president. Within a brief period, the boundaries of negotiation, the procedures, and the likely agenda had changed.[28]

Simultaneously, the United States began to explore the attitudes of the Soviet Union in order both to constrain its ability to obstruct and to encourage it to help resolve the procedural issues and to bring pressure to bear on Syria. Washington and Moscow agreed on a joint communiqué, which was issued as the United States was formalizing a draft statement on procedures for a multilateral conference at Geneva. The publication of the communiqué led to strident political criticism from Israel's supporters in Washington, a secret meeting between Dayan and Vance and Carter, and a joint statement by Israel and the United States. Although the substance of the statement involved little change in Carter's position, its publication created an impression of domestic political weakness and lack of resolve.

By early October, American officials had come to the con-

---

27 In an interview with Quandt, Usama al-Baz, a senior adviser to the president, said that Sadat wished to find out if Israel was serious about peace. See Quandt, *Camp David*, 111, note 20.

28 Despite their mutual agreement not to do so, both Egypt and Israel informed the United States of their secret meeting. Dayan told Vance and an aide to Sadat informed the United States ambassador to Egypt, Herman Eilts. Eilts felt that if the meeting had been serious, a representative far more senior than Tuhamy would have been sent. *Ibid.*

clusion that the process of prenegotiation had to be brought to an end. Further progress on substantive issues, Carter and Vance argued, could be made only when a negotiating process that directly involved the parties to the conflict had begun. At the same time, Egypt too had become convinced that the process of prenegotiation was no longer of use. Sadat was convinced that domestic political pressures in Washington would constrain Carter, that a unified Arab delegation would obstruct progress, and that Syria would not co-operate. His trip to Jerusalem was designed explicitly to abort the ongoing process of prenegotiation about a multilateral conference. As he subsequently observed:

The Syrian Baath party will not go to Geneva, and if it did, the picture would be like this: The Soviet Union has the Syrians in its pocket and Syria has the Palestinians in its pocket also. In Geneva, we would busy ourselves with all the things we have had enough of – semantic and legalistic arguments, the modalities, and the names of the topical, geographic, and historical committees. All this, in addition to what we know about the nature of the Syrian Baath party. And the result would be that the Geneva Conference would greatly add to our level of disillusionment.[29]

Effectively, exploration of the possibility of a multilateral format to negotiate a comprehensive settlement had ended.

Although this prenegotiation failed, it had a significant impact both on the process of negotiation that followed and on the more limited process of prenegotiation that would begin in January. Egypt, Israel, and the United States had all learned a great deal. They had explored the likely zone of agreement, examined the bargaining range, made preliminary judgments about the critical minima, and assessed the likelihood of requitement. As a result, negotiating boundaries were narrowed, procedures were fundamentally altered, and important parties to the conflict were excluded from the process. Most important, two of the central participants, the United States and Egypt,

29 *Oktubar* (Arabic), 25 December 1977, 15.

abandoned the pursuit of a comprehensive settlement of the
Arab-Israeli conflict; Israel's leaders had never considered a
general settlement an appropriate objective. Well before Sadat's
visit to Jerusalem, experts in the State Department and the
National Security Council had begun to doubt the feasibility of
a settlement of one of the central issues, the future of the Palestinians. The secretary of state summarized the extensive in-
house deliberations in August of 1977:

Over the previous several weeks, Atherton, Saunders, Quandt, and I
had exhaustively studied all the parties' positions and statements about
Palestinian self-determination and the status of the West Bank. We
had come to the conclusion that solving this emotion-laden issue in a
single negotiation was not feasible ... We concluded that some form
of transitional arrangement was needed ... My initial idea was a UN
trusteeship under joint Israeli-Jordanian administration, leading to a
plebiscite and Palestinian self-determination after several years.[30]

The summary is instructive. Egypt, Israel, and the United States
had effectively excluded a settlement of the future of the
Palestinians from the immediate negotiating problem. At best,
Egypt and the United States now defined the problem as the
design of transitional arrangements which would, in Carter's
language, 'enable the Palestinians to participate in the determination of their own future.'[31] Israel defined the problem even
more narrowly: the negotiation of transitional arrangements
which left the outcome open, to be determined by the parties
at the end of the transition.

The reshaping of the boundaries of the negotiating problem
and the narrowing of the agenda were not confined to the issue
of the future of the Palestinians. Syria was effectively excluded
as a participant. The deliberate exclusion of Syria by Egypt took
the disposition of the Golan Heights off the agenda and further
narrowed the scope of the problem to be negotiated. As the
problem was narrowed and potential participants were ex-

30 Vance, *Hard Choices*, 187.
31 Aswan Declaration, 4 January 1978, in *New York Times*, 5 January 1978.

cluded, the role of the Soviet Union also became increasingly peripheral. Once the first process of prenegotiation ended in the abandonment of a multilateral conference, the United States emerged as the pivotal party among those that returned to prenegotiation in January 1978 after the attempt at negotiation failed.

Within a matter of weeks after President Sadat's trip to Jerusalem, the secretary of state concluded that a multilateral conference was unlikely. In a memorandum written on 24 November, Vance estimated that Egypt and Israel would likely move towards a bilateral agreement and defined the central question as how, or whether, their move would be tied to progress in working out an interim agreement on the West Bank and Gaza.[32] This question defined the boundaries of the process of prenegotiation that began in January 1978 and, indeed, of the negotiation that took place at Camp David. Until formal negotiation began nine months later, discussion revolved around the issue of what kind of agreement, if any, on the Palestinian issue should accompany an Egyptian-Israeli peace treaty.

Senior American officials have acknowledged that the United States had no strategy as the second process of prenegotiation began. Brzezinski and Quandt urged a strategy of collusion with Sadat to extract concessions from Begin. In a memorandum Quandt drafted for Brzezinski on 12 January, he argued that the United States should not try to paper over disagreements between Egypt and Israel, but allow the impasse to develop into a stalemate: 'In total confidence, we should develop a strategy for developing a mini-crisis, which will be resolved by an American proposal which Sadat will accept.'[33] President Carter agreed that the next step should be to restore a close working relationship with Sadat.

The two leaders met at Camp David on 3 February. Brzezinski prepared a nine-point draft of a final agreement between Egypt and Israel and recommended that Egypt be asked to

32 Vance, Hard Choices, 195.
33 Quandt, Camp David, 163, note 31, and Brzezinski, Power and Principle, 240-2.

provide its own proposal, which Israel, of course, would reject, allowing the United States to put forward its draft. The two delegations agreed on a joint scenario of a visit by Dayan to Washington, a return trip by Roy Atherton of the State Department to the Middle East, a visit by Begin to Washington, a proposal from Egypt, followed finally by an American proposal.[34]

At the same time as the two leaders agreed on a strategy of coalition formation, they began informally to consider an even narrower definition of the problem, an agreement between Egypt and Israel connected only loosely to an attempt to negotiate an agreement on the Palestinian question. On his return from Camp David, the president asked his national security adviser to prepare an analysis of the consequences of a such a bilateral treaty. Brzezinski suspected that the request was motivated by the president's private discussions with Sadat.[35] A short time later, in response to an explicit question from Carter, the Egyptian president replied that if Egypt and Israel could agree to a strong declaration of principles governing future negotiation and King Hussein remained unwilling to participate, he would go forward with the negotiation himself. Jordanian participation would be helpful, but was secondary to a statement of principles.[36] The boundaries of the problem and the participants in the negotiation had been narrowed further.

By mid-May 1978 American officials became concerned about the lack of progress. The Egyptian proposals that Carter had requested as part of a joint American-Egyptian strategy were disappointing and Israel's suggestions about how the future of the West Bank and the Gaza Strip was to be decided after a transitional period were, in Quandt's language, 'useless.'[37] Even more alarming was a letter from Sadat telling Carter that an American proposal based on the nine-point draft discussed at

34 Brzezinski, *Power and Principle*, 243-4; Quandt, *Camp David*, 171-2, 175; Kamil, *Lost Peace*, 140-1.
35 Brzezinski, *Power and Principle*, 244.
36 Quandt, *Camp David*, 181.
37 *Ibid*, 190.

Camp David in February could have negative repercussions for Egypt in the Arab world.[38] The strategy of explicit collusion between the United States and Egypt during the process of prenegotiation appeared to be breaking down. In a memorandum drafted on 17 May for Brzezinski, Quandt analysed the dilemmas confronting the United States. On the central issue of the Palestinians, he argued, the PLO had been eliminated and King Hussein was pessimistic about the prospects of negotiation; only Sadat remained to negotiate with Israel over the future of the West Bank and Gaza. Without a clear commitment from Israel to withdraw, the only alternatives were continuing stalemate or a bilateral Egyptian-Israeli agreement on the Sinai. The memorandum concluded on a pessimistic note: 'Time is working against us and against moderation and flexibility ... At some point we may have to ask ourselves whether a bilateral deal is better than none at all.'[39]

President Sadat was even more pessimistic. A meeting of the foreign ministers of Egypt, Israel, and the United States at Leeds Castle in mid-July broke little new ground. In a cable from Cairo on 30 July, the American ambassador reported that Sadat was agitated about the lack of progress and that Saudi Arabia was urging him to terminate the process entirely.[40] In his memoirs, Carter emphasizes that Sadat had warned him that if no progress were made by the anniversary of the Sinai agreement in September 1978, he would consider resigning or perhaps reverting to belligerency.[41] That same day Carter therefore decided to invite Prime Minister Begin and President Sadat to Camp David to negotiate an agreement.

In deciding to push for a negotiation at the summit, the president chose to pursue the possible, rather than the preferred. The prospect of failure, as we shall see, was politically

38 Kamil, *Lost Peace*, 263-4.
39 Quandt, *Camp David*, 192-3.
40 *Ibid*, 202.
41 Jimmy Carter, *Keeping Faith: Memoirs of a President* (New York: Bantam Books 1982), 315-16.

unacceptable to Carter. To improve the prospects of success, he restricted the participants to Egypt and Israel and used his estimates of the critical minimum of each to determine the agenda. The agenda for Camp David was restricted to a bilateral Egyptian-Israeli agreement loosely tied to a transitional arrangement for the West Bank and Gaza. Finally, Carter drastically narrowed the boundaries of the negotiating problem. As Quandt observes, whatever Begin could be brought to accept without a confrontation would determine the outer limits of the agreement.[42]

Strategies of prenegotiation: the politics of coalition formation
Both processes of prenegotiation were unusual in that a party that was not a principal to the dispute was the initiator of the process and played the most important role. In the first one, the United States began the exploration of the attitudes of the principal parties to negotiation through an extended series of bilateral meetings. Almost to the end, all the traffic of prenegotiation went through Washington in a series of sequential bilateral discussions. This process of prenegotiation was not one carried on among equals; rather, it was orchestrated, managed, and controlled by a powerful outsider to the dispute with strong interests in the outcome.[43] Assessments of the attitudes of the other principals were done largely by President Carter and his

---

42 Quandt, *Camp David*, 204.
43 It is a matter of some controversy whether the United States should be included as a participant in the processes of prenegotiation even though it was an outsider to the dispute. Zartman argues that the United States is best treated as an outsider in the negotiations between the United States, Israel, and Egypt from 1973 to 1975: see I. William Zartman, 'Explaining disengagement,' in Jeffrey Rubin, ed, *Dynamics of Third Party Intervention: Kissinger in the Middle East* (New York: Praeger 1981), 156. In the process of prenegotiation that preceded Camp David, he suggests that an agreement between the United States and either of the two parties would not have been sufficient to get the parties to the table, while an agreement between Egypt and Israel was necessary to move the process of prenegotiation to the table. Therefore, the United States is best treated as an interested outsider in the process. (Zartman, personal communication, May 1988.) Harold Saunders argues, to the contrary, that the United States was a 'full partner' (personal communication). While the United States was not a

advisers, as were the early definition of the issues at stake and the delineation of appropriate procedures. Indeed, only when it disagreed with the direction provided by the United States, did Egypt take unilateral action to change the trajectory of the process.

In the second process of prenegotiation, the strategies of the parties were more sharply defined as the boundaries of negotiation were narrowed and the number of participants reduced. The role of the United States in this second process was enhanced; it was the pivotal party in a triadic process. Its leverage derived not only from its capacity to reward and punish the other two, but also from its crucial position as coalition-maker. Although direct talks did occur between Egypt and Israel, the critical importance of the United States as the third party predisposed both to seek to secure the support of the United States to form a coalition and, equally important, to prevent Washington from joining in coalition with the adversary. Insofar as these dynamics operated in the process of prenegotiation, the United States acquired substantial leverage in agenda setting, in the definition of the issues through its control of the paper traffic, and in channelling the scope and pace of the process.

When the process of prenegotiation began again in January of 1978, the United States moved explicitly to a strategy of coalition with Egypt in order to extract concessions from Israel. In large part because Sadat proved an unpredictable coalition partner, President Carter modified this strategy near the end of the process to work through rather than around the prime minister of Israel. In so doing, he introduced greater fluidity into the process and expanded the possible coalitions. The president best describes how well each of the parties understood the pivotal role of the United States as coalition-maker and how

---

direct party to the dispute, the evidence suggests that it was a principal in the process of prenegotiation. Indeed, throughout much of the process, it was the engine.

astute they were about the rules by the end of the second process of prenegotiation:

[Begin] pointed out that there had to be two agreements ... the most important was between the United States and Israel, and the other, of secondary importance but obviously also crucial, was between Israel and Egypt. The most important one would have to come first. He wanted the world to know that there were no serious differences between Israel and the United States.

It was true that the relationship between our two nations was vital to Israel, but I also knew it was a good negotiating tactic by either Sadat or Begin first to reach agreement with me and then to have the two of us confront the third. Sadat had understood this strategy before he arrived at Camp David.

...

In my private visits with Sadat he emphasized again and again that his main concern was about me ... It was imperative to him that the United States and Egypt stand together.[44]

Once the boundaries of the negotiating problem had been narrowed, the number of participants reduced to three, and the agenda limited, the strategies of Egypt and Israel can best be explained by the logic of coalition politics, with the United States as the pivotal party. In this case, the process of prenegotiation dictated not only the definition of the problem, the delimitation of the agenda, and the selection of the participants, but their strategic behaviour as well.

The impact of domestic politics

The importance of domestic politics during both processes of prenegotiation cannot be overstated. Domestic politics operated in two crucial ways: first, the major parties were all constrained at various times by their political constituencies; second, they designed their strategies to influence both their own political environment and the domestic politics of others. The process

44 Carter, *Keeping Faith*, 366, 418.

of prenegotiation permitted leaders to structure as well as to respond to domestic politics.

The leader most obviously constrained was President Carter who continually adjusted his strategy to accommodate domestic politics and, indeed, spoke openly to others of the political constraints he faced. The evidence of the pervasive impact of domestic politics is overwhelming. In September of 1977, for example, in a private meeting with the Egyptian foreign minister, Carter explained that he could not put any additional pressure on Israel to modify its positions; to do so would be 'political suicide.'[45] On the basis of this conversation, the foreign minister concluded that the president was weak. Similarly, in his meeting with Israel's foreign minister following publication of the Soviet-American communiqué in October, Carter shifted the conversation from the substantive issues to his domestic political problems. He explained that the attack on his policies by American Jews and Congress was of some concern; in effect, he asked Dayan for help in managing his domestic political environment. The result was the joint United States-Israel statement which gave the Arab world, particularly Egypt, the impression that Carter was politically weak. Paradoxically, leaders in the Middle East judged Carter's resolve not by his past behaviour, or by his repeated commitments, but by his response to domestic political imperatives.[46] Indeed, President Sadat aborted the first process of prenegotiation in part because of his concern about the weakness of President Carter – his lack of resolve and his inability to transcend his political constraints.

Domestic politics were important not only in the shaping of American tactics during the process of prenegotiation but also in the determination of strategic decisions. That same September, Carter and Vance concluded that the process of prenegotiation had to be brought to an end, in large part because it was eroding the president's political support at home. If the

45 Quandt, *Camp David*, 115.
46 Janice Gross Stein, 'Domestic politics and international conflict management,' *International Security* 12(spring 1988), 361-82.

administration was to press Israel on Palestinian rights, it could do so only if Arab leaders were actively involved in direct negotiation with Israel. Otherwise, the political costs of a dialogue between Israel and the United States on this issue were simply too great for the president to accept.[47]

Domestic political considerations were even more important in the second process of prenegotiation than they were in the first. When President Carter considered initiating a second process in January of 1978, he was strongly influenced by the obvious political benefits of a foreign policy success. He had invested considerable time and political capital in the earlier process of prenegotiation, with little return. His desire for political gain was an important motivating factor in his decision to recommit his resources.

Political concerns were even more salient in the summer of 1978 as the president considered his alternatives in the face of the stalemate between Egypt and Israel. Carter held a crucial meeting with his advisers on 6 July, a few weeks before he made his decision to invite Sadat and Begin to Camp David. Brzezinski defined the alternatives as a confrontation with Israel or withdrawal from the process. The forthcoming congressional elections were discussed. Hamilton Jordan, a political adviser, argued strongly that Carter could rebuild his ties with the American Jewish community only if he successfully mediated an agreement; only positive results, he insisted, could help the president politically.[48] On 30 July Carter decided to risk negotiation at a summit meeting. He did so in part because a success of any kind was a political necessity.[49] The imperative of a political success in an election year was an important component in the president's willingness to narrow the boundaries of negotiation, limit the agenda, and restrict the participants. The choice of a summit, as Brzezinski notes, was dictated in part by Carter's hope that it would have a dramatic political impact.[50]

47 Quandt, *Camp David*, 131.
48 *Ibid*, 197.
49 *Ibid*, 204-5.
50 Brzezinski, *Power and Principle*, 250-1.

Domestic politics affected Egypt and Israel as well, albeit in different ways. In the first process of prenegotiation, the domestic weakness of the Rabin government in Israel and its deep internal divisions constrained its ability to commit itself to negotiation. Estimates of the adverse electoral consequences of the concessions required to agree on a negotiating formula loomed large. In Egypt, however, domestic political weakness was an incentive rather than a constraint in the process of prenegotiation. Of all the parties to the conflict, President Sadat pressed hardest for negotiation, in large part because of his estimate of the adverse political consequences of a continuing stalemate. His unwillingness to tolerate deadlock was due in part to the intense domestic pressure created by Egypt's economic crisis.

The intersecting political and economic crises in Egypt had intensified by the summer of 1978. Increased budget deficits eroded Egypt's ability to negotiate a long-term loan from the International Monetary Fund. Mohamed Heikal returned to Egypt from abroad and urged President Sadat to end discussions with the United States and Israel.[51] In response to the growing political pressure, Sadat restricted editorial criticism in Egypt's newspapers and held a national referendum to endorse further repressive measures against 'extremists' who challenged his strategy. After the referendum on 21 May, Sadat ordered a crackdown on opposition groups: he recalled over thirty Egyptian journalists stationed abroad, disbanded the Wafd whose activities he had encouraged a year earlier, and imposed severe restrictions on political dissent.[52]

Although the constraints in Jerusalem were considerably less than in Cairo and Washington, Prime Minister Begin was also under greater political pressure than he had been when he assumed office a year earlier. One of the important parties in his governing coalition had split, in large part over the slow

51 See *New York Times*, 30 April 1988.
52 See R. Michael Burrell and Abbas R. Kelidar, *Egypt: The Dilemmas of a Nation, 1970–77* (Beverly Hills CA: Sage 1977), 17-18, and Friedlander, *Sadat and Begin*, 179.

pace of the prenegotiation process, and the peace movement in Israel was organizing large demonstrations.[53] At the same time, leaders on the right fought the army to establish unauthorized settlements in the West Bank as well as in the Sinai.

For all three leaders, the opportunity costs of failure increased the longer the process of prenegotiation went on. This was especially so for the presidents of Egypt and the United States. In the final stage, the anticipation of failure drove the process forward and encouraged both Carter and Sadat to define the boundaries and limit the agenda to meet the critical minimum set by Begin.

In the context of political constraints, leaders at times designed their strategies to compensate for political weakness at home. In September 1977, for example, Israel's foreign minister presented a proposal to Carter for slowing the pace of settlement in the West Bank. Because he knew that Begin was certain to object, Dayan urged the United States to present the proposal as an American suggestion and 'force' it on Israel.[54] In this instance, Israel's foreign minister attempted to use the United States as a resource to circumvent the limits of Israel's domestic politics. The use of outsiders to compensate for political weakness at home is generally a neglected dimension in the analysis of both prenegotiation and negotiation.

It is not only leaders' assessments of their own political constraints and opportunities that are important. Their evaluation of the political situations of others can be critical; the political weakness of one can create opportunities for another. When Begin, for example, considered that Carter was politically vulnerable and in need of a success, he toughened his demands in an attempt to exploit that weakness. Egypt's president, politically vulnerable at home and sensitive to the political weakness of Carter, made important concessions during the second process of prenegotiation. And, indeed, Sadat explained his

<hr>

53 Yigal Yadin lost control of the Democratic Movement for Change. At the same time Peace Now joined the chorus of criticism.
54 Quandt, *Camp David*, 113.

trip to Jerusalem at the end of the first process of prenegotiation as, in part, an attempt to reduce the impact of political groups that were constraining President Carter. His target was American as well as Israeli public opinion.

Domestic politics were an important factor at the beginning, at the end, and throughout the two processes of prenegotiation. Domestic political incentives were significant in the initiation of both processes of prenegotiation and in both decisions to terminate and to proceed to negotiation. During the process of prenegotiation, the impact of domestic politics varied, depending in part on political constraints and in part on leaders' strategic calculations. At times, political weakness constrained leaders, as it did Rabin in Israel and Carter in Washington, and at times it increased the incentive to negotiate, as it did with Sadat in Cairo. Leaders' assessments of the political constraints faced by other parties and the opportunities they provided also had a critical impact on the strategic decisions that they made during the process of prenegotiation. Finally, to the extent that the political costs of failure grew as prenegotiation proceeded, leaders had a greater incentive to get to the table.

EXPLAINING THE OUTCOME OF PRENEGOTIATION

Analysis of these two processes of prenegotiation has identified the first as a technical failure and the second as a success. It is more useful, however, to see the two as a sequence, which was interrupted briefly by an attempt at negotiation that failed but culminated in a negotiation that succeeded. Even though the result was unintended and unplanned, that the first process led to direct negotiation in November 1977 is unprecedented in the protracted and bitter history of the Arab-Israeli conflict. Looking at the process as a whole, prenegotiation contributed in important ways to the negotiation that began at Camp David in September 1978.

In explaining the outcome of prenegotiation, four central factors stand out. First, all the major participants attached a high cost to stalemate and immobilism; the perpetuation of the

status quo was unacceptable. For Egypt, the choice was negotiation or a renewal of war. In the light of the 1973 war, President Sadat was both pessimistic about the prospects of military
success and unwilling to risk the tangible gains he had reaped
after the war. The United States also feared the consequences
of a renewed round of warfare. Israel, too, was pessimistic about
the stability of the status quo and recognized that its perpetuation was unlikely. The shared perception of the instability of
the status quo was reinforced by a mutual aversion to war.
Neither Egypt nor Israel wanted war and the United States very
much feared a war. These estimates provided the processes of
prenegotiation with a dynamism and a purpose. They not only
triggered prenegotiation, but drove the process through many
of the critical turning points.

Second, as the process proceeded, significant learning occurred. Prenegotiation reduced uncertainty by narrowing the
number of participants, limiting the agenda, and setting the
boundaries of the table. Risk management was especially important to Egypt because of the real costs attached to negotiating
with Israel. The process also permitted and encouraged leaders
to clarify their core interests. The principal parties did not
change their definition of their interests substantially during
prenegotiation, but they did clarify their priorities and face up
to the difficult trade-offs. Prime Minister Begin attached greatest priority to maintaining Israel's presence in the West Bank
and Gaza and President Sadat gave overwhelming weight to
the return of the Sinai. The process of prenegotiation sharpened these priorities in the minds of each leader and clarified
the importance of each goal to the other party. This clarification
was critically important in establishing a zone of agreement.
Only after uncertainty and complexity were significantly reduced were the parties able to commit to negotiation.

Third, the domestic political weakness of the leaders of Egypt
and the United States was important in pushing the process of
prenegotiation forward. Paradoxically, the constraints imposed
by politics at home created a strong incentive for Carter to

persist in the search for a foreign policy 'success.' Indeed, in the summer of 1978, the president and his advisers weighed the alternatives of withdrawing from the process or pushing it forward to negotiation. The need for a dramatic achievement in the context of forthcoming congressional elections was the determining factor. President Sadat well understood the enormous political cost of failure, both in Egypt and in the Arab world as a whole. Indeed, the costs of failure grew commensurately with the growth of political opposition as the process proceeded. Domestic political pressure was an important lubricant of prenegotiation at various critical turning points.

Finally, the overlapping roles of the United States as a participant, with strong and obvious interests of its own, and as a 'third party' were essential to the success of the process. Even after the zone of agreement was apparent to Egypt and Israel, following the secret meeting between Dayan and Tuhamy in September 1977, the two parties were unable to negotiate their differences directly. Their negotiation broke down in January 1978, and indeed the process of prenegotiation would in all likelihood have collapsed again in July without the active intervention of the United States. Distrust, inability to communicate, misunderstanding, and cultural barriers were insuperable obstacles even within the framework of a zone of agreement. Without the United States as interpreter, facilitator, intermediary, and committed participant, the second process of prenegotiation would in all likelihood have failed.

These four factors were all necessary to the success of prenegotiation. Without a shared aversion to war, reinforced by estimates of the unacceptability and the instability of the status quo, leaders would have had little incentive to explore the prospects of negotiation. If leaders had not clarified their own priorities among their interests and identified the trade-offs that conceivably could produce an agreement, they would have been unlikely to take the risk of negotiation. If some had not been driven by domestic political weakness and the need for an agreement, they would have been unlikely to sustain the process of prenegotiation through to the table. And, without the assistance of a powerful, wealthy, and committed third party, Egypt and Israel alone would not have been able to get to the table. The passage through prenegotiation was strewn with obstacles that were overcome only by the reinforcing impact of a complex set of variables.

DID PRENEGOTIATION MATTER?

Prenegotiation can matter in three important ways. First, it can significantly affect the process of negotiation which follows. Second, it can influence the long-term relationship among the parties if learning occurs; the relationship can be modified, redefined, weakened, or reinforced. Third, it can have important consequences that are independent of what happens at the table.

We have already demonstrated the overwhelming impact of the process of prenegotiation on the negotiation that followed at Camp David. It defined and narrowed the boundaries of the problem, reduced the number of participants, set the agenda by eliminating many of the most difficult items, identified the trade-offs, clarified the zone of agreement, and structured the bargaining strategies of the remaining participants. Its impact was pervasive on almost every critical dimension of the subsequent negotiation.

Prenegotiation also had important effects independent of the process of negotiation that followed. The wide-ranging exploration of the attitudes of important parties to the conflict persuaded the United States that progress was unlikely except between Israel and Egypt. President Carter also learned that there were important domestic political costs of failure. Consequently, he made no serious attempt to renew the process of prenegotiation after Camp David. In particular, the future of the Palestinians received far less attention and no further attempt was made to involve the PLO in a process of prenegotiation. The successor administration in Washington made no serious effort to explore the prospects of negotiation until war erupted over Lebanon. In effect, American officials learned about the obstacles to further progress and the domestic political risks of trying.

The extra-negotiatory effects of the prenegotiation process were both significant and unanticipated. In the short term, the clarification of their priorities by the leaders of Egypt and Israel made a bilateral agreement easier but a comprehensive settlement of the Arab-Israeli conflict more difficult. Egypt acquired tangible benefits in the negotiations that followed and, consequently, became less willing to risk these benefits in a pursuit of a wide-ranging settlement. Prime Minister Begin and his governing coalition considered that they had ceded the Sinai in return for continued control over the West Bank and Gaza.

The achievement of a limited agreement thus reduced the likelihood of a broader settlement. Insofar as prenegotiation was successful, it reduced the incentives of the two principal parties to broaden the process. And insofar as it failed, it educated everyone about the serious obstacles to further progress. Recalling the deliberations that preceded the president's decision to push the process of prenegotiation forward to negotiation, William Quandt subsequently explained American reasoning to members of the Egyptian opposition: 'We had to choose between two things: no agreement at all or settling one aspect of the problem. We made the decision that it was preferable to settle one aspect of the problem now, then to settle the other aspects later. There is a French proverb which says, "The best is the enemy of the good." We decided that the good was preferable to nothing at all.'[55] Quandt's analysis is apt. The process of prenegotiation revealed that the best was the enemy of the good and that the choice was, indeed, between failure and the good. Paradoxically, analysis of the long-term consequences of these processes of prenegotiation also demonstrates that the good can be the enemy of the best.

55 'On the shaping of United States' Middle East policy: William Quandt and the Egyptian opposition, a dialogue,' *Middle East Review* (spring 1980), 31-7.

One final caveat. This analysis has identified the necessary preconditions for the success of prenegotiation in this case. The preconditions are demanding and difficult to achieve: a shared aversion to war, an unstable status quo, a capacity to identify and make important trade-offs, domestic political incentives that favour negotiation, high opportunity costs of failure, and a powerful and committed third party that can overcome psychological and cultural obstacles to communication as well as reward concessions.[56] The analysis is sobering in that it highlights the obstacles to success. It is also sobering because it suggests that the failure of prenegotiation can be costly. It can be costly not only because of the negative 'learning' that may occur during the process, but also because failure can alter the strategic calculations of the participants in favour of a use of force.

In 1971 and 1972, the United States explored the willingness of both Egypt and Israel to consider negotiation of a limited agreement on the opening of the Suez Canal. Israel's government, politically secure at home and confident of its deterrent strategy abroad, saw no reason to make the concessions required for negotiation to begin. President Sadat, however, was under intense domestic pressure and pessimistic about the consequences of a use of force. He therefore agreed to exploratory, informal talks with the American secretary of state and, through the 'back channel,' with the president's national security adviser. Only when these exploratory talks exposed the serious obstacles to negotiation, did Sadat commit himself fully to a use of force. Here, the failure of prenegotiation in the context of acute domestic pressure was the catalytic factor in the choice of war. The evidence thus suggests that prenegotiation should not be undertaken lightly; its failure may be expensive. It should not be used as a stop gap, as a diversion, or as an alternative to doing nothing. Especially when the use of force is a viable option in the context of an acute and protracted conflict, the risks of prenegotiation must be considered along with its benefits.

56 William Zartman identifies similar conditions in *Ripe for Resolution: Conflict and Intervention in Africa* (New York: Oxford University Press 1985).

Evidence from the Arab-Israeli conflict highlights the paradoxical consequences of prenegotiation. In the short term, it can be dangerous if it fails insofar as it makes war more likely; if it succeeds, however, it can significantly reduce the likelihood of war, as it did between Egypt and Israel in 1978. In the longer term, prenegotiation can be successful in narrowing the parameters of a problem and subdividing a complex conflict into its component parts. Insofar as it fractionates a conflict to make agreement easier on one part of the problem, however, it can complicate the prospects for the negotiation of other parts. For policy-makers, the dilemmas are acute and the trade-offs real and painful. The dilemmas are real and painful because, as evidence from the analysis of its role in the Arab-Israel conflict suggests, prenegotiation matters, whether it succeeds or fails.

7. Prenegotiation Problem-solving Discussions: Enhancing the Potential for Successful Negotiation

RONALD J. FISHER

The world is beset by a host of severe and protracted communal and international conflicts that appear intractable. Traditional approaches to conflict management have proven ineffective, and the parties pursue with intransigence their strategy of threat, intimidation, and violence in attempts to attain their goals. Negotiation, mediation, or arbitration are difficult to implement or fail when attempted. There appears to be a gap in both the thinking of conflict theorists and the practice of diplomatic practitioners with regard to the question of how to facilitate movement towards negotiation which is meaningful and ultimately successful. More specifically, there is a lack of knowledge and expertise regarding the process of prenegotiation by which hostile parties move from stalemate to negotiation.

Effective negotiation is difficult, if not impossible, in the poor relationship which is typical of a protracted conflict. Mistrust, selective and distorted perceptions, negative attitudes or images, poor communication, and a competitive win-lose orientation that attempts to force or extract capitulation from the adversary all undermine negotiations in such circumstances. The negotiators are usually under pressure to maintain and operate from the views held by the constituencies to which they are responsible. Thus positive changes in the perceived or actual

Professor of Psychology and Coordinator of the Applied Social Psychology Graduate Program, University of Saskatchewan, Saskatoon, Saskatchewan; research fellow, Canadian Institute for International Peace and Security, 1989-90; author, inter alia, of *The Social Psychology of Intergroup and International Conflict Resolution* (forthcoming 1990).

social relationship by both influential constituents and negoti-ators should have a constructive influence on negotiation. A shift towards more accurate perceptions and images, more fa-vourable attitudes, more open and accurate communication, increased trust, and a co-operative win-win orientation would augur well for a meaningful and successful negotiation. The formidable challenge is how to facilitate the changes necessary to bring forward such qualities in the relationship.

This article examines the manner and degree to which prob-lem-solving discussions focussing on their basic relationship might facilitate the decision of parties to move into prenegotiation or from prenegotiation to negotiation. It is proposed that such discussions can have a useful influence on perceptions, atti-tudes, and orientations in ways that will improve both the prob-ability of negotiation occurring and the likelihood of its success. Two originators of the problem-solving approach to conflict, Herbert Kelman and Stephen Cohen, suggested that such dis-cussions might serve as a preparation for and a supplement to negotiation. Problem-solving discussions could be used to create an atmosphere conducive to negotiation and to help to establish an appropriate framework for negotiation.[1] Particularly during the prenegotiation process, problem-solving workshops can provide the parties with an opportunity to evaluate the feasi-bility of more formal negotiations and to determine the basis for future activity. Workshops provide a unique forum for low-risk exchanges.

A variety of informal initiatives have been proposed and implemented in an effort to improve the relationship between

---

[1] For a comprehensive rationale and description of problem-solving workshops and the interactional approach to conflict resolution, see Herbert Kelman and Stephen Cohen, 'The problem-solving workshop: a social-psychological contri-bution to the resolution of international conflict,' *Journal of Peace Research* 13(no 2, 1976), 79-90, and Herbert Kelman and Stephen Cohen, 'Resolution of inter-national conflict: an interactional approach,' in Stephen Worchel and William Austin, eds, *Psychology of Intergroup Relations* (2nd ed; Chicago IL: Nelson-Hall 1986).

parties engaged in international conflicts.[2] Carolyn Stephenson divides alternative (that is, non-military) approaches to security into two broad complementary clusters: world law/world government/international organization and non-violent conflict resolution. The second cluster includes a variety of unofficial initiatives which most frequently take one of two forms: third-party conciliation or mediation directed towards a specific conflict, and regular conferences involving nationals from countries engaged in hostile relationships. The former is exemplified by the Quaker approach to peacemaking as described by Adam Curle and, more recently, by Mike Yarrow.[3] The latter is represented by the well-known Pugwash and Dartmouth Conferences focussing on East-West relations and, more specifically, on Soviet-American tensions.[4] Most of these approaches are now captured under the label of track two diplomacy, a term coined by Joseph Montville and his associates to denote 'unofficial, informal interaction between members of adversary groups or nations which aims to develop strategies, influence public opinion, and organize human and material resources in ways that might help resolve their conflict.'[5] In this context, Montville identifies the problem-solving workshop as a distinct methodology designed to bring together informal representa-

---

2 See Carolyn Stephenson, ed, *Alternative Methods for International Security* (Lanham MD: University Press of America 1982), Maureen Berman and Joseph Johnson, eds, *Unofficial Diplomats* (New York: Columbia University Press 1977), and John W. McDonald Jr and Diane Bendahmane, eds, *Conflict Resolution: Track Two Diplomacy* (Washington: Foreign Service Institute, Department of State, 1987).

3 See Adam Curle, *Making Peace* (London: Tavistock 1971), and Mike Yarrow, *Quaker Experiences in International Conciliation* (New Haven CT: Yale University Press 1978).

4 See Norman Cousins (interview), 'The Dartmouth Conferences,' in Berman and Johnson, eds, *Unofficial Diplomats*, and Philip Stewart, 'The Dartmouth Conference: U.S.-U.S.S.R. relations,' in McDonald and Bendahmane, eds, *Conflict Resolution*.

5 Joseph Montville, 'The arrow and the olive branch: a case for track two diplomacy,' in McDonald and Bendahmane, eds, *Conflict Resolution*, 7. See also William Davidson and Joseph Montville, 'Foreign policy according to Freud,' *Foreign Policy*, no 45(winter 1981-2), 145-57, in which the term 'track two diplomacy' was first used.

tives of conflicting parties in facilitated discussions in the hope of bringing them to a better understanding of the dimensions of the conflict and of helping them to develop joint strategies directed towards a mutually acceptable solution. This form of unofficial interaction is not geared to the settlement of specific disputes, as is third-party conciliation, or towards a general exchange of views on topical issues, as are regular conferences. In contrast, the problem-solving workshop focusses the analysis directly on the nature of the relationship between the parties, their perceptions and attitudes, and the underlying causes of the conflict.

Although the problem-solving workshop as an approach to negotiation is only now gaining acceptance among social scientists and some recognition from diplomatic practitioners, its creation and development go back over two decades to the pioneering efforts of John Burton, Leonard Doob, and Herbert Kelman.[6] I have reviewed and evaluated these initiatives under the rubric of *third-party consultation*, in order to emphasize that the discussions are organized and facilitated by social scientists/practitioners who play an essential consulting role as impartial analysts and intermediaries.[7] The objectives of the problem-solving approach include realizations about the sources and nature of the conflict, positive attitude change, improvements in the relationship, and the generation of creative solutions.

6 John Burton, *Conflict and Communication: The Use of Controlled Communication in International Relations* (London: Macmillan 1969); Leonard Doob, ed, *Resolving Conflict in Africa: The Fermeda Workshop* (New Haven CT: Yale University Press 1970); Herbert Kelman, 'The problem solving workshop in conflict resolution,' in Richard Merritt, ed, *Communication in International Politics* (Urbana: University of Illinois Press 1972). Also for seminal work in organization development on the social technology of intergroup conflict resolution, see Robert Blake, Herbert Shepard, and Jane Mouton, *Managing Intergroup Conflict in Industry* (Houston TX: Gulf 1964).

7 For a selective review and initial development of the model of third-party consultation, see Ronald Fisher, 'Third party consultation: a method for the study and resolution of conflict,' *Journal of Conflict Resolution* 16(March 1972), 67-94. For a comprehensive and evaluative review, see Ronald Fisher, 'Third party consultation as a method of intergroup conflict resolution: a review of studies,' *Journal of Conflict Resolution* 27(June 1983), 301-34.

The model I have developed emphasizes the identity, strategies, and behaviour of the third-party consultant whose primary functions are to induce motivation for problem-solving, improve communication, assist in the diagnosis of the conflict, and regulate the interaction. The intent is to aid the representatives of the parties to analyse and deal with the underlying attitudes and basic issues in their relationship. Although the results are promising, much work in the area is of a pilot nature and few outcomes have been successfully transferred to the wider relationship and conflict between the parties. Further theoretical development and additional demonstration research are needed before it will be possible to assess the efficacy of the problem-solving approach in prenegotiation.

In pursuing developments in both theory and practice it is important to distinguish third-party consultation from mediation, a more widely accepted and understood type of intervention in difficult negotiations.[8] Briefly, consultation or problem-solving involves the intervention of a skilled and impartial third party who attempts to facilitate creative problem-solving through communication and analysis. In contrast, mediation involves the intervention of a competent and trusted intermediary who facilitates a negotiated settlement on a set of specific, substantive issues through reasoning, persuasion, the control of information, and the suggestion of alternative compromises. This distinction is related to the fundamental view that one takes of social conflict and its management. Many believe the sources of conflict lie both in the incompatibility of goals and values (the objective side) and in the misperception and misunderstanding between the parties (the subjective side). While both are usually present in any conflict, third-party interventions differ in the emphasis they give to each. The problem-solving approach places more emphasis on the subjective factors, highlighting social-psychological elements such

---

8 For an initial distinction, see Fisher 'Third party consultation as a method of intergroup conflict resolution'; for a detailed comparison, see Ronald Fisher and Loraleigh Keashly, 'Third party interventions in intergroup conflict: consultation is *not* mediation,' *Negotiation Journal* 4(October 1988), 381-93.

as perceptions, attitudes, communication, and various characteristics of the relationship. Mediation emphasizes the objective side and attempts to work around the subjective elements even though it is cognizant of them and their effects. Thus, mediation accepts a competitive, win-lose, power orientation and works towards compromise by eliciting concessions. It is typically directed towards settlement of substantive issues. Consultation, however, is directed towards the de-escalation and resolution of the conflict through an improved relationship and functional co-operation. It is therefore seen as more useful in the early prenegotiation process while mediation is more relevant to negotiation. Thus these two different third-party approaches are complementary.

The potential that the problem-solving approach has for contributing to prenegotiation by facilitating de-escalation and creating movement towards negotiation in protracted conflicts will be explored through a number of avenues. First, the theoretical premises or rationale of the problem-solving approach in terms of social-psychological concepts will be explained. Second, the distinctions between the nature and effects of consultation and of mediation will be supported through research utilizing a complex laboratory simulation of intergroup conflict. Third, the work of Kelman on the Israeli-Palestinian conflict will provide an illustration of how problem-solving workshops might create the conditions conducive to movement towards negotiation. Fourth, a general consideration of traditional diplomatic activity within the Commonwealth will be used to examine the utility of problem-solving discussions as an important forerunner to substantive negotiation. Fifth and finally, a concluding analysis of potential applications will examine the relevance of the problem-solving approach to the stages of prenegotiation and to three of the cases presented in this volume.

THE SOCIAL-PSYCHOLOGICAL RATIONALE OF THE PROBLEM-SOLVING APPROACH

Two questions immediately directed towards any innovation are: How is it different and why should it work? With regard to the problem-solving approach to conflict resolution, the answer to both questions is to be found in underlying concepts drawn largely from social psychology. Kelman and Cohen argue that although problem-solving workshops overlap with other efforts to promote communication among conflicting parties, crucial differences exist:

What is unique about the problem-solving workshop is that it represents a systematic effort to utilize social-psychological principles in achieving a specific set of effects, both within the communication situation itself and within the larger conflict system. Social-psychological principles enter into the formulation of the structure, the process, and the content of the problem-solving workshop: The structure is based on analysis of the place of the workshop within the larger social system in which the conflict takes place. The process is designed to create the conditions conducive to establishing and maintaining certain patterns of social interaction and to utilize the ongoing interactions themselves as raw materials for gaining greater understanding of the dynamics of the conflict. The content focuses to a considerable degree on social-psychological analyses of collective experiences and processes, such as mutual perceptions and images, national self-images and national identity, sources and forms of nationalist ideology, interaction processes conducive to the escalation of conflict, and structural changes conducive to its perpetuation.[9]

The social-psychological rationale of the problem-solving approach assumes that conflict is always partly and at times predominantly a subjective, phenomenological, social process. Thus, the perceptions and behaviours of the parties in a conflict are affected by psychological and social processes at a number of levels of analysis including the individual, the interpersonal, the group, the intergroup, and the larger social system in which the conflict is embedded. What follows is a selective treatment of concepts which can be usefully invoked at these different levels of analysis.[10]

9 Kelman and Cohen, 'Resolution of international conflict: an interactional approach,' 340.
10 For a basic coverage of relevant social-psychological concepts, principles, and

At the level of the individual, the concept of attitude and the process of attitude change, which have received a great deal of attention in social psychology, are relevant to problem-solving interventions. Basically, third-party consultation is directed towards shifting the attitudes of the parties to each other in more veridical and positive directions. It is assumed that face-to-face interaction is necessary to break down rigid and simplified stereotypes and to provide undeniable information about the other group on which attitude change may then be based. The concept of attitude is typically defined as an individual's tendency to evaluate and respond to a social object in a consistently favourable or unfavourable way and is often seen to be comprised of a cognitive, an affective, and a behavioural component. The objectives of third-party consultation include attitude change towards a more realistic cognitive component, a more positive affective component, and a more co-operative behavioural orientation, all arising from favourable interaction with the other party. It is further assumed that attitudinal change will subsequently affect the perceptions, cognitions, and behaviours that characterize the relationship between the parties, at least for those individuals who have been participants in the consultation. Reduced selectivity and distortion in perception, increased complexity and flexibility in cognition, and a wider range of behavioural options would be predicted on the basis of positive attitude change. Whether these changes will in fact occur, particularly in the behavioural domain, of course depends on the host of other factors in the social environment of the individuals. How these changes might unfold is informed by a number of other social-psychological concepts and processes in areas such as cognitive consistency, attribution theory, and the functional theory of attitudes. Suffice it to say that a variety of useful ideas exist to help explain why consultation is predicted to have beneficial effects on individuals involved in a protracted and intractable social conflict.

---

theories organized by level of analysis, see Ronald Fisher, *Social Psychology: An Applied Approach* (New York: St Martin's Press 1982).

At the level of interpersonal relations, the interaction among participants in a third-party consultation allows certain processes to occur that may have beneficial effects. The sharing of perceptions and ideas about the conflict and the other party leads to a considerable amount of self-disclosure in a manner that is typically absent in the wider relations between the parties. The consistent research finding (as predicted by theory) is that this mutual and respectful self-disclosure will lead not only to greater understanding but also to increased trust among the participants. Furthermore, the opportunity to share similarities (as well as differences) is predicted to lead to an increased sense of social attraction and thereby greater receptivity to the ideas of the other party. This is in stark contrast to the usual relationship between parties engaged in conflict wherein similarities are ignored or glossed over while differences are exaggerated. In a similar vein, the more open and accurate communication which consultation endeavours to create allows the parties to see each other's intentions more clearly and fully and thus to evaluate their own interpretations and reactions more critically. This can lead to a much greater degree of congruence in the communication process as compared to the barriers and breakdowns characteristic of severe and protracted conflicts. Finally, the norm of reciprocity in interpersonal relations predicts beneficial outcomes from consultation. When, with third-party assistance, participants from one party share their views and analyses in a relatively respectful and objective fashion, representatives from the other party feel an obligation to do the same. Thus, a commitment to a mutual co-operative exchange develops which helps to move the participants towards the ultimate objective of solving the problem. In sum, a number of principles of interpersonal relations increase our understanding of how consultation differs from more traditional interactions (for example, from negotiation) between representatives of parties engaged in conflict.

At the level of group processes, some theoretical work indicates that the small informal nature of interaction in consultation should create a climate conducive to attitude and behavioural changes congruent with de-escalation. Theories of group development predict that the agenda and atmosphere which consultation provides should lead the parties through a number of stages to the creation of a new, and of course temporary, social reality. This reality involves a shared approach to analysing the conflict in a mutual and co-operative manner. Thus, a set of group norms comes into existence which supports and influences behaviours that are typically proscribed in the wider relationship between the parties. In terms of social process, consultation blends human relations training with small group problem-solving. Thus, meetings are not simply sensitivity sessions, although the increased openness and flexibility of interaction parallel the norms of such sessions to some degree. Social structure is added to consultation by an adherence to the sequence of problem-solving with consideration being given to both task and process requirements. Thus, the consultant facilitates movement of the discussions through problem identification and diagnosis to the creation and selection of alternatives that might assist in the de-escalation of the conflict. The fact that the participants are functioning as a single group in this experience ensures that a mutual and collaborative approach will accrue to some degree. Hence, a number of influential group dynamics are capitalized on by the design and implementation of consultation sessions.

At the intergroup level, social psychologists have distilled a considerable amount of research and theorizing on intergroup contact into a set of conditions under which interaction is predicted to lead to positive attitude changes and constructive behaviours. First, a setting which allows a high degree of 'acquaintance potential' by which participants from different groups become familiar with each other in a personal way helps to break down stereotypes and barriers to further interaction. Second, equal status is essential to respectful and productive interaction. Third, the social norms of the interaction, particularly those supporting friendliness, respect, openness, and trust, will

have important effects on both the expectations and the behaviour of the participants. Fourth, the involvement of participants in a co-operative task and reward structure will tend to
build a collaborative atmosphere that will support positive attitude change and problem-solving behaviour. Fifth, the characteristics of individuals will affect the process and outcomes
of intergroup contact. Participants need to be generally competent and secure and should not be so extreme in their attitudes that change is unlikely. The design and implementation
of consultation sessions need to be considered carefully in light
of these conditions so that their influence can be maximized
within appropriate constraints.

At the international level, social psychologists have emphasized the importance of nationalism, or the ideology of the state,
in affecting interactions between individuals from different
countries. Nationalism involves a favourable attitude towards
one's country and a predisposition to support its interests in
international relations. Advanced in a competitive fashion, nationalism thus works against international co-operation and collaborative approaches to conflict resolution in particular. The
state is seen to possess the supreme authority to protect and
advance the national interest in opposition to the interests of
other nations. Often, nationalism is linked to a sense of cultural
identity which embodies the unique history and way of life of
the people who constitute the majority of the state's population.
This element may be expressed as ethnocentrism, in which the
national or ethnic group is seen as superior to others. This
collection of sentiments must be analysed so that their effect
on behaviour between parties is understood. Thus, many of the
procedures employed in the problem-solving consultation encourage participants to examine jointly their national images
and ideologies to gain a sense of how these factors influence
policy development within nations and interaction, including
negotiation, between states.

The increased awareness and attitudinal changes sought by
the problem-solving approach underlie the 'perceptual shift'

that is required to initiate prenegotiation and negotiation. That is, both parties must come to see that negotiation has some potential for seriously addressing the conflict and for moving them towards their goals. This includes a 're-perception' or 're-imaging' of the adversary as a party that is reasonable and trustworthy to some minimal degree, and a reassessment of the stakes such that the potential benefits of negotiating now outweigh the risks and costs. There are indications that such changes in perception do occur for participants in problem-solving workshops. However, for these changes to lead to a perceptual shift among decision-makers and a consequent move to prenegotiation, they must have an impact on the wider relationship between the parties. And so we come to the crucial question of the transfer of effects on workshop participants to decision-makers back in the home setting.

This question has been addressed by all the major investigators of the problem-solving approach. The selection of participants, the design of the workshops, and their interface with the wider relationship are all important facets of the transfer question. The consensus is that for maximal impact, participants should be influential yet informal representatives of the parties to the conflict. These individuals should be members of decision-making élites (academics, advisers, ex-officials, retired or out-of-power politicians) who have the potential to influence policy but are not directly accountable for policy decisions. Their agenda following the workshop would be to convince actual decision-makers that a perceptual shift and a change in policy regarding negotiation of the conflict in question are desirable and realistic. Thus, it is essential that the design of the workshops confront reality squarely and comprehensively, including the domestic and international political constraints that bear upon the parties. The analysis of the conflict and any creative alternatives that are generated must be realistic and transferable to the wider relationship. The setting for a workshop is usually an isolated one, to maximize unfettered and creative discussion, but the connections to the real world must not be lost. This is particularly important in designing a re-entry or transfer component in which participants discuss their learning and its potential applications, including the constraints and risks. Finally, any consultation initiative that proposes to influence the wider relationship must comprise an extended, long-term programme of workshops and a host of supplementary activities. Such a programme can adapt to the political reality of the conflict and over time might influence a large enough number of influential individuals that the decision-making élite will modally experience a perceptual shift towards negotiation. When these and other aspects of transfer are considered and appropriate strategies are implemented, the problem-solving approach holds the possibility of moving beyond pilot work to a programme of action research that has the potential of facilitating de-escalation and a move towards constructive negotiation.

CONSULTATION VERSUS MEDIATION IN THE INTERGROUP CONFLICT SIMULATION

Although third-party consultation and mediation have been conceptually distinguished, there has been some blurring of the boundaries between the two methods.[11] Unfortunately, some recent literature has categorized the problem-solving approach as mediation, even though the former focusses largely on subjective elements and is directed towards relationship change rather than substantive settlement. On the research side, the difficulty is compounded because there exist no comprehensive data-based, rigorous comparisons between the two types of intervention. The development of the Intergroup Conflict Simulation (ICS) at the University of Saskatchewan provided the opportunity to assess the relative effects of consultation and mediation within the context of a realistic and yet manageable conflict between groups. This comparative evidence is important because it demonstrates the positive impact of consultation on relationship variables such as attitude and orientation. While

---

11 See Fisher and Keashly, 'Third party interventions.'

the generalization of laboratory results to the real world is difficult, the relatively high external validity of the ICS engenders optimism about the relevance of the findings for international conflicts.

The ICS was developed to provide an operating analogue of the essential processes and outcomes of intergroup conflict in a holistic, systematic, and controlled manner.[12] The ICS is a strategic simulation in which conflict is created by imposing a situation of scarce resources over which the parties negotiate their differences.[13] The overall design covers the phases of group development, intergroup conflict, and conflict resolution. Representatives from two groups negotiate over differences linked to an economic and value conflict involving real threat, potential escalation, and alternative outcomes. Following the escalation of the conflict and initial negotiation, consultation or mediation is introduced and the relative effects of each on perceptions, attitudes, the relationship, and further negotiation are assessed. (The ICS is described in detail in the annex at the conclusion of this article.)

The differential effects of consultation and mediation on the perceptions and attitudes of the participants were dramatic. Groups exposed to the consultation intervention showed significantly increased liking and trust towards each other as measured by rating scales administered prior to and after the intervention. These differences held over time to the point of

---

12 For a description and evaluation of the Intergroup Conflict Simulation, see Ronald Fisher, Peter Grant, Donald Hall, Loraleigh Keashly, and Ruth Kinzel, 'The development and testing of a complex strategic simulation of intergroup conflict,' unpublished manuscript under review, University of Saskatchewan (1988). For details on the design of the ICS, see Donald Hall, 'The Development of a Comprehensive Simulation of Intergroup Conflict,' doctoral dissertation, University of Saskatchewan, Saskatoon, 1986. For details on the design and effects of the third-party interventions, see Loraleigh Keashly, 'A Comparative Analysis of Third Party Interventions in Intergroup Conflict,' doctoral dissertation, University of Saskatchewan, Saskatoon, 1988.

13 For a distinction among the different types of simulations used to study intergroup negotiations, see Richard Klimoski, 'Simulation methodologies in experimental research on negotiations by representatives,' *Journal of Conflict Resolution* 22(March 1978), 61-78.

post-settlement. On a standard measure of intergroup attitudes composed of semantic differential scales, groups subject to consultation showed significantly increased positive evaluations towards the other group while those subject to mediation did not. These differences also held through settlement. With respect to perceptions of the intergroup relationship, the consultation intervention resulted in significant increases in perceived collaboration whereas the mediation intervention did not. On a set of semantic differential scales evaluating the intergroup relationship, consultation groups showed significantly more positive evaluations following the intervention than did mediation groups. These differences on the perceived relationship also held through to post-settlement. In sum, these results are the first indications from a systematically controlled and moderately complex laboratory study that basic social-psychological elements of an intergroup relationship have been positively affected by a problem-solving intervention.

Unfortunately, these positive changes did not directly affect the negotiation sessions following the intervention. On a relatively detailed and sophisticated coding scheme, the behaviour of negotiators from consultation groups did not differ from that of negotiators from mediation groups. It may be that within the moderate but limited intensity of the ICS, negotiation was already going well enough so that the interventions had no discernible effect. Nor did the interventions differ in their effect on outcomes, as measured by pay-off matrices, even though mediation was hypothesized to be superior because of its focus on substantive issues. In conclusion, the positive effects of consultation on perceptions, attitudes, and the intergroup relationship augur well for the potential of problem-solving as a prenegotiation methodology which may produce the perceptual shift required for progress towards negotiation.

PROBLEM-SOLVING AS A PATH TO ISRAELI-PALESTINIAN NEGOTIATIONS: THE WORK OF HERBERT KELMAN

The interactional, problem-solving approach developed by Herbert Kelman of Harvard University and his associates is at the forefront of applications designed to increase the likelihood and potential of negotiation in a protracted conflict. In his initial conceptual work, Kelman compared and evaluated the approaches of two other pioneers in the area, John Burton and Leonard Doob, and integrated these into the concept of the problem-solving workshop.[14] This term was used to indicate the utilization of 'workshop' techniques, but to stress that the emphasis is on problem-solving rather than personal growth or sensitivity training. Kelman considered that the unique strength of the workshop approach was its provision of a novel context for certain processes of communication which are practically impossible to achieve in more public and formal settings. He also saw, as others have seen, that the primary limitation of the workshop approach centres on the question of transfer and proposed, as noted above, that the ideal workshop participants are influential members of their societies who can have an impact on foreign policy but are not directly responsible for making or implementing policy. Those so responsible are not only less likely to experience changes in the workshop but are also less able to bring about changes in policy.

Kelman, Cohen, and other associates have built upon Kelman's initial work to develop a wider interactional approach to international conflict resolution in which problem-solving workshops play a central role, with the Middle East conflict as the primary focus of their efforts. An early prototype workshop, held in 1971, brought together Palestinian and Israeli nationals living in the United States with the goal of inducing effective communication and objective analysis of the conflict.[15] Preworkshop sessions were held with each group to enhance commitment to the workshop and to provide the third party with

14 Kelman, 'The problem solving workshop in conflict resolution.'
15 In addition to the general description provided in Kelman and Cohen, 'The problem-solving workshop: a social-psychological contribution,' and 'Resolution of international conflict: an interactional approach,' see Stephen Cohen, Herbert Kelman, Frederick Miller, and Bruce Smith, 'Evolving intergroup techniques for conflict resolution: an Israeli-Palestinian pilot workshop,' *Journal of Social Issues* 33(no 1, 1977), 165-89, for a detailed presentation of the prototype workshop.

information to plan the sessions. A statement on the legitimacy of Palestinian nationalism became the focus of the workshop and an amended version was eventually agreed upon. The third-party team perceived the workshop as offering useful insights into the conflict and follow-up contacts with participants indicated increased understanding and support for further workshops.

Since then Kelman has organized and facilitated numerous workshops bearing on the Middle East conflict and the Israeli-Palestinian relationship in particular. Participants have included both 'pre-influentials' (often graduate students in the context of a Harvard University seminar) and influentials (present and former officials, parliamentarians, and advisers who have input into the policy process). The broader context for these initiatives is provided by the interactional approach which asserts that social interaction between the parties is often a necessary (though not sufficient) condition for the resolution of international conflict. Thus, this action research approach focusses the interaction on a mutual analysis of the conflict, promotes a collaborative problem-solving process, and uses social scientists in a third-party role designed to facilitate the interaction. The broader thrust of the interactional approach involves a variety of activities to enhance the third-party role and to identify opportunities for improving communication within and among the parties. This includes organizing workshops and meetings, recruiting and training potential third-party team members with a view to ethnic balance, widening contacts with a range of decision-makers and élites, developing policy analyses, and conducting research on the conflict.

Based on this extensive background of activities, Kelman has increasingly turned his attention to the ways in which problem-solving could identify the psychological prerequisites for mutual acceptance and create the conditions for Israeli-Palestinian negotiations.[16] Thus, he 'conceptualizes a *prene-*

16 See Herbert Kelman, 'Israelis and Palestinians: psychological prerequisites for

gotiation process designed to create the political and psychological conditions for beginning Israeli-Palestinian negotiations toward a mutually satisfactory settlement, conducive to stable peace and reconciliation.'[17] Kelman assumes, as many others do, that the competing territorial claims of these two parties are the core issue in the larger Middle East conflict and that there can be no resolution until the basic needs and concerns of both Palestinians and Israelis are addressed.[18]

For negotiation to be successful, Kelman maintains that it must aim for a *resolution* of the conflict, that is, an outcome that involves compromise but leaves both parties better off and is responsive to their basic needs and consistent with their sense of justice. Negotiation must therefore build trust and produce outcomes to which the parties are committed. Thus, it is essential that negotiation involve direct communication, focus on developing a formula for sharing the land between the two people (with sensitivity to the parties' sense of injustice, quest for security, and national identity and to current political realities), and enable each party to achieve and benefit from national and international legitimacy. Based on these assumptions, Kelman provides an analysis of the prospects for negotiation which links prenegotiation tendencies to current events in the area. Mobilizing existing incentives in the face of severe constraints requires steps that increase the 'sense of opportunity' and lessen the 'sense of danger' associated with negotiation. Unfortunately, any such initiatives immediately confront a fundamental dilemma: neither side is willing to accept the national identity or

mutual acceptance,' *International Security* 3(summer 1978), 162-86; Herbert Kelman, 'An interactional approach to conflict resolution and its application to Israeli-Palestinian relations,' *International Interactions* 6(no 2, 1979), 99-122; Herbert Kelman, 'Creating the conditions for Israeli-Palestinian negotiations,' *Journal of Conflict Resolution* 26(March 1982), 39-75; Herbert Kelman, 'The political psychology of the Israeli-Palestinian conflict: how can we overcome the barriers to a negotiated solution?' *Political Psychology* 8(September 1987), 347-63.

17 Kelman, 'The problem-solving workshop in conflict resolution,' 39. Emphasis added.

18 Herbert Kelman, 'The palestinianization of the Arab-Israeli conflict,' *Jerusalem Quarterly* 46(spring 1988), 3-15.

to recognize the legitimate rights of the other; such acceptance and recognition are perceived as threats to one's own identity, a compromise of one's own legitimacy, and an abdication of one's own rights. The psychological essence of the conflict is a zero-sum clash between two nationalist movements each struggling for national identity and existence and making claims on the same territory. If one side concedes that the other has rights, its own claims become more ambiguous. Each group believes that the ultimate intention of the other is to destroy it. In this context, a dramatic initiative (such as Sadat's visit to Jerusalem) which might remove the barriers to negotiation cannot be taken without the initiator paying a heavy political price. Thus, a process of successive approximations is required which enables each party to offer sufficient reassurances to the other so that communication can be initiated without threatening its own vital interests.

The central question is how might such a process of pre-negotiation or 'pre-prenegotiation' (depending on the definition adopted) be instituted in a way that overcomes the barriers to negotiation? Kelman proposes that hopes must be raised and fears lowered through communication involving reassuring messages that are not too threatening *to the sender* and yet invite reciprocation by the receiver. Such communication would need to start at a low level of commitment and gradually move towards increasingly concrete negotiations. According to Kelman:

Gradually, if the communication is carried out in a problem-solving mode, it should facilitate both the emergence of new ideas and the development of mutual trust, allowing the parties to offer each other increasingly greater degrees of reassurance and encouragement. At some point, these should be sufficient to enable them to enter into official negotiations, designed to produce formal mutual recognition as the final outcome. Thus, I am envisaging a process of communication that may enable the parties to move toward the recognition that each needs from the other but is afraid to give to the other by successive approximations, in which levels of reassurance are continually calibrated to correspond to levels of commitment.[19]

Kelman argues that the problem-solving approach is uniquely suited to facilitating the type of prenegotiation process that is required. Direct interaction between the parties is essential, and in the early stages of low commitment, the participants would ideally be influentials chosen by their groups but possessing no official standing who could feed the results back into the policy process. The norms and procedures of the problem-solving workshop and the facilitative interventions of a third party provide a context in which the principals can share perspectives and concerns, exchange signals, explore the range of satisfactory solutions, and identify steps for breaking the impasse. Such a prenegotiation process also allows the image of the enemy as a monolithic camp to be undermined and the other side to be perceived as possessing both negative and positive characteristics. Ultimately, the interaction allows the parties to explore the feasibility of creating an understanding that might serve as a framework for beginning negotiation. If successful, the conclusion that a framework is possible could then be injected into the domestic political process of the parties. If a political climate favourable to the understanding can be created, further discussions involving quasi-official representatives would then be held to move the prenegotiation process another step forward.

Kelman does not anticipate that such an understanding would be easy to obtain and identifies numerous pitfalls in the process. However, he believes that through sensitivity to certain criteria, such as the importance of simultaneous announcements, the barriers to negotiation might be overcome. The type of understanding that he envisages consists of concrete, descriptive undertakings rather than statements of principles and rights. Kelman believes that important segments in both the Israeli

19 Kelman, 'Creating the conditions for Israeli-Palestinian negotiations,' 68.

and Palestinian communities have strong incentives to achieve a negotiated settlement. Thus, there is a chance that a communication process along the lines of the problem-solving approach might ultimately contribute to the resolution of the conflict through the initiation of prenegotiation.

THE COMMONWEALTH AS A FORUM FOR PRENEGOTIATION PROBLEM-SOLVING

In the practice of international diplomacy, the Commonwealth of Nations may provide one of the most appropriate forums for the pursuit of the problem-solving approach. In 1985, the first secretary-general of the 'new' Commonwealth, Arnold Smith, made a strong case for the unique value and potential of the association as an alternative vehicle for conflict resolution.[20]

Smith contends that the value of the Commonwealth for international consultation and co-operation derives from the unique nature of its membership and the intimacy and informality of its procedures. The heterogeneity of its almost fifty members is evident in a number of basic dimensions including size, level of economic development, nature of economic activity, race, and religion. In short, the association provides a representative cross-section of humankind and its problems. At the same time, there is considerable homogeneity – a common language (English), shared traditions and habits of administration, the widespread use of English common law, similar principles and methods of education, and significant elements of a shared history.

The meetings of the Commonwealth, whether involving heads of government, ministers, or officials, are typically seen by the participants as occasions for informal consultation and the ex-

20 For a concise description of the Commonwealth 'approach,' see Arnold Smith, 'Commonwealth cross sections: prenegotiation to minimize conflict and to develop cooperation,' in Arthur Lall, ed, *Multilateral Negotiation and Mediation: Instruments and Methods* (New York: Pergamon and the International Peace Academy 1985); for details on particular meetings, see Arnold Smith, with Clyde Sanger, *Stitches in Time: The Commonwealth in World Politics* (Don Mills, Ont: General 1981).

change of views rather than for negotiation. Roundtable discussions following the model of a cabinet meeting are preferred to prepared speeches. The tradition of closed meetings has supported a degree of informality, frankness, and flexibility that is simply not possible in many other forums. Particularly in the smaller meetings and retreats of heads of government and the secretary-general, with no other ministers or advisers present, this climate can facilitate the spontaneous expression of fresh and creative ideas to deal with difficult and contentious problems. According to Smith: 'Participants in Commonwealth meetings, especially at the head of government or ministerial or "senior official" level, seldom think of themselves as negotiating but rather as discussing; but the purpose is the exchange of views, and when it seems desirable and practicable, the result is agreements or undertakings, often informal but usually nonetheless effective, for harmonized and, often, for cooperative actions. Because of the shared characteristics referred to earlier, the informality of Commonwealth procedures usually greatly enhances the effectiveness of this type of multilateral discussion.'[21]

The role of the secretary-general in Commonwealth meetings is that of a facilitator of discussion and appears to be closer to that of a third-party consultant than a traditional mediator. The relationship between the secretary-general and the participants must be one based on trust, understanding, and fairness if the discussions are to be profitable. The secretary-general chairs the meetings, supporting the norms of informality and flexibility, occasionally encouraging questions and interjections, and facilitating the discussions towards understanding and agreement.

Decisions are not taken by a formal vote, but by an undefined 'consensus,' in which the decision has the support of a large and representative majority and is not rejected by any member. This approach to decision-making allows greater flexibility, more effective implementation, and less rigidity and abuse

21 Smith, 'Prenegotiation,' 70.

than formal voting systems, weighted or otherwise. In Commonwealth meetings, it is not the practice to put forward formal resolutions or to work towards specific agreements. General agreements are often forwarded for study or action or both to an appropriate body such as the secretariat or a meeting of ministers, officials, or technical experts. In addition, the secretary-general may follow up or play a continuing role, by providing good offices or mediation in conflicts among members or related states.

In sum, the Commonwealth may be one international forum in which a problem-solving approach to conflict resolution would seem to be natural. It should be noted, however, that the focus of discussion in Commonwealth meetings generally tends to be on substantive issues rather than on the process issues which are given emphasis in third-party consultation. In addition, the Commonwealth is a continuing forum for discussion and thus quite unlike the situation in a protracted conflict where the parties have often ceased to communicate. Nonetheless, it is likely that such discussions have served an important function compatible with prenegotiation. They certainly demonstrate how group problem-solving by consensus can influence the move towards bilateral negotiations.

Discussions at a Commonwealth heads-of-government meeting played a crucial role in moving the Rhodesia/Zimbabwe conflict through the prenegotiation process to negotiation.[22] In post-colonial Rhodesia, a white minority, descendants of British settlers, controlled the government, while the majority of black Africans increasingly attempted to gain equal rights.[23] The in-

22 Credit for successful prenegotiation as well as the eventual settlement has of course been claimed by and given to a variety of actors and processes, including the Lusaka Commonwealth conference, and the proportion of credit to be attributed to any one source is impossible to estimate. For a description of these various forces and individuals, see Colin Legum, 'The road to and from Lancaster House,' *Africa Contemporary Record* 12(1979-80), A3-A31.

23 For a concise description of the Rhodesia/Zimbabwe conflict, see George Betts, 'The Lancaster House Conference: a game theoretical explanation of the outcome,' master's thesis, Carleton University, Ottawa. As Betts and others point out, in the context of the decolonization period following World War II, Britain

ternal settlement and elections of 1978, which yielded a parliamentary majority to blacks but kept judicial, administrative, and police power in white hands, set the stage for the Lusaka Commonwealth conference in August of 1979. In the background was a military conflict whose increasing costs had led to exhaustion, frustration, and stalemate on both sides.

Britain's role was critical. Prior to the Lusaka meeting, it appeared that the newly elected Conservative government of Margaret Thatcher would agree to independence and the lifting of sanctions, as the régime of Bishop Muzorewa and its white backers wanted. However, the Conservative cabinet, and particularly the foreign secretary, Lord Carrington, prevailed over their party's election platform, and Thatcher went to Lusaka with a renewed concern about genuine majority rule and international support for any settlement.

The Commonwealth setting was propitious because it included the leaders or representatives of the front-line African states supporting the Zimbabwean Patriotic Front as well as aides to Mugabe and Nkomo, the leaders of the Front. As background to the conference, the Commonwealth secretariat had

refused to grant independence to Rhodesia unless the white minority accepted the principle of majority rule. White Rhodesian frustration and desire for statehood led to the Unilateral Declaration of Independence by the régime of Ian Smith in 1965. The response of the Zimbabwean nationalists was to escalate the guerrilla war against this illegal government. The two major nationalist movements, the Zimbabwe African National Union, led by Robert Mugabe, and the Zimbabwe African People's Union, led by Joshua Nkomo, joined forces in 1976 as the Patriotic Front, which represented the nationalist position in the negotiation and ultimate settlement at Lancaster House in 1979. In the interim, the conflict played itself out in several forms. In addition to the escalation of military operations, the Smith régime faced international condemnation and the increasing application of sanctions. Supported by South Africa, the rebel régime was resourceful in evading sanctions and building self-reliance while increasing internal repression and control. For a discussion of these aspects of the conflict, see Douglas G. Anglin, 'Zimbabwe: retrospect and prospect,' *International Journal* 35(autumn 1980), 663-700. While there were repeated attempts at mediation, primarily British and American, Smith was particularly adept at evading serious negotiations in his struggle to preserve the status quo. For a description of various failed attempts at settlement, see Robert O. Matthews, 'Talking without negotiating: the case of Rhodesia,' *International Journal* 35(winter 1979-80), 91-117.

published a detailed critique on the constitutional defects of the internal settlement. Thatcher, in her opening comments, indicated her acceptance of the critique by stressing Britain's commitment to genuine black majority rule and to bringing Rhodesia to independence on a basis acceptable to the Commonwealth and the international community.

An initial understanding now existed, and the prenegotiation process moved to the smaller, informal weekend meeting of the so-called contact group of eight chaired by the secretary-general, Shridath Ramphal. In addition to Thatcher and Carrington, this group included Kenneth Kaunda of Zambia, Julius Nyerere of Tanzania, Henry Adefope of Nigeria (federal commissioner for external affairs), Malcolm Fraser of Australia, and Michael Manley of Jamaica; thus, the concerns of a number of the principals in the conflict were directly or indirectly represented. The informal yet serious problem-solving atmosphere of Commonwealth meetings, along with impartial third-party assistance, moved the parties through the process of prenegotiation. According to Arnold Smith, this group worked out the framework that led to the formal negotiation at Lancaster House.[24] The consensus of the group, facilitated by the efforts of the secretary-general, was that it was Britain's responsibility to grant independence based on genuine majority rule and that a settlement must involve all the parties concerned and must include a democratic constitution and elections with Commonwealth observers. The understanding was unanimously approved by all heads of state in attendance and was included in the final communiqué of the conference.

The initial change in the position of the British government made it possible to move towards consensus on the basic principles of a resolution. The multilateral conference at Lusaka was then instrumental in producing the perceptual shift required for negotiation to be seen as a viable option. Although considerable persuasion was still required to get the parties to

24 Smith, 'Prenegotiation.'

Lancaster House, the Commonwealth conference provided a crucial opportunity for successful prenegotiation.[25] The spirit of the Lusaka communiqué was strongly evident in the final settlement, and the prenegotiation process at the Commonwealth conference can be regarded as a significant turning point in the resolution of the conflict.

CONCLUSION: POTENTIAL APPLICATIONS

Destructive intergroup and international conflict is the most serious and difficult problem facing humankind. Traditional approaches to conflict management seem to have a limited capacity to deal with protracted conflict, and it is therefore appropriate to search for new analyses and approaches. It appears particularly useful to explore mechanisms that could help parties move towards negotiation; thus, the process of prenegotiation takes on a special significance. The innovative approach of problem-solving workshops is a potentially useful prenegotiation strategy.

Problem-solving or third-party consultation is a relatively new and unexplored approach to conflict resolution, particularly in the international system. Initial theories on its practice are disproportionately based on experimental and pilot work, and there is need for much more research and theory development. Nonetheless, the approach finds a strong rationale in social-psychological theory and can be clearly distinguished from other alternatives for improving relationships and other forms of third-party intervention, particularly mediation.

The potential of the problem-solving approach as a prenegotiation strategy has been demonstrated through three different avenues. First, the different effects of consultation and mediation have been clearly demonstrated within a complex laboratory simulation of intergroup conflict. Consultation had superior effects on intergroup perceptions, attitudes, and re-

25 See Jeffrey Davidow, *A Peace in Southern Africa: The Lancaster House Conference on Rhodesia, 1979* (Boulder CO: Westview 1984), for a discussion of how the Lusaka conference set the stage for the Lancaster House negotiation.

lationship qualities. Second, the work of Herbert Kelman provides an excellent example of problem-solving as a prenegotiation
strategy designed to bring about negotiation in an intractable
conflict – that in the Middle East. Kelman has produced a clear
and detailed statement of the psychological prerequisites for
mutual acceptance and the conditions for acceptable negotiations between Israelis and Palestinians. Third, the Commonwealth appears to provide an appropriate forum for problem-
solving discussions that serve a prenegotiation function. Based
on the description of a former secretary-general and an analysis
of the Commonwealth's involvement in the Rhodesia/Zimbabwe
conflict, it appears that the organization might well pursue this
role with greater vigour and direction.

It is useful to ask how third-party consultation might be
applicable both to the individual stages of prenegotiation and
to certain of the cases described in this volume.[26] In problem
identification, the first stage of prenegotiation described by
Tomlin, consultation would focus on perceptions and attitudes
to facilitate the start of the perceptual shift required for the
parties to proceed. The emphasis would be on breaking down
stereotypes and building differentiated and more realistic intergroup images while inducing increased flexibility in behavioural orientations. The parties might then come to see each
other as minimally reasonable and trustworthy and begin to
consider negotiation as a viable option. Analysis of the conflict
could be profitably directed towards the underlying causes, particularly in terms of the basic needs of the parties for recognition, identity, and security.[27] The parties must come to see
that the use of force will only suppress and frustrate basic needs
and that, in addition, the continuing costs of the conflict are

26 For a model of the stages of prenegotiation, see Brian Tomlin, 'The stages of
   prenegotiation: the decision to negotiate North American free trade,' in this
   volume.
27 The importance of understanding basic needs in the analysis of conflict has
   been emphasized in Edward Azar and John Burton, eds, *International Conflict
   Resolution: Theory and Practice* (Brighton, England: Wheatsheaf 1986).

unacceptable while the benefits of a negotiated settlement are attractive.

In the second stage of prenegotiation, the search for options, the focus of discussion would move to the final phase of the perceptual shift in which the parties would gain a clearer picture of each other's intentions and behaviour. The realization that negotiation might be a superior option for expressing intentions and achieving goals would underlie the conclusion that negotiation is a viable option and promote the decision to negotiate. The focus would move to the qualities of the relationship and how they affect the potential for negotiation. In particular, an examination of perceptions of the actual versus ideal relationship would be a useful exercise.

In the third stage, commitment to negotiation, each party would need to acknowledge its acceptance of the identity and legitimacy of the other as part of the fundamental understanding on which negotiation is based. Additional discussion would be directed towards the basic issues on which negotiation is to be conducted: what is negotiable and what is not. In the fourth stage, agreement to negotiate, informal channels established through consultation could be used to reach agreement before public announcements are made. In discussions proper, it would be useful for parties to consider how national ideologies and group cultures will affect negotiation. Such an analysis could prevent misunderstandings that might arise at the table. In the final stage, setting the parameters, the emphasis would be on establishing the substantive framework for negotiation: What are the relevant issues and how should they be ranked? Thus, further analysis of the conflict and the drawing of important distinctions between issues, interests, and positions would be valuable. Finally, discussion could directly acknowledge the utility of the facilitative conditions of intergroup contact that had been established and consider how these qualities could be transferred to the formal negotiation.

In sum, problem-solving discussions could facilitate movement through the stages of prenegotiation. However, this approach departs from existing practice in at least two important respects. First, it would involve social scientists/practitioners moving into a consultation role which involves more direct intervention than usual. This raises a host of professional and ethical issues, and while these considerations have received much attention in the basic problem-solving literature, they require further consideration and analysis specifically directed towards involvement in the process of prenegotiation.[28] Second, in line with the rationale of consultation, prenegotiation discussions would involve representatives of the parties meeting together rather than separately as is the usual mode of operation. That is, as opposed to working separately, the parties would jointly consider the various issues and questions involved in moving through the stages of prenegotiation. This mutual problem analysis and decision-making is a core strength of the consultation approach.

The applicability of consultation can be further explored by a brief and speculative analysis of its potential relevance to three of the cases of prenegotiation presented in this volume: the Arab-Israeli conflict discussed by Stein, the Soviet-American prenegotiation of arms control analysed by Griffiths and by Hampson, and the Canada-United States prenegotiation on free trade described by Tomlin.[29]

The Arab-Israeli conflict represents a protracted, severe, complex, multiparty dispute that is extremely resistant to de-escalation and resolution. Thus, it is not surprising that there have been more failures of prenegotiation than successes. The prenegotiation discussed by Stein which led to the Camp David negotiation was 'successful' because it simplified the conflict, particularly by reducing the number of parties and eliminating

28 For a concise and explicit presentation of ethical guidelines in problem-solving, see John Burton, *Resolving Deep-Rooted Conflict: A Handbook* (Lanham MD: University Press of America 1987).

29 See Janice Stein, 'Prenegotiation in the Arab-Israeli conflict: the paradoxes of success and failure,' Franklyn Griffiths, 'The Soviet experience of arms control,' Fen Hampson, 'Headed for the table: United States approaches to arms control prenegotiation,' and Tomlin, 'The stages of prenegotiation,' all in this volume.

many of the most difficult items from the agenda. This pre-negotiation also succeeded, as traditional negotiation and mediation often do, by working around underlying issues rather than tackling them head on as prescribed by consultation. A problem-solving approach would focus discussions in prenegotiation on perceptions, attitudes, and qualities of the relationship that impede movement towards de-escalation and negotiation. The high degree of mistrust, the lack of meaningful and direct communication, and the cultural differences in language use are among the obstacles that require attention and analysis. They would need to be approached through joint discussions involving all or most of the parties rather than the type of 'shuttle process' and fractionation that were practised by the United States in the period preceding Camp David. Moreover, this form of intervention would need to occur earlier in the process of prenegotiation and would require a longer time line and greater investment by the third party. Prenegotiation might then succeed not by reducing the number of parties and issues but by increasing mutual understanding and acknowledging basic needs. The complexity and intensity of the Arab-Israeli conflict makes it highly appropriate for consultation while rendering the probability of success extremely low.

The relationship between the Soviet Union and the United States represents a protracted, escalated, and yet relatively stable conflict in which arms control is one major issue. The complexity of the conflict is partly expressed through linkages to a variety of domestic influences and the international agendas of both superpowers. Given their past experience of interaction and a moderate degree of direct communication, there appears to be less need for problem-solving in prenegotiation than in the Arab-Israeli conflict. Nonetheless, consultation could profitably be directed towards such crucial issues as how cultural differences and unrealistic images affect negotiating styles, and how the intentions of each party are often misinterpreted by the other through selective and distorted perception of behaviour. Increased mutual understanding of these kinds of processes should have beneficial effects on both prenegotiation and negotiation.

The relationship between Canada and the United States is characterized by moderate to high degrees of co-operative interdependence, open and direct communication, familiarity and trust, and cultural similarity. Within this relatively positive context, the prenegotiation process of free trade was essentially 'business as usual' in bilateral relations, even though, as Tomlin points out, it involved a significant redefinition of the relationship by Canada. The high degree of power asymmetry in the relationship is indicated by the one-sidedness of the prenegotiation process in which internal dialogue in Canada was stimulated by the external actions of the United States. In this situation, in which subjective and cultural obstacles are minimal, problem-solving during prenegotiation focussing on process issues would have little utility. If problem-solving discussions had been instituted as part of prenegotiation they would most likely have taken a task focus, considering items such as the parameters, issues, priorities, and agenda. These activities would differ from typical prenegotiation mainly in the nature of the joint analysis that would be involved. How realistic and attractive the parties would have found such an intervention, however, is uncertain.

This limited analysis of these few cases raises the question of the general applicability of problem-solving discussions in the prenegotiation of different kinds of conflict. Conflicts can be assessed on a number of central dimensions, including intensity, complexity of sources, frustration of basic needs, degree of subjectivity, extent of cultural differences, and power symmetry. When all these indicators are high, as in severe protracted conflict, problem-solving discussions could be most useful in facilitating the prenegotiation process, although implementation would be most problematic. When these indicators are low, there would be less need for and utility in such interventions during prenegotiation. The Arab-Israeli conflict is the most appropriate situation for consultation, the Soviet-American conflict somewhat less so, while the case of Canada-United States free trade is the least appropriate. Paradoxically, consultation may be most difficult in the prenegotiation processes in which it is most needed. However, this is true of most conflict resolution strategies. The problem-solving approach deserves to be subjected to further analysis and evaluation as potentially useful both in encouraging the onset of prenegotiation and in facilitating progress through its stages.

ANNEX

The Intergroup Conflict Simulation (ICS) consists of five two-hour sessions spread over a two-week period in which male university undergraduates serve as participants. In the first year of development, 8 complete runs of the ICS were carried out and following minor modifications, 16 further runs, which included the third-party interventions, were completed. In Session 1, participants are randomly assigned to five-person groups, and structured discussions are used to develop group cohesion and identity. In Session 2, participants work on a land development task out of which the resource and value conflict between the groups emerges. Groups are provided with a map of a land area having a variety of resources and are asked to develop a plan to support a viable community. Through different but not contradictory information, one group is led to take a conservationist or renewable resource approach, the other an exploitive or non-renewable resource approach to development. The groups are then required to negotiate the division of five specific land tracts on which their preferences lead to initial dividing lines which are diametrically opposed. The outcomes of negotiations are based on a payoff matrix in which more points are awarded to the more valued tracts and for proximity to the original dividing lines. In Session 3, the groups plan their negotiation strategy and selected negotiators then meet for two negotiation periods each, followed by group caucuses. In Session 4, further strategy planning and an initial negotiation period are followed by the third-party intervention. In Session 5, strategy planning is followed by three negotiation periods interspersed with caucuses and after agreement is reached, the simulation experience is debriefed. Throughout the simulation, a variety of measures are taken at the individual, group, and intergroup levels, and all sessions are videotaped.

Analysis of results from the 24 runs of the ICS indicates that it captures the essence of intergroup conflict in a manageable and observable fashion. Indices of group development show high levels of cohesion and identity, and adequate intensity of conflict is demonstrated by moderate levels of perceived threat, anger, and frustration. Thus, the ICS is a reliable and valid representation of intergroup conflict within which the comparative effectiveness of different types of third-party intervention can be gauged. Consultation and mediation were introduced by random assignment into the 16 later runs of the ICS. The operationalization of consultation was based on Fisher's model, while the design of the mediation intervention was drawn from generic treatments primarily in labour-management and international relations, particularly Deborah Kolb, *The Mediators* (Cambridge MA: MIT Press 1983) and James Wall Jr, 'Mediation: an analysis, review, and proposed research,' *Journal of Conflict Resolution* 25(March 1981), 157-80. In consultation, the third party worked separately with the two groups to articulate their images of each other, the intergroup relationship, and the progress of negotiations. These perceptions were then exchanged and clarified in a joint meeting, and the consultant provided ideas on the nature and escalation of intergroup conflict. Finally, the participants discussed the characteristics of an ideal relationship and the implications of this for negotiation. In mediation, the third party asked the groups to identify the main issues and their perception of the other group's positions. The mediator then analysed this information and reported to each group the similarities and differences in positions and the potential points of movement. Finally, the mediator provided ideas on negotiation as a process of successive concession-making, and the groups were instructed to reconsider their positions and to develop their next proposal for negotiation.

8. *Getting to the Table: The Triggers, Stages, Functions, and Consequences of Prenegotiation*

JANICE GROSS STEIN

Comparative examination of our cases of prenegotiation enables us to identify a number of important attributes of the process of getting to the table. We look first at the factors that trigger active consideration of negotiation as one among an array of options. We then explore the pattern of progress through the stages of prenegotiation as leaders approach and avoid the table. We turn next to the functions that a process of prenegotiation performs. By comparing the evidence from cases where the parties reached the table, we then attempt to identify the conditions of getting to the table. Finally, we explore the larger significance of prenegotiation as a process of learning and of conflict management.

TRIGGERS: WHY DO PARTIES CONSIDER GOING TO THE TABLE?

The beginning of a process of prenegotiation is generally marked by a turning point in the relationship between the parties, an event or change in conditions that triggers a reassessment of alternatives and adds negotiation to the strategies of conflict management that are seriously considered.[1] In most of the cases

Professor of Political Science, University of Toronto, Toronto, Ontario and co-ordinator of the Project on Prenegotiation of the Canadian Institute of International Affairs and the Centre for International Studies of the University of Toronto.

1 For a discussion of crises and turning points in the process of negotiation, see Daniel Druckman, 'Stages, turning points, and crises: negotiating base rights, Spain and the United States,' *Journal of Conflict Resolution* 30(June 1986), 327-60, and I. William Zartman, 'Common elements in the analysis of the nego-

examined in this study, either a recent crisis or the attempt to avoid an impending crisis was the most important turning point that prompted serious consideration of negotiation as one among a series of options. Comparative evidence from these cases suggests, first, that prenegotiation is triggered by an attempt to prevent a crisis or to manage a relationship in the wake of a recent crisis.

In the Canadian-American relationship, as Brian Tomlin argues, the acute conflict that developed in 1981 over Canadian energy and investment policies and the probability of American retaliatory measures triggered a crisis in Canada. American threats to the security of Canada's access to a market on which it was overwhelmingly dependent increased uncertainty in Canada about the future of the bilateral economic relationship and provoked a reassessment of Canadian strategy. This led to a redefinition of the problem and consideration of the option of negotiating a trade agreement.

The context of prenegotiation in the General Agreement on Tariffs and Trade (GATT) could not differ more sharply from that of free trade in the Canadian-American relationship. As Gilbert Winham notes, negotiation is routine behaviour in this highly institutionalized régime. Consequently, prenegotiation can almost be considered 'business as usual,' as part of a cyclical process in régime maintenance. Yet even within the GATT, it was a perception of threat by important members which triggered consideration of this particular prenegotiation. Members anticipated an erosion of the régime as a result of extra-legal actions taken by member-governments. The strong perception of impending trouble triggered consideration of a new round of negotiations as a strategy of crisis avoidance.

Crisis avoidance and management were somewhat less apparent as triggers in the onset of prenegotiations on arms control between the Soviet Union and the primary adversary. In

---

tiation process,' *Negotiation Journal* 4(January 1988), 31-43. Our evidence suggests that crisis avoidance is as important a trigger of prenegotiation as is crisis itself.

his examination of Soviet prenegotiations, Franklyn Griffiths identifies a pattern of broad policy failure interacting with a perception of opportunity. Under Lenin, the failure of the socialist revolution to spread lent urgency to an embattled leadership's search for strategies to moderate the hostility of its adversaries. In 1963, the memory of the Cuban missiles crisis was vivid. In 1969, even though the relative strength of the Soviet Union had increased, the Brezhnev-Kosygin régime faced the shadow of policy failure in the Soviet economy. Under Mikhail Gorbachev, an acute economic crisis was one important trigger of Soviet interest in prenegotiation. Policy failure, interacting with identification of opportunity, led Soviet leaders to reframe their problem and consider negotiation actively. In each case, however, the Soviet leadership considered negotiation not only, or not even necessarily, because it promised agreement but because the process of getting to the table was expected to have important political and strategic benefits that were largely independent of a negotiated agreement. Under these kinds of conditions, Soviet leaders considered what type of negotiation was most likely to bring the broad political and strategic benefits they wanted.

In the United States it was perceptions of threat interacting with perceptions of opportunity which promoted active consideration of negotiation. In Washington, a mixture of strategic crisis and domestic political pressure triggered processes of prenegotiation. In 1921, as Fen Osler Hampson notes, the threat of a new naval arms race among the great powers was an important motivating factor in American considerations. Even then, the need to come to terms with Congress was the catalyst. Harding's calculus of the relative costs and benefits of negotiation of a naval arms control agreement was tipped by the exigencies of domestic politics. In 1963 the experience of the Cuban crisis was central in prompting active American consideration of negotiation. President Kennedy wrote to President Khrushchev in the immediate aftermath of the crisis that 'perhaps now, as we step back from danger, we can make some real progress in

this vital field.'[2] Both leaders seized on the prospect of negotiating a test ban treaty as an important symbol of de-escalation.

In 1969 President Nixon and his national security adviser,
Henry Kissinger, responded both to the threat they perceived
from Soviet strategic parity and to the opportunity to link progress in arms control to broader changes in Soviet behaviour.
Crisis avoidance was an important impetus to the consideration
of negotiation. Only under President Reagan did the United
States consider negotiation largely in response to domestic and
allied pressures rather than as a strategy of post-crisis management or crisis avoidance. In that case, consideration of negotiation was prompted largely by the important side-benefits it
was expected to bring.

The importance of crisis avoidance as a trigger is most strikingly apparent in the case of the processes that preceded the
negotiation at Camp David in 1978 on the Middle East. The
first process of prenegotiation was initiated in early 1977 by the
new president of the United States as a deliberate strategy of
crisis avoidance. Carter began this process because of his memory of the adverse consequences of the war between Egypt,
Israel, and Syria in 1973, the priority he gave to the development of a comprehensive energy policy to prevent renewed 'oil
shocks,' and his fear of the consequences of renewed war. He
and his advisers were convinced that the status quo was inherently dangerous; in Zartman's terms, there was an unstable and
hurting stalemate.[3] Only progress in negotiation could avoid a
slide towards war. Arab leaders, especially in Egypt, also anticipated a crisis if progress were not made before the expiry of
the second disengagement agreement then in place between
Egypt and Israel in September 1978. The deadline served as
the 'forcing mechanism' to a process of prenegotiation. The
urgency of negotiation was multiplied by the domestic crisis in

2 Quoted by Glenn T. Seaborg, *Kennedy, Khrushchev, and the Test Ban Treaty*
(Berkeley: University of California Press 1981), 176.
3 I. William Zartman, *Ripe for Resolution: Conflict and Intervention in Africa*
(New York: Oxford University Press 1985).

Egypt. Food riots, student strikes, and growing political opposition to the régime intensified the need for a strategy of
crisis avoidance in Cairo. An option of negotiation became especially attractive because the obvious alternative, renewal of
military action, was unappealing in the light of the mixed military outcome of the 1973 war. Israel's leaders also faced an
intensifying domestic crisis. Its balance-of-payments deficit had
soared and inflationary pressures were particularly acute for
Sephardi voters in the large cities. The Rabin government was
weak and bitterly divided. Thus, in Jerusalem, in Cairo, and in
Washington, domestic and strategic factors interacted to promote active consideration of negotiation.

When the negotiation which issued from the first prenegotiation failed, sunk political costs increased the attractiveness
of a second attempt at prenegotiation in January 1978. Domestic political incentives were greater than they had been a
year earlier in both Washington and Cairo. President Sadat had
incurred heavy costs, at home and abroad, as a result of his trip
to Jerusalem. To counter these pressures, he encouraged the
resurgence of nationalist parties that supported the return of
the Sinai. Consequently, a negotiated agreement had become
even more important in January 1978 than it had been a year
earlier. In Jerusalem, Prime Minister Begin faced increased
domestic opposition, both from the Labour party to his left who
opposed the return of the airfields in the Sinai on security
grounds and from leaders on the right who urged the establishment of more settlements in the West Bank. In Washington,
the president was increasingly anxious for a visible foreign policy success to offset domestic criticism. Under these conditions,
Egypt and Israel, followed by the United States, reframed the
problem and began again to consider actively the option of
negotiation.

This comparative review of evidence across a variety of issues suggests that either recent or anticipated crisis, or a paired
perception of threat and opportunity, was the most important
catalyst of a process of prenegotiation. Under these conditions,

exploration of the option of negotiation was attractive for several interrelated reasons. Most directly, as Zartman argues, mutual perception of a hurting stalemate informed by a recent or impending crisis leads policy-makers to consider actively the option of negotiation.[4] At a minimum, introduction of this additional option changes the relative weighting of the options already under consideration. At a maximum, consideration of negotiation as one among several options encourages leaders to think about the advantages of a co-operative solution in comparison to unilateral action.

Consideration of a co-operative solution can encourage leaders to frame the problem differently. Experimental evidence from the laboratory suggests that, contrary to the expectation of rational models, decision-makers' choices are not invariant. As Ronald Fisher notes, when the same problem is framed differently, people shift their preferences.[5] Evidence from these cases suggests that the intensity of the perception of impending crisis may affect the way leaders frame their problem.

Impending crisis was most acutely perceived by leaders in Canada in the 1980s and in Egypt and Israel in the wake of the war in 1973. Leaders in these countries gave greatest weight to a joint solution; neither side anticipated that it could avoid a crisis through escalation and both expected a unilateral strategy of conflict management to be ineffective. In these cases, getting to the table was a principal purpose of prenegotiation. The reframing of the problem was extensive, as leaders seriously considered the benefits of a joint solution. Although the problem was identified and reframed, however, the problem diagnoses of the participants in the process differed widely.

Where perception of impending crisis was not so great, as in Moscow and Washington when they considered negotiation

---

4 *Ibid*, 25ff, and I. William Zartman and Maureen R. Berman, *The Practical Negotiator* (New Haven CT: Yale University Press 1982), 52-70.

5 See also George A. Quattrone and Amos Tversky, 'Contrasting rational and psychological analyses of political choice,' *American Political Science Review* 82(September 1988), 719-36.

of arms control agreements, getting to the table was only one among several purposes of the process. In Moscow, particularly, the attractiveness of prenegotiation was in large part a function of the political benefits it promised, benefits which were largely independent of the outcome of negotiation. As Griffiths argues, although the table was in the foreground of Soviet calculations, it is the background which merits serious attention. When Soviet leaders identified and reframed the problem, they paid attention not only to the benefits of a joint solution but also to the anticipated benefits of the process of prenegotiation itself, over and above whether it culminated in an agreement at the table. The same held for members of the Reagan administration in Washington when they considered the prospect of negotiating an arms control agreement with the Soviet Union. As Zartman suggests, the perception of the consequences of stalemate and the positioning of the impending crisis or the conjunction of threat and opportunity affect the framing of the problem and the salience of negotiation as an option.[6]

Prenegotiation was also attractive to leaders for other reasons. It can be an effective strategy of risk management, especially for leaders whose principal purpose is a negotiated agreement. It can permit the parties to reduce uncertainty and to manage complexity at lower levels of risk than a formal commitment to a strategy of negotiation would allow. Leaders who agree only to explore the option of negotiation can begin to assess the intentions and objectives of other parties without public commitment to a process of negotiation.

A process of prenegotiation also allows leaders to make preliminary judgments about the bargaining ranges and reservation points of others, again without publicly committing themselves to a negotiation. It allows the exploration of requitement and assessment of the likelihood of reciprocity, again at a lower cost. Reciprocity is in part a function of the way problems are framed, the attribution of others' intentions and motives, and

6 I. William Zartman, 'Prenegotiation: phases and functions,' in this volume.

the degree of trust.[7] Prenegotiation can serve as a useful diagnostic instrument by providing valuable information that leaders need to make judgments about the likely risks and benefits of negotiation.

The reduction of uncertainty is especially important in an adversarial relationship, when there can be both strategic and political costs to a strategy of negotiation. In Cairo, for example, there were important domestic and 'reputational' costs to negotiation with Israel. Prenegotiation minimized these costs as President Sadat acquired valuable information about Israel's intentions, strategies, bargaining range, and critical minimum for a negotiated agreement.

Prenegotiation can also provide a valuable opportunity to manage complexity when there is a multiplicity of interests, parties, and roles. When leaders first consider going to the table, it is frequently unclear who will come, what their roles will be, how the table will be structured, and what will be on and off the agenda. The answers to these questions are important components of leaders' decisions to commit to negotiation. This kind of complexity was prominent in the multilateral prenegotiation of economic issues for the Uruguay Round and in the prelude to Camp David, where participants and roles were undefined at the outset. Indeed, President Carter structured the preliminary rounds of prenegotiation to acquire and share information. In brief, prenegotiation promises to lower the cost of critical information. In so doing, it is attractive to leaders as a strategy of risk management in situations of uncertainty and complexity.

Prenegotiation is attractive as well because it promises lower exit costs than formal negotiation does. Leaders make a com-

7 See Deborah Welch Larson, 'The psychology of reciprocity in international relations,' *Negotiation Journal* 4(July 1988), 281-301; James K. Esser and Stuart S. Komorita, 'Reciprocity and concession making in bargaining,' *Journal of Personality and Social Psychology* 31(1975), 864-72; Dean Pruitt, *Negotiation Behavior* (New York: Academic Press 1981); Robert Axelrod, *The Evolution of Cooperation* (New York: Basic Books 1984); and Robert O. Keohane, 'Reciprocity in international relations,' *International Organization* 40(winter 1986), 1-28.

mitment to explore negotiation, not to negotiate. The option to withdraw remains open, and leaders can exercise that option before domestic political interests have had the opportunity to organize and mobilize, either on behalf of or against negotiation. Prenegotiation is usually a less public process than is negotiation and interested outsiders have less access to critical information. The exploratory process is better insulated from political interests and, in this sense too, leaders can acquire critical information at lower cost. The political costs of information are less at the outset of prenegotiation than in negotiation. As Israel's leaders anticipated, for example, interested publics had almost no access to information through the early stages of the process of prenegotiation in 1977.

Finally, prenegotiation is attractive to leaders whose interest is not exclusively in a negotiated agreement as the outcome. Hampson suggests, for example, that President Reagan valued the benefits that an exploration of negotiation would bring to his relations with allies and his image with domestic publics. Similarly, Soviet leaders anticipated broad political benefits independent of agreements that might result should prenegotiation succeed. Under these conditions, prenegotiation is an attractive political strategy for the management of a continuing adversarial relationship. At the extreme, exploring the possibility of going to the table can be a preferred alternative to getting there.

Evidence from our cases suggests that leaders have decided to consider negotiation when they see the need for a strategy of crisis avoidance or post-crisis management or when they see a conjunction of threat and opportunity, when prenegotiation promises to reduce some of the risks associated with negotiation, and when they anticipate benefits from the process which are largely independent of whether or not it culminates in agreement. The limited evidence we have does not permit us to establish whether these three conditions are all necessary or, indeed, whether they are sufficient; more work is needed. In all the cases examined, however, more than one of these conditions was present. Indeed, when they reinforced one another, they made exploration of negotiation an attractive option.

THE STAGES OF PRENEGOTIATION

A recent review of analyses of international negotiation concludes that attempts to model deductively the outcome of negotiation from a clearly defined set of initial conditions have generally proved unsatisfactory. Daniel Druckman and P. Terrence Hopmann note that the outcome of a negotiation on an international issue is generally determined through the process itself.[8] This observation is even more pertinent in the analysis of prenegotiation. The process of prenegotiation is less structured, less governed by norms, and less regulated by rules than is negotiation. Indeed, as we have argued, prenegotiation is attractive at the outset in part because it is open-ended and fluid.

The process of prenegotiation has not received a great deal of attention from analysts of negotiation. Those who have acknowledged its importance have tended generally to treat it as the first phase of a larger process. William Zartman, in his introductory article to this volume, considers prenegotiation as a critical diagnostic phase that precedes negotiation. Harold Saunders conceives of the first stage of the process of negotiation as a shared definition of a problem and the second as a commitment to a negotiated settlement where parties conclude that a fair settlement is likely. The third stage consists of arranging the negotiation and, in the fourth stage, the negotiation begins.[9] The integration of prenegotiation into a phased model

8 Daniel Druckman and P. Terrence Hopmann, 'Behavioral aspects of negotiations on mutual security,' in Paul Stern, Jo. L. Husbands, Robert Jervis, Philip Tetlock, and Charles Tilly, eds, *Behavior, Society, and Nuclear War* (New York: Oxford University Press 1989, forthcoming).

9 See Harold Saunders, 'We need a larger theory of negotiation: the importance of pre-negotiating phases,' *Negotiation Journal* 1(July 1985), 249-62. Zartman and Berman (*Practical Negotiator*) identify the diagnostic phase as the first of their three phases of negotiation. It is followed by the formula phase, when each party perceives the other to be serious about finding a negotiated solution. The third phase is that of negotiation itself. Only Zartman and Druckman focus

of negotiation can blur the distinction between the two processes and mask the important analytic differences. And, as we have argued, for some of the participants, some of the time, negotiation is not the principal purpose of prenegotiation.

To model the process of getting to the table, Tomlin suggests that prenegotiation proceeds through five stages, two of which precede the formal onset of prenegotiation. If, in the initial stage of problem identification, at least one of the parties adds negotiation to the array of options under active consideration, the process moves to the next stage. In the search for options, the second stage, leaders consider their options and choose negotiation as the preferred one, at least for the moment. The third stage, when one party makes a commitment to negotiate, marks the shift from whether to negotiate to what will be negotiated. At this point, Tomlin suggests, the preoccupation of the leaders with internal dynamics gives way to increased attention to the interests of other parties to the negotiation as leaders begin to try to define the scope of the negotiation. The beginning of the fourth stage is signalled by the communication of a desire to negotiate by one of the parties to the others. In this stage, the parties must agree to go to the table. The fifth and final stage of prenegotiation is dominated by the setting of parameters for the negotiation to follow. This stage may shade into the first stage of the negotiation process.

Tomlin's model nicely illuminates the process of prenegotiation between Canada and the United States as the parties proceeded sequentially through the stages towards negotiation on free trade. It works especially well because the initiative was

---

explicitly on the 'diagnosis' phase or prenegotiation and its appropriate contextual conditions. See Daniel Druckman, 'Prenegotiation experience and dyadic conflict resolution in a bargaining situation,' *Journal of Experimental Social Psychology* 4(1968), 367-83. Brian Tracy, 'Bargaining as trial and error,' in I. William Zartman, ed, *The Negotiation Process: Theories and Applications* (Beverly Hills CA: Sage 1978), includes many of the structuring activities which are better characterized as part of a process of prenegotiation in negotiation. His analysis collapses many of the functions of prenegotiation into the negotiation process itself.

taken by Canada which perceived a strong threat, was most anxious to avoid an anticipated crisis, and yet had considerable time to mobilize its policy-making resources to consider its options. As Tomlin expects, the third stage of commitment to negotiate was the most protracted as the two governments explored their options and simultaneously negotiated with important constituencies at home. Indeed, as governments explored their options, at times in public, opposition from powerful bureaucracies and interest groups grew. In part because of the intensified perception of a threat of protectionist legislation by the United States, and in part because no other option appeared as promising as a strategy of conflict management, the two governments nevertheless agreed in principle to bilateral negotiation. Tomlin finds that for the United States, it was the dim prospects of multilateral solutions that made a bilateral agreement attractive. In Canada, the flaws of a sectoral strategy moved the government incrementally towards a comprehensive strategy. The evidence suggests that the process of prenegotiation proceeded to agreement to negotiate through the progressive elimination of alternatives. Only after agreement in principle to negotiate did the two governments turn to the creation of the structures and boundaries of the negotiation to follow.

The process was much messier in the other cases examined in this volume. In 1985 the United States secretary of state and the Soviet foreign minister specified the structure and the boundaries before they committed to negotiation. By contrast, only after the Strategic Arms Limitation Talks (SALT) negotiation began in 1969 did the parties specify the boundaries and the agenda. In the process that preceded the negotiation of the test ban treaty, the United States first developed a broad definition of the problem and then a narrow definition as a fallback position. In the Middle East, neither Israel nor Egypt would commit to negotiate until the risks of a negotiation were reduced through the clarification of the participants, the boundaries of negotiation, and the agenda.

Analysis of these cases suggests that the sequencing of stages in a process of prenegotiation needs further examination. In all cases, definition of a problem, although not shared diagnoses, and a search for options constituted the first two phases of the process of getting to the table. The placement of the commitment to negotiate in the sequence is more troublesome. The evidence suggests that when leaders consider the process of negotiation a high-risk option, with potentially large costs, the reduction of uncertainty will dominate the process and order the phases.

The management of complexity and competing trade-offs is also important in the progress of prenegotiation. In the prenegotiation of the Uruguay Round, for example, agreement to negotiate came only at the end, after much of the structuring of trade-offs had taken place. As Winham points out, the commitment to negotiation came in the final hours of the process of multilateral consultation; the third stage followed all the others.

Examination of the evidence from our cases also suggests that domestic politics affected the ordering of the stages of prenegotiation in different ways. In some cases, domestic pressures tended to intensify as prenegotiation proceeded and opposition forces had the opportunity to organize and coalesce; as they did, trade-offs sharpened and complexity grew. In the prenegotiation process before Camp David, for example, the political costs of prenegotiation intensified over time for Egypt, Israel, and the United States; sunk costs grew as the process proceeded. Commitment to negotiation became more difficult until the trade-offs were clear. Under these conditions, leaders tried to maintain their option to exit at the lowest possible cost by delaying the commitment to negotiate. In the prenegotiation of Canada–United States free trade, by contrast, the support of an influential commission created by the government and of important elements within the business community and the bureaucracy in Canada facilitated an early commitment to negotiate.

Both the reduction of uncertainty and the management of

complexity appear to be critical determinants of the ordering of the stages of prenegotiation. Uncertainty and complexity were functions, moreover, not only of the issues likely to be on or off the table, but also of the anticipated domestic consequences. The limited evidence we have suggests that the sequencing of prenegotiation appears to be highly context-dependent.

THE FUNCTIONS OF PRENEGOTIATION

We distinguish the process of getting to the table from that of negotiation by an important difference in their functions. Generally, as Zartman argues, prenegotiation focusses on the promotion of a joint solution and a commitment to negotiate, although, as we have seen, this is not always the aim of some participants in the process. It does so by attempting to create structures for negotiation which make a commitment to negotiate possible or attractive to those considering the option. Analysis focusses then not on integrative or distributive bargaining, or on processes of concession-convergence, but rather on creating the structures in which these kinds of activities can take place.

Analysis of our cases suggests that prenegotiation structures the negotiation which follows in several important ways. Indeed, some of this structuring activity, which is usually considered a part of negotiation, might be better located within the process of prenegotiation. As we have noted, prenegotiation is attractive in part because it reduces uncertainty and manages complexity at lower cost. It provides valuable information and reduces risk by defining the structure of negotiation through the specification of the boundaries, the participants, and, at times, even the agenda for the negotiation that may follow.

Boundaries

In most of the cases examined in this volume, prenegotiation was critical in specifying the boundaries of the negotiation to follow. In getting to the table to negotiate free trade, the United

States and Canada agreed on a comprehensive framework for negotiation. They eliminated sectoral negotiations or ad hoc bilateral arrangements and committed both governments to a comprehensive strategy. In the multilateral process that preceded the Uruguay Round, the declaration of principles similarly set the framework and the formula for the complex negotiation to follow. Although less extensive, boundary setting was also important in Soviet and American prenegotiation of arms control issues. As Griffiths and Hampson demonstrate, what was excluded from the framework during the process of prenegotiation set the broad boundaries for the processes that followed.

Nowhere was the importance of boundary setting more important than in getting to Camp David. The first process of prenegotiation was dominated by the search for principles to guide the negotiation of a comprehensive settlement of the Arab-Israeli conflict. Extensive exploratory discussions revealed that no agreement was possible; without such an agreement on boundaries to reduce the risks, none of the principal parties was willing to make a commitment to negotiate. The failure of the first process of prenegotiation led the parties to explore a negotiation with much more narrowly defined boundaries in the second round.

Participants

Generally, the participants were obvious and non-controversial in the cases examined in this volume. In the bilateral discussions between Canada and the United States, in the exploratory multilateral process that preceded the Uruguay Round, and in Soviet and American consideration of negotiation of arms control agreements, the participants were generally not at issue. In the prenegotiation of the limited test ban treaty, the process quickly produced agreement on the appropriate participants. In the process of getting to Camp David, however, the selection of participants was critical.

The first process of prenegotiation included a wide range

of participants: the United States, the Soviet Union, Egypt, Syria, Jordan, Saudi Arabia, leaders of the Palestine Liberation Organization, and Israel. Both Egypt and Israel, for quite different reasons, found some of these participants unacceptable and, as the prenegotiation proceeded, discovered their convergence of interest in eliminating those who, in their judgment, were most likely to obstruct an agreement. Only after unacceptable participants were eliminated in the second round did the two, at the urging of the United States, agree to negotiate.

Agenda

In almost all the cases we examined, prenegotiation was critical in setting or delimiting the agenda for the negotiation that followed. Agenda formation differed across processes of prenegotiation in two distinct ways. First, in some of the cases, prenegotiation proceeded through its stages by enlarging the agenda and creating bundles for future negotiation and trade-offs. In others, what was kept off the table was far more important than what was put on; prenegotiation significantly narrowed the agenda and, in so doing, reduced both uncertainty and risk. More important, in some cases the agenda was largely defined by the process of prenegotiation, while in others significant issues of agenda formation spilled over into the process of negotiation.

In the prenegotiation of the Uruguay Round, participants began the process by creating an exhaustive inventory of the agenda items in preparatory committees. In the early stages of the process, those developing countries opposed to the inclusion of services on the agenda succeeded in creating a separate negotiating structure for services independent of goods. As Winham observes, however, pyramidal relations among the participants increasingly structured the agenda as the process of prenegotiation proceeded. By the end of the process, the agenda created packages of items which will subsequently permit trade-offs among the major coalitions in the complex multilateral process of negotiation to follow. The process of prenegotiation between Canada and the United States similarly broadened the agenda.

Agenda formation in the process of getting to the table at Camp David was dramatically different. When the process began, the agenda was diffuse and uncertain and it was progressively narrowed as the principal parties proceeded through the stages of prenegotiation. By the end of the second prenegotiation, the most controversial issues had been eliminated or postponed and the agenda for the meeting at Camp David had been basically set. Indeed, Stein finds that the narrowing of the agenda through the elimination or the postponement of the most controversial issues was a critical component in the lessening of uncertainty and complexity and in the reduction of the anticipated costs of negotiation for Israel. Agenda definition was an important part of risk management and a critical prerequisite of the commitment to negotiate.

The politics of agenda formation were most obvious in Soviet strategy during the process of prenegotiation. The role of politics differed, however, depending on the internal and external constraints and opportunities. In the first case examined by Griffiths, he finds that Lenin and his associates were unprepared to go to the negotiating table with its proposed agenda. On the contrary, Soviet leaders designed their strategy to modify the agenda by creating political pressure on western governments. The extra-negotiatory side-benefits, however, were far more important than progress at the table; the agenda was a vehicle rather than a target. By contrast, Khrushchev was willing to narrow the agenda on a test ban in order to improve Kennedy's bargaining situation as well as his own. Even then, however, what would happen at the table was not Khrushchev's only concern. As Griffiths observes, Khrushchev needed measures that constrained conservatives simultaneously in the United States and the Soviet Union. In Soviet strategy, politics were generally more important than reduction of uncertainty and risk management in agenda formation.

The process of prenegotiation differed not only in whether

the agenda was narrowed or expanded but also in whether it came to be inclusive or indeterminate. This latter difference is more important analytically than the former. Irrespective of whether an agenda is narrowed or expanded, as long as it is set it reduces uncertainty and risk for the participants. Consistent with our argument that prenegotiation is attractive in part because it serves to reduce uncertainty and risk, we would expect that in the majority of cases, prenegotiation would set or at least delimit the agenda for the negotiation to follow before the parties committed themselves to negotiation. Although there are important differences in degree, the evidence that is available from our cases generally sustains this expectation.

As we have seen, during the process that preceded Camp David, the agenda was agreed before the parties arrived. Similarly, Winham finds that the multilateral process of prenegotiation virtually set the agenda for the negotiation to follow during the Uruguay Round. The agenda for the negotiation of the limited test ban treaty was also established by the wide-ranging process of consultation that preceded the formal session. As Hampson observes, the agenda was narrowed by both external and domestic constraints.

In the process that preceded the negotiation of the SALT I agreement, however, only a rough agenda emerged after exploratory talks between the Soviet and American delegations. The agenda was even less defined as the Soviet Union and the United States began the negotiation in the Strategic Arms Reduction Talks. Important struggles within the bureaucracy, congressional and public pressures, and allied demands shaped the outlines of an agenda for the United States. Equally important, however, was the determination of the Reagan administration to define the agenda differently, to emphasize reductions rather than the limitations or ceilings which were characteristic of SALT. Agenda formation proceeded by the elimination of alternatives; the agenda was delimited by what it would not include.

In the prenegotiation of free trade between the United States and Canada, both committed themselves to negotiation before they defined the agenda. Differences between the two parties as to what should be put on and what should be kept off the agenda were not resolved before the start of the formal negotiation in Ottawa. The divergence flowed from different diagnoses of the problem and from the way the prenegotiation process developed. Serious structuring activity began only late in the process. As Tomlin notes, these differences would subsequently become major obstacles in the negotiation itself.

Where negotiation was not perceived as an inherently risky process in and of itself, the parties gave correspondingly less attention to the reduction of uncertainty through the specification of the agenda. In a process like the one that preceded Camp David, however, where the major participants anticipated serious costs to entry into negotiation, they gave far greater attention to structuring activity. The evidence suggests, moreover, that when the parties made a commitment to negotiate without some structuring of the agenda, the negotiation that followed was far more likely to reach impasse and deadlock.

A comparative analysis of the evidence suggests that the process of prenegotiation was generally characterized by important structuring activity. It set broad boundaries, identified the participants, and, in at least half the cases, specified the agenda for negotiation. Even in those cases where it produced only a rough outline of the agenda, it nevertheless reduced uncertainty and complexity by establishing what would be kept off the table. In every case, prenegotiation framed the problem and set the limits of the negotiation to follow. Without an analysis of the process of getting to the table, we cannot explain the shape of the table, who gets there and who doesn't, what is on the table and, equally important, what is kept off.

Management of domestic politics and coalition-building
Analysts of the process of international negotiation have long recognized that bargaining takes place not only among the par-

ticipants in the process but also within each party as representatives try to manage their domestic constituencies and to build
support for anticipated agreements. Indeed, as Robert Putnam
argues, the politics of many international negotiations can usefully be conceived as a two-level game.[10] Domestic politics, however, does not only constrain; leaders are not passive in their
domestic arenas. The process of prenegotiation permits political
leaders to perform important structuring activity in the domestic as well as in the international arena. It enables leaders
not only to manage domestic constituencies but also to attempt
to structure domestic coalitions.

In many of our cases, political structuring, both at home
and across borders, was an important function of the process
of prenegotiation. In the process of getting to the table with
the United States, a task force created by the Department by
External Affairs in Ottawa, an independent bipartisan royal
commission set up by the government, and a series of government reports and statements were all important in legitimating
the option to negotiate free trade among the Canadian public.
In Egypt, prenegotiation permitted Sadat, at least for a time,
to neutralize growing domestic political opposition through the
manipulation of elements within the coalition that provided
critical support. Begin was even more adept at using the process
of prenegotiation to restructure and broaden the base of his
political support in Israel. Domestic political management was
also evident in American strategy. As Hampson notes, domestic
pressure played a decisive intervening role in processes of prenegotiation. Indeed, Washington frequently explored negotiation to deflect strong public, congressional, and bureaucratic
pressures.

---

10 Robert Putnam, 'Diplomacy and domestic politics: the logic of two-level games,'
International Organization 42(summer 1988), 427-53. Putnam argues that within
issue-areas, bargaining games are played simultaneously at two levels, domestic
and international, and that successful initiatives must be in the 'win-sets' of both
games. See also Daniel Druckman, 'Boundary role conflict: negotiation as
dual responsiveness,' in Zartman, ed, *The Negotiation Process*; Pruitt, *Negotiation
Behavior*, 41-3; and Gilbert R. Winham, 'Negotiation as a management process,'
World Politics 30(October 1977), 87-114.

Domestic political management was most striking, however, in Soviet strategy. Indeed, the structuring of domestic politics, both at home and abroad, was often the most important purpose of Soviet participation in a process of prenegotiation. As Griffiths concludes, the underlying pattern in Soviet strategy is one of tendency shifts in processes of internal bargaining whose outcomes favour reformist approaches to negotiation. External bargaining has not been unimportant; typically Soviet leaders have engaged in simultaneous internal and external bargaining as they contemplate moving to the table. The essence of Soviet prenegotiatory behaviour, however, is internal bargaining which serves to build critical political support for action by the régime. Lenin had to manipulate and reconcile conflicting predispositions within the régime to move the Soviet Union to the table in 1922. Khrushchev propelled the Soviet Union to the table in part to strengthen his weakened internal bargaining position. The prenegotiation of SALT was characterized by active structuring by Brezhnev of coalition politics to build support for reformative tendencies in the Soviet Union. Again, under Gorbachev, active consideration of going to the table has been used as much to strengthen and consolidate political support as it has been to change the texture and direction of the relationship with the United States. It seems that Soviet behaviour during processes of prenegotiation can be understood as much as a strategy of domestic restructuring as of external bargaining. The process gave Soviet leaders the opportunity to manipulate constraints and structure coalitions at home. These benefits were largely independent of what happened at the table.

Putnam has also observed that the representative of one side has a strong interest in the political strength of the other; in two-level games, there are synergistic linkages in which strategic moves in one game facilitate unexpected coalitions in the other.[11] A process of prenegotiation not only permits leaders to build political support at home but also to build transnational coalitions.

11 Putnam, 'Diplomacy and domestic politics,' 451.

The building of transnational coalitions was important in the process of prenegotiation between the United States and Canada. It was facilitated, of course, by the permeability of the border, the easy access each has to the communications network of the other, and the strong transnational ties that characterize the relationship. Summit meetings between the leaders, addresses in each other's capitals, and testimony of experts were all designed to build political support on the other side of the border as well as at home.

Among our cases, attention to transnational coalitions is most pronounced in Soviet behaviour. As Griffiths observes, Soviet exponents of negotiation with the United States have found themselves engaged in informal alliances with counterparts on the other side. Consistently in the four cases he examines, Griffiths finds Soviet leaders designing their strategy to strengthen constituencies in the primary adversary and among its allies who favoured accommodation. They did so to reduce political opposition to the pursuit of negotiation; in this sense, prenegotiation can be conceived as a process of building transnational coalitions to circumvent domestic political obstacles which threatened the process of getting to the table. Even more important, Soviet leaders designed their strategy to strengthen political coalitions abroad which were likely to support changes in the general direction of the Soviet-American relationship over time. These were not extra-negotiatory effects but fundamental and important purposes of Soviet participation in prenegotiation. The model of prenegotiation that emerges from Griffiths' analysis is one of highly informal transnational coalitions of people in the United States and the Soviet Union who pursue broad and parallel goals in separate internal bargaining exercises loosely linked by external bargaining.[12] The object of prenegotiation was not primarily to get to the table but to manage an adversarial relationship.

---

12 For a formal analysis of the determinants of the 'win-sets' of simultaneous domestic and international bargaining, the implications for transnational coalition-building, and the counter-intuitive implications for strategy, see the excellent analysis by Putnam, in *ibid.*

In sum, the process of getting to the table performs an important structuring activity as leaders explore an option of negotiation. It reduces uncertainty, clarifies risks and costs, and manages complexity as leaders contemplate the boundaries of the table, who is likely to be there, the rules, and what is likely to be put on and kept off the table. Equally important, the possibility of going to the table permits leaders to structure domestic activity and to build transnational coalitions as the process proceeds. At times, however, as leaders looked over the heads of other leaders to constituencies abroad, the table did not loom very large.

EXPLANATION OF THE OUTCOME

Our evidence does not permit us to draw more than tentative conclusions about when and why parties get to the table. In virtually all the cases examined in this volume, the parties did get to the table. A more robust explanation of 'successful' pre-negotiation must await detailed comparative examination of processes that failed to culminate in negotiation. Given this caveat, some suggestive preliminary propositions emerge from this comparative examination of successes.

If success is defined, technically, as getting to the table, ear-lier analyses of prenegotiation have suggested that the process is most likely to succeed when the parties assure each other that they will bargain in 'good faith,' when negotiation promises to help them avoid a mutually unsatisfactory breakdown in their relationship, and when parties focus on the issues and avoid intensive preparation of strategy.[13] Our analyses suggest a broader analytic perspective.

At the outset, the parties considered the status quo unac-ceptable; they anticipated high costs, even crisis, if existing trends

13 John Thibaut, 'The development of contractual norms in bargaining: replica-tion and variation,' *Journal of Conflict Resolution* 12(March 1968), 102-12; Druck-man, 'Prenegotiation experience and dyadic conflict resolution in a bargaining situation'; B.M. Bass, 'Effects on subsequent performance of negotiators of studying issues or planning strategies alone or in groups,' *Psychological Mono-graphs*, no 614(1966); and Druckman and Hopmann, 'Behavioral aspects of negotiations on mutual security,' 82.

continued. They also hoped to change or at least to modify the overall direction of their relationship and they identified an opportunity to do so. These expectations not only triggered a process of prenegotiation but helped to propel it through its stages.

As the process of prenegotiation proceeded, the reduction of central uncertainties and the specification of the critical trade-offs were associated with arriving at the table. In most of the cases we examined, the definition of the boundaries, the iden-tification of the participants, and the delimitation of the agenda were important in moving the parties to the table. Not only were core interests clarified as parties considered the alterna-tives, but each learned about the core interests of others. While keeping the costs of exit down, especially in the early stages, the participants acquired crucial, relatively low-cost information about others' bargaining ranges, critical minima, and reserva-tion points and were able to explore the likelihood of reci-procity. Finally, leaders at times not only responded to domestic constraints and inducements but also actively manipulated the process of prenegotiation to build political coalitions in support of negotiation.

Only in three cases did prenegotiation fail to perform all of these critical functions. In the first multilateral attempt at pre-negotiation of the Arab-Israel conflict, the parties could not define the boundaries or agree on the appropriate participants; ultimately, the process was aborted by the party most interested in a negotiated agreement. In the process that preceded SALT, only a very rough agenda emerged after exploratory discus-sions. In the prenegotiation of the free trade agreement be-tween the United States and Canada, the parties delimited the agenda, but they did not define its contents. Indeed, they did not try to do so until very late in the process. Ironically, as Tomlin concludes, it may well have been the failure of the two countries to address a prospective negotiating agenda in detail until late in the process of prenegotiation which enabled them to begin formal negotiation. Here, the masking of some of the

complexity was an important component of success. Nevertheless, even in these cases, the process of prenegotiation did perform other critical functions.

Across the cases, our evidence suggests generally that the
greater the anticipation of crisis and the greater the incentive
to avoid crisis, the greater the identification of threat and opportunity, the greater the reduction of uncertainty and complexity through the specification of boundaries, participation,
and agenda, the greater the identification and clarification of
trade-offs, and the greater the structuring of domestic support,
the smoother the progress through the stages of prenegotiation
to the table. Whether all these conditions are necessary and
whether, together, they are sufficient to get the parties to the
table remains a subject for further research.

WHY PRENEGOTIATION MATTERS

From several perspectives, reaching the table is too narrow and
technical a criterion of success. Prenegotiation matters both
when parties get to the table and when they do not. It matters
because the process provides the participants with significant
opportunities for learning, both about themselves and about
others. It matters because it permits the participants to learn
about the preconditions for and possibilities of both a negotiated agreement and an alternative management of their relationship. Finally, and paradoxically, prenegotiation matters even
when the outcome of the negotiating process does not. Some
analysts of arms control, for example, have argued that the
outcome of any given negotiation is not intrinsically important,
but that the learning it engenders and its consequences for the
management of the larger relationship between the United States
and the Soviet Union are.[14] In this sense, the process of 'getting
to the table' is inherently valuable and significant irrespective
of whether the table figures in its outcome.

14 Franklyn Griffiths, 'Limits of the tabular view of negotiation,' *International
Journal* 35(winter 1979-80), 33-46.

Analysts of international relations differ substantially in their concept of learning. Some suggest that leaders learn insofar as they seek to reduce uncertainty and improve predictability in a loosely structured international environment. Others contend that learning is demonstrated by greater cognitive complexity or knowledge about means-ends relationships. This kind of learning may overcome the obstacles to co-operation created by anarchy and self-help. New technical information, shared knowledge, the development of common expertise, and better knowledge of cause-effect relationships may alter policymakers' beliefs and expectations.[15] Leaders may be able to revise stereotypical images, to develop new vocabularies and new kinds of discourse, and, optimally, to reframe the problem they confront. Finally, analysts suggest that leaders learn as they redefine their interests over time.[16]

Cognitive psychology cautions, however, against overly optimistic estimates of the capacity to learn. It identifies serious obstacles to learning at the individual level. Generally, people assimilate new information to existing beliefs; they are 'cognitive misers.' Until and unless the information is sufficiently discrepant, they are unlikely to 'learn.' Leaders are most likely to learn when they repeatedly encounter strongly discrepant information that challenges fundamental beliefs. Only then are they likely to reformulate their beliefs about others and reframe the problem.[17]

---

15 See Joseph S. Nye Jr, 'Nuclear learning and U.S.-Soviet security regimes,' *International Organization* 42(summer 1987), 371-402; Joseph S. Nye Jr, 'Neorealism and neoliberalism,' *World Politics* 40(January 1988), 235-51; and Robert O. Keohane and Joseph S. Nye Jr, 'Power and interdependence revisited,' *International Organization* 41(autumn 1987), 725-53. The different conceptions of learning are discussed in Deborah Welch Larson, 'Learning in U.S.-Soviet relations: the Nixon-Kissinger structure of peace,' paper delivered at the annual meeting of the American Political Science Association, Washington, September 1988.

16 See, in particular, Nye, 'Nuclear learning and U.S.-Soviet security regimes,' and Axelrod, *The Evolution of Cooperation*.

17 See, for example, Robert Jervis, *Perception and Misperception in International Politics* (Princeton NJ: Princeton University Press 1976); Robert Jervis, 'Cognition and political behavior,' in R.R. Lau and D.O. Sears, eds, *Political Cognition* (Hillsdale NJ: Lawrence Erlbaum 1986); Daniel Kahneman, Paul Slovic, and

Consistent with this cautionary note, analysts of institutions are also pessimistic about the capacity of 'states' to learn. They suggest that states do not adapt well to changes in their environment. Élites resist changes that threaten their interests, and bureaucratic organizations proceed routinely through highly institutionalized procedures. When learning occurs, it is a sporadic response to crisis, not a smooth incremental process of structural adaptation.[18]

Analyses of processes of prenegotiation in this volume suggest that recent crises did promote substantial learning which facilitated the process of getting to the table. The shared experience of the Cuban missiles crisis encouraged Soviet and American leaders to reframe the problem and to seek to stabilize their relationship through negotiation. In the aftermath of the October War in 1973, leaders in Egypt learned that a renewal of war was unlikely to achieve their minimum objective of regaining the Sinai and Israel's leaders learned that even superior military capability and a robust deterrent reputation could not prevent costly and unwanted war. Crisis provoked important and far-reaching changes in fundamental beliefs which permitted a reframing of the problem and the active consideration of negotiation.

Substantial learning also occurred as the participants proceeded through the phases of prenegotiation. The impact of scientific and technical information is most obvious. Winham notes the exhaustive enumeration and analysis of technical issues in the early phases of the prenegotiation within the GATT. The technical information was critical to the structuring of the

---

Amos Tversky, *Judgment Under Uncertainty: Heuristics and Biases* (New York: Cambridge University Press 1982); Deborah Welch Larson, *Origins of Containment: A Psychological Explanation* (Princeton NJ: Princeton University Press 1985); Richard Ned Lebow, *Between Peace and War: The Nature of International Crisis* (Baltimore MD: Johns Hopkins University Press 1981); and Robert Jervis, Richard Ned Lebow, and Janice Gross Stein, *Psychology and Deterrence* (Baltimore MD: Johns Hopkins University Press 1985).

18 Robert O. Keohane reviews this literature in 'Reciprocity, reputation, and compliance with international commitments,' paper delivered at the annual meeting of the American Political Science Association, Washington, September 1988.

agenda and to the commitment to negotiate the Uruguay Round. In the process of getting to the table to negotiate the Limited Nuclear Test Ban Treaty, an accumulation of scientific evidence highlighted the dangers of nuclear testing in the atmosphere. Moreover, the absence of progress in the testing programmes of the two superpowers removed a potential constraint to progress towards the table. As Hampson observes, however, there were also limits to learning: although the destabilizing consequences of the technology of multiple independently targeted re-entry vehicles were understood during the process of the SALT prenegotiation, the limitation of MIRVs was not included on the agenda. Generally, however, in all four processes of prenegotiation on arms control, expert knowledge and a growing understanding of the implications of new military technologies for crisis and arms race stability generated significant learning and facilitated progress towards the table.

Griffiths finds even stronger support for the impact of generalized learning on processes of prenegotiation. He argues that the most important obstacle to getting to the table was the stubborn and unrealistic optimism among Soviet leaders in estimating their capacity to transform their external environment. When this optimism was punctured and unrealistic expectations were revised, Soviet leaders moved through the stages of prenegotiation not only for its side-effects but to get to the table.

Our analysis has also demonstrated that significant and differentiated learning occurred during the process of prenegotiation. Leaders developed more informed assessments of the intentions of others, of their reservation points and bargaining ranges, and of the likelihood of requitement and reciprocity. Moreover, they learned not only about others but also about themselves. Although the degree of learning differed, in all the processes of prenegotiation we examined leaders clarified the trade-offs they were likely to confront, the risks, the opportunity costs of alternatives, and the nature of their domestic constraints and opportunities. They learned not only how to manage but also how to shape their political environment to facilitate a commitment to negotiation. In addition, they were able to do so incrementally and at lower cost than in a formal process of negotiation.

Griffiths concludes that learning by Soviet leaders occurred largely during the process of prenegotiation. Much the same holds for the Egyptians and Israelis; they learned far more as they approached the table than they did at Camp David. Fisher argues that the prenegotiation process is especially conducive to the kind of fundamental learning that is required to move parties to a highly escalated and protracted conflict towards alternative strategies of conflict management. A shift towards more accurate perceptions, more veridical images, better communication, and a co-operative framing of shared problems, although extraordinarily difficult under any circumstances, is more likely to occur in the fluid process of prenegotiation than at the table.

Both the experimental and historical evidence reviewed by Fisher and the comparative analysis of cases suggest that prenegotiation can be usefully conceived as a process of learning. In this sense, the process has intrinsic merit, whether or not it culminates at the table. Indeed, cognitive psychology suggests that we learn more from failure than we do from success. Evidence from the only 'failure' examined in this volume, the prenegotiation process between the Arabs and the Israelis in 1977, suggests both that leaders did learn and that what they learned was critical to the subsequent prenegotiation that culminated at Camp David. Success does not equate with significance.

Analysts have suggested at times that when a conflict is 'not ripe,' the parties should stay away from the table because of the significant costs of failure.[19] The same proposition may hold, albeit to a lesser degree, for prenegotiation. As Stein points out in her analysis of the Israel-Egypt relationship, President Sadat

19 See, for example, Richard Haass, 'Ripeness and the settlement of international disputes,' *Survival* 30(May/June 1988), 232-51, and David A. Lax and James K. Sebenius, *The Manager as Negotiator: Bargaining for Cooperation and Competitive Gain* (New York: Free Press 1986), 59.

learned in 1971 about the bargaining range of his adversary and the risks of negotiation and concluded that negotiation was unlikely to produce an agreement; in consequence, war became a more attractive option. In a highly escalated conflict, the risks are real that the failure of prenegotiation can alter leaders' calculations in favour of intensified conflict. Prenegotiation matters both when it succeeds and when it fails.

If leaders are to overcome deadlock and impasse in a protracted and dangerous conflict, however, there is little alternative to learning. David Lax and James Sebenius warn of the risks of the table when a conflict is not ripe but urge that the parties move away from the table to consider actions that can reshape perceptions and promote alternative definitions of their problem.[20] The analyses in this volume suggest strongly that the process of prenegotiation provides an environment especially conducive to this kind of learning.

Our analysis of prenegotiation was stimulated in large part by the call for a broader theory of negotiation which integrates the processes that precede it with bargaining at the table. The evidence in this volume suggests overwhelmingly that prenegotiation triggers, shapes, and structures the negotiation that follows. The process of getting to the table defines the boundaries, identifies the participants, and shapes the agenda at the table. A valid theory of prenegotiation can make an important contribution to the larger theory of negotiation. Our analyses also suggest that much of what is important in the management of international conflict and much of the significant learning that does occur happen as leaders approach and avoid the table. Whether they get to the table and what they do there may be less important for the management of international conflict than what leaders learn and do as they consider going to the table. Good theories of prenegotiation are important even when negotiation does not follow.

20 Lax and Sebenius, *The Manager as Negotiator*, 59.

Index